# EXPLORING HUMAN VALUES

# EXPLORING HUMAN VALUES

Psychological and Philosophical Considerations

Richard A. Kalish
Kenneth W. Collier

Brooks/Cole Publishing Company
Monterey, California

*Brooks/Cole Publishing Company*
*A Division of Wadsworth, Inc.*

Printed in the United States of America

10 9 8 7 6 5 4 3 2 1

Library of Congress Cataloging in Publication Data:

Kalish, Richard A
    Exploring human values.

    Bibliography: p.
    Includes index.
    1. Values.    I. Collier, Kenneth W., joint author.
II. Title.
BF778.K34        128        80-21875 √
ISBN 0-8185-0331-9

Acquisition Editor: *Claire Verduin*
Production Editors: *John Bergez and Stacey C. Sawyer*
Interior and Cover Design: *Ruth Scott*
Typesetting: *Computer Typesetting Services, Inc., Glendale, California*

# PREFACE

The origins of the field of psychology are rooted deeply in the field of philosophy. As recently as 50 years ago, many academic psychology programs were still housed in philosophy departments. Over the years, however, psychology seems to have set its own course, and now only in an occasional advanced course is the connection between the two fields clearly made.

In this book, we focus on personal and social values from both psychological and philosophical points of view. We discuss a selection of issues that are relevant to human behavior and mental health, probing into each in some depth, looking at the values and assumptions that underlie different positions, and then pulling back without trying to offer neat and clean answers. Our main goals are to open up issues for exploration and to urge examination of much of what we ordinarily take for granted.

The specific issues are varied: the meaning and purpose of life, the nature of freedom, the potential for personal growth, the biological limitations of competence, the impact of early socialization, the nature of psychological defenses, the implications of mental-health services, the obligations of the children of elderly persons. In each instance we ask readers to examine their own values and the implications of their values. What does it mean to believe that the purpose of life is to serve God? What does it mean to believe that all individuals are born with virtually no differences in intellectual potential? What does it mean to believe that society is corrupting and that people are better off in a state of nature?

There is tension in this book, because we have discussed issues that provoke tension. In fact, we ourselves are not always in agreement, and we have indicated some of our disagreements in the book. Even where we do agree, we may well be wrong, or we may be presenting opinions as facts, or we may have lost our objectivity. We state exactly what we believe; it is up to our readers to find out what they believe.

The possible student audiences for this book are varied. Although we wrote the book primarily for courses in psychology and human development, counseling and education, and philosophy, we believe it will be extremely helpful in any course in which students are asked to seriously reevaluate their views about themselves and their world. Some of the specific courses for which it is appropriate are psychology of adjustment, applied philosophy, mental health, counseling theory, psychology of personality, foundations of education, and human development. The book could also be used as an ancillary text in introductory courses in psychology and philosophy that focus on probing underlying values; the same is true of courses in theology, social work, and sociology. Finally, we hope that on some campuses faculty from different departments—perhaps counseling and philosophy or psychology and social work—will co-teach courses that are stimulated by this book.

So here is the book, a mixture of data and speculation, of psychologizing and moralizing, of history and contemporary issues, of many questions and a few attempts at answers. It is a personal book, representing where we—a social psychologist interested in human values and a philosopher now entering the ministry—are today. We may not be in the same place tomorrow, but we assume that the same issues and the same concerns will still be cogent, and that understanding what our values really are will still be important.

Many people contributed to this book in many ways. We specifically want to thank Ann Johnson Silny, Sheila Fabricant, Lee Dunn, and "Charlie" Ho, who read drafts of the manuscript, commented, typed, inspired, and encouraged. For their thoughtful reviews and suggestions, we are grateful to Charlotte Blee, Tallahassee Community College; Sandra LaFave, Orange Coast Community College; James Peterson, University of Vermont; Ronald Roussève, University of Oregon; and Cyril Svoboda, University of Maryland.

*Richard A. Kalish*
*Kenneth W. Collier*

# CONTENTS

PART FOUR
**MENTAL HEALTH AND HUMAN VALUES/217**

# EXPLORING HUMAN VALUES

# INTRODUCTION

If you don't know where you're going, any road will take you there.

Let us be more concrete: This book is about human values and their relationship to behavior. It is based on the assumption that an understanding of the significance of values—of *your* values—enables you to be a better person, to behave more effectively, to be more successful. Some questions arise immediately: *Better* as defined by whom? *Effective* in whose eyes? *Successful* for what?

Such notions as effective behavior, success, and goodness are all value-laden concepts. We believe that you must define them for yourself, even though your definitions inevitably reflect your history and your present environment. You must give some thought to where *you* are going, or you may spend most of your life walking along a road that leads to the wrong town. If we write a book that directs you to our town, and if your instructor or employer requires you to read it because it is also his or her town, and if some policymakers like it because it is also their town, you may arrive after a long and arduous walk only to find that you're not at all where *you* want to be. You feel like a stranger, an alien, successful in the eyes of others yet knowing yourself to be something different. You feel alienated both from yourself and from others.

Being successful according to your standards, on the other hand, gives you a sense of integrity, of being a whole person. "To thine own self be true," Polonius advises in *Hamlet*, but to do so you must know who you are and who you want to be. This is not to say that it doesn't matter what you do so long as you decide for yourself that you'll do it. It *is* to say that what you do is, for good or ill, *your* responsibility.

In this book we invite you to explore the values and beliefs that guide your behavior. We make no special effort to be "objective": like you, we have feelings and opinions, emotions and thoughts, and we make no apology for letting them show. We believe it would be less than honest to pretend to be something we're not. We hope that by letting our academic guard down we'll challenge you to respond. Whether or not you agree with our thoughts, you should submit them to the most critical scrutiny.

In writing a book like this one, it's impossible to explore all the alternatives to a given concern or to indicate all the shadings along a continuum. You'll often realize that your views don't fit into the alternatives we offer, and you'll need to adapt the discussions to fit your own unique circumstances. That is, we believe, as it ought to be. Please think up your own alternatives.

Before plunging into specific issues, however, we must take a look at the concept of *value*—a concept that pervades this book as it pervades society. The obvious question to ask at the outset is what values are. Unfortunately, this is probably the most difficult question to answer without prejudicing our responses to many of the questions we want to raise.

Let us say starkly that, as we use the term, *values* refers to criteria according to which some things are judged to be more desirable than others. Having said that, let us quickly point out what we have *not* said. For example, this characterization (it is not a definition) sidesteps the issue of whether there are *absolute* values, or values that exist independently of whether anyone happens to hold them. An absolute value would be one that everyone *should* abide by in all circumstances. Our characterization also sidesteps the issue of whether some things are *intrinsically* valuable, without reference to some other desirable goal. We've left such questions open on purpose, not because they're unimportant, but because we think their solutions must be discovered rather than stipulated.

Notice that our characterization does not square in every respect with the way the term *values* is used in everyday speech. If we ask you what your values are, you might answer in terms of principles or criteria, but you might also answer in terms of the things you value, such as personal freedom or authenticity. As is often the case, ordinary usage is, in this instance, ambiguous. Part of the task of scholarship is to examine such ambiguities and to define terms clearly in order to avoid misunderstandings. In this case, we're concerned with *why* some things are judged more desirable than others, not with *what* things you should desire.

The importance of values in the sense of criteria is underscored in a story told by the medieval philosopher Buriden. An ass stands halfway between two identical stacks of hay. Since there is nothing to distinguish one stack of hay as more desirable than the other, the ass cannot make up its mind which one to eat. In the end the unfortunate beast starves to death.

If we had no values, we would have no basis for choosing one thing over another, and we would be immobilized like Buriden's unfortunate ass. In this sense, our values (in the sense of criteria) determine what things we find desirable. If a society judges actions according to whether they contribute to one's material well-being, then it will consider getting a well-paying job to be more important (or better) than doing low-paying work one happens to enjoy. Thus, you can discover what values people hold by looking at what they like.

Although the values people hold determine what they think of as desirable, and although these values differ from person to person and from society to society, it does not follow that all values are relative. It is still an open question whether there are absolute values. If there are such values, then people who hold values inconsistent with them make mistakes, judging certain things to be desirable or undesirable when, in a deeper sense, they are not. At this point, we will have nothing to say about this issue, important though it is. Most of our attention in the book will be on values as people hold them.

All too often, of course, actions and even judgments are inconsistent. At one time a person may act as though money and power are the most desirable of all things and at other times as though the love and esteem of others are the most desirable of all things. This suggests that people frequently hold inconsistent values or are unclear or confused about their values.

In the last ten years or so, a process has been developed to help people resolve this kind of confusion. It is called "values clarification" (Raths, Harmann, & Simon, 1966; Simon, Howe, & Kirschenbaum, 1972). Basically, values clarification involves trying on various values to see how they fit. The process proceeds on two fronts. First, it points out that, according to a given set of values, certain things are desirable. Second, it requires you to consider whether or not you agree that these things really are valuable. Thus, you might be invited to imagine yourself caught up in some situation. Then you'd be asked to think through the implications of certain values, always keeping in mind your own feelings about these implications.

Notice something very important about this process. It is *not* concerned with discovering what absolute values there may or may not be. Instead, it is designed to help you clarify what values you actually hold, whether or not these values are absolute or relative, right or wrong. This means that values clarification does not replace such philosophical disciplines as ethics, aesthetics, and political theory. It is, however, what might be called "applied philosophy"—that is, the application of philosophy to real people's real problems.

In industry, engineers have learned that they can make an electronic model of an industrial process on a computer and then use the computer model to see what happens when they allow certain variables to fluctuate. It's much less expensive to accidentally blow up a plant on a computer than it is to blow up a real one! Values clarification is something like that. It's a lot easier—and probably more effective—to try on competing values in the safety of the classroom or counselor's office than it is to bumble through life never quite knowing what your values are.

In a sense, this entire book is an exercise in values clarification.

We discuss different roads and different communities, and we briefly explore the history of some of these roads and the philosophies of some of these communities. Although reading this book is no substitute for a serious study of history and philosophy, we frequently refer to certain prominent thinkers to provide historical perspective on contemporary issues. We present many conflicting and competing points of view, each of which is fraught with values, and we challenge you to become as clear as you can about what *you* think of them.

You may find answers to some of your questions by reading this book, and you'll probably discover new questions that require answers—at least we hope you do. We want to stress that the many questions we raise are *not* rhetorical; we ask you to think carefully about every one of them. Often enough we don't know what the answers are. More importantly, we aren't interested in serving up the Truth for you; we *are* interested in helping you to discover your own truth for yourself. When you think about it, that's rather ambitious.

## REFERENCES

Raths, L. E., Harmann, M., & Simon, S. B. *Values and teaching*. Columbus, Ohio: Charles E. Merrill, 1966.

Simon, S. B., Howe, L. W., & Kirschenbaum, H. *Values clarification*. New York: Hart, 1972.

# PART ONE

## MEANING, FREEDOM, AND VALUES

# CHAPTER 1

## INTRODUCING MEANING

Our discussion begins with the meaning of life. A grandiose notion? Most certainly. An impossible task? No, because our plan is only to open the matter for consideration, not to close it with an answer. An irrelevant question? Emphatically not! The meaning you discover or create determines what goals are truly relevant for you. If an advertising executive designs an excellent campaign to boost sales, but her client is really more concerned with the company's status in the community, she might see the contract given to another agency. Her plan is a good one, but it achieves an irrelevant goal. The success of a nursery school director who does an excellent job of teaching art appreciation may cost him his job if what the parents care about is whether their children learn how to read. Similarly, if you define effectiveness in terms of creativity but are persuaded to seek social acceptance, or if you value warm family relationships but find yourself trying to avoid demanding involvements, then you may succeed gloriously—in achieving an irrelevant goal. You'll have successfully found your way to the wrong town.

## MEANING AND PURPOSE

Sometimes a tiny shift in the sense of a word or phrase alters the entire significance of a statement. Specifically, finding a meaning or purpose *in* life is quite different from finding a meaning or purpose *of* life. The latter phrase refers to the ultimate meaning or purpose of human existence; the former phrase refers to what particular individuals find to be relevant within their own lives—a more personal, less cosmic notion (Choron, 1964). Although these two concepts are related, they are far from identical. You may find a purpose *in* life through being of service to others, even though you believe that life itself has no ultimate purpose or meaning. For some people, the purpose *of* life might coincide with their purpose *in* life; for instance, you may feel that service to God is the ultimate reason for existence and at the same time derive a personal purpose or meaning from serving God. On the other hand, you might also find meaning in life through reading, painting, backpacking, or relating sexually to another person, but it's unlikely that you would accept any of these activities as being the ultimate purpose of life. In the following discussion, it's important to keep in mind this distinction between the purpose or meaning *of* life and a purpose or meaning *in* life.

☐ Do you live your life for your own personal satisfaction and gain? For persons or causes outside yourself, such as your country, your family, your fellow human beings? For more cosmic purposes, such as serving God or being at one with nature? Do you believe that the purpose of life is expressed through what you do each hour of the day, or do you believe that life is without purpose? It's not at all unusual or blameworthy if you're inconsistent in your beliefs, if you vacillate back and forth, or if you aren't fully committed. Openness and flexibility can be desirable. ☐

## PERSONAL SATISFACTION AND GAIN AS THE PURPOSE OF LIFE

According to the Greek philosopher Epicurus (341/40–270 B.C.), personal happiness is the only sensible goal of human existence. Since you as an individual are powerless to change the world, and since you're not obligated to try, you should be encouraged to increase your pleasures and diminish your pains, thus producing the greatest possible happiness for yourself (Greer, 1968). For some people, acceptance of this view would lead to hedonism—to seeking pleasure through enjoyment of food and wines and sex—without particular regard for others. (It is important to note, however, that for Epicurus the greatest pleasure lay in serenity.) A similar but modified viewpoint has been attributed to Rousseau (1712–1778) and other philosophers, in particular John Stuart Mill (1806–1873). According to Randall (1940), these thinkers recommended that "every man seek as many pleasures and as much happiness as he can, *without depriving his fellows of their share*" (p. 370; italics ours).

□ How would each of these two views, both centered on obtaining happiness and pleasure for oneself, affect the behavior of the owner of a small business? A social worker? A college student? A policeman whose beat was the most impoverished section of town? Also think about which vocational fields a person espousing each of these views should pursue and which ones he or she should avoid. □

"Eat, drink and be merry" is not the only purpose of life that is self-centered. The notion that life should be devoted to personal growth and development, to maturing and becoming a better person, to realizing one's potential also assumes that the purpose of life is individual satisfaction and gain. *Self-actualization* is the term we will use to embrace this concept, and we'll return to this theme frequently in later chapters.

Although both hedonism and self-actualization are self-centered approaches, hedonism is frequently thought of as less noble or less worthy than self-actualization. Why? Partly, we think, because of the enormous influence of Plato (428/7–358/7 B.C.), who believed that the only things of permanent value exist in a suprasensual realm that can be apprehended only by the mind. If we turn our attention solely to satisfaction of the senses, Plato taught, we fail to realize our unique human potential.

Hedonism ordinarily espouses the pleasures of the senses; self-actualization is much more likely to be thought of as mental and spiritual. For this reason, self-actualization is much more acceptable as a purpose of life to those of us whose upbringing has been influenced greatly by Plato—and, to some degree, that includes all of us. This theme of conflict between the spirit and the body, the mental and the physical, recurs throughout the history of thought in both East and West. You've probably been affected by it in the way you've been taught about love (spiritual) and sex (physical), about white-collar work (mental) and blue-collar work (physical), or about reading good books (mental and slightly spiritual) versus watching television (rarely either mental or spiritual). Christianity generally tends "to place spirit above matter" (Greer, 1968) and occasionally takes the extreme position that the body is base and of the devil.

We are, of course, making a generalization; and you might wish to consider some exceptions and the values upon which they are based. You might contend that Western civilization is extremely materialistic and that business people are more influential in most circles than are teachers, artists and writers. Although we would agree with this contention, we'd also point out that much of our religious and secular literature inveighs against this emphasis upon materialistic motives and gain. The conflict between the spiritual and the bodily, the mental and the physical, seems to be a pervasive theme in human life.

## LOVE AND HUMAN
## RELATEDNESS AS THE PURPOSE OF LIFE

The search for meaning beyond the self can lead to the belief that relationships with other people constitute the purpose for living. The Bible says to love thy neighbor as thyself. Such love can be thought of as the love of one person for another or as the love of humanity, a much more sophisticated concept. For many people, such oneness with the world or attunement to life may serve as a purpose in and of life. Further, once this kind of awareness develops, the individual will find peace and knowledge within, thus becoming free to make the most of life on earth.

## SOCIAL CAUSES AS
## THE PURPOSE OF LIFE

Social causes have provided a purpose *in* life for a great many people. Sometimes a specific cause—or the general feeling of serving humanity—is considered the purpose *of* life. Among the causes that have received considerable attention during the past decade are international peace, improved interpersonal relations, elimination of poverty and hunger, an improved physical environment, and equality for all people regardless of ethnic background, sex, or sexual orientation.

Throughout the world, many people want their nations to be morally righteous, regardless of the cost in money or image. Others adhere more closely to the "my country right or wrong" position, whose master, Machiavelli (1469–1527), was able to say "When the entire safety of our country is at stake, no consideration of what is just or unjust, merciful or cruel, praiseworthy or shameful, must intervene . . . that course alone must be taken which preserves the existence of the country and maintains its independence" (Randall, 1940, p. 195). Relatively few persons would accept the need to sacrifice all morality to the cause of nationalism. However, before assuming that you could never be machiavellian, substitute the name of your favorite cause for the word *country*.

For some people, crusading for causes can provide a sense of vitality and a temporary escape from the awareness of meaninglessness in their lives. In addition, perhaps "the hard core of people who show up time after time at virtually any and all movements" (Maddi, 1970, p. 147) simply enjoy the process of crusading. The excitement of crusading can thus become more important than the nature of the cause.

People are more likely to consider working for a cause to be the purpose of life when they feel that the impact of their efforts will be felt in the future, beyond their own life span. Then they can see their work as improving not only the condition of their contemporaries but the condition of humanity. Horace Mann captured this sentiment in a commencement address at Antioch College: "Be ashamed to die until you have won some victory for humanity" (Mann, 1859).

☐ Does it matter whether a person's motive in joining a cause is to avoid feelings of meaninglessness or to accomplish something for posterity? When we question a person's motives for supporting a cause, might we really be expressing disagreement with the cause or dislike of the person? ☐

## WORK, ACHIEVEMENT, AND ACCOMPLISHMENT AS THE PURPOSE OF LIFE

"Blessed is he who has found his work; let him ask no other blessedness" Thomas Carlyle wrote in 1843, reflecting the high regard in which work has been held in Western society (Carlyle, 1870). A similar idea was expressed by William Osler, a famous British physician, who said that work "is the open sesame to every portal, the great equalizer in the world, the true philosopher's stone which transmutes all the base metal of humanity into gold" (Osler, 1903). Hard work and its fruits are still valued highly in Western culture, despite some contemporary questioning of this attitude.

Choron (1964) suggests that our society places tremendous emphasis upon work in order to avoid having to deal with questions of ultimate meaning. If you work hard enough and long enough, work becomes your ultimate goal, and you'll probably be too tired and too involved to become disturbed over the possibility that your existence is meaningless. Perhaps some of the people who exhaust themselves through community work, humanitarian endeavors, or the quest for power or wealth are hiding from the question of what meaning their lives have.

☐ Do you know people who are so totally involved in activity that they may be avoiding the distressing notion that life is not only finite but without ultimate meaning or purpose? If so, are their achievements any less important or worthy? ☐

Lifelong commitment to work has been, for perhaps most people, the only way to attain such basic biological requirements as food, shelter, and clothing. Something that initially serves the purpose of survival may eventually take on the mystique of value in itself. Whether or not the value attributed to work originated in this way, work does provide many with a purpose *in* life and a few (who may not even realize it) with a purpose *of* life. People expend great effort to attain such concrete symbols of work achievement as goods or capital, track records, books published, and tributes from the Chamber of Commerce or the union local. The satisfaction arising from a job well done or an important service provided, although not involving visible rewards, also reflects an effort that can readily become a purpose in life. Although perhaps few people would claim that work is the purpose of life, many behave as though they lived in order to work.

## SALVATION AND OTHER COSMIC PURPOSES OF LIFE

Serving God in the anticipation of some form of immortality or salvation has provided many people with a purpose in living and, for some, has constituted the purpose of life. Throughout a great deal of Western history, it was taken for granted that the purpose of existence was to serve God and attain salvation. Life on earth was simply a test of faith that determined a person's fitness for an eternal life of grace and oneness with God. (A somewhat similar notion is found in the East, especially in the branch of Hinduism called *Bhakti Yoga*.) We can trace at least some elements of this idea of cosmic purpose back to Plato, several centuries prior to the advent of Christianity. He believed that everything has a unique purpose, a special function for which it is especially fit. The function of humans is to come to know the eternal reality that stands behind this sensed world of appearances. Cornford (1941), in his notes on Plato's *Republic*, puts it this way: "[Plato] held that man's happiness consists in the full realization of his characteristic virtue and function, and that his virtue, as a rational being, is a clear insight into the end of life, 'knowledge of the Good,' the Good being for Plato the highest reality" (p. 8).

Perhaps you agree with the poet James Montgomery (1771–1854), who wrote in "The Issues of Life and Death":

> Beyond this vale of tears
> There is a life above,
> Unmeasured by the flight of years;
> And all that life is love.

Or, perhaps you take a more optimistic view of potential enjoyment in this life, believing that you serve God best by serving others or by actualizing your potential as a person. Either way, it seems natural to hope that being on earth has meaning or purpose that extends beyond your own relatively brief existence. Self-centered purposes cease with death—the self-actualizing you do, the goods you accumulate, your sexual prowess, all afford you nothing after your death. Social causes last longer, but eventually they succeed, change, or cease to be important. What you produce or create rarely has permanence, and eventually you will cease to exist even as a memory.

In the absence of a cosmic purpose, then, the significance of what you do in your life may end with your death. In fact, some writers feel that the lack of a sense of cosmic purpose accounts for the considerable fear of death evident in our culture (Becker, 1973). A cosmic purpose can diminish the awesomeness of death by giving your life meaning into infinity. If, for example, the Judaeo-Christian God exists, then by serving God and satisfying God's purpose, you can spend your life on earth in tune with the universe, on a mission of infinite importance. And even if there is no such God, there might still be a cosmic purpose of life. According to the Eastern concepts of karma and reincarnation, our selves predate and outlive our bodies, but the things we do affect our future state. Thus the Hindu tells us that each life can move the self closer to Ultimate Reality. If this is right, then our lives do have cosmic purpose, and our actions reach far into the future.

□ But is the Judaeo-Christian God real? How can you know? And in the face of doubt, where, if anywhere, can you look for meaning? The idea of reincarnation sometimes sounds very plausible, but is there any real reason to think it is correct? Or is it just wishful thinking, a whistling-in-the-dark hope for immortality? □

## PERHAPS LIFE HAS NO ULTIMATE PURPOSE

Perhaps you're wondering at this point why we should bother searching for an ultimate meaning. Why not just live life without all this intellectual fuss? No problem—if you can do it. The difficulty is that many people feel the need for a purpose of life in order to give meaning to their brief visit to earth. For many people, a sense of meaninglessness is a very distressing and even devastating feeling.

Nevertheless, some existentialist authors, such as Sartre and Camus, have contended that people should have the strength to admit that the only purpose of life is living. The existentialists contend that an individual who can accept the meaninglessness of life is better able to deal with the present moment as it goes by, since that moment exists for itself and is unrelated to some ultimate purpose.

Much of the strength of the existentialist point of view developed during and just after World War II, when death was imminent for so many people as the result of a chance encounter with violence. Perhaps living under the constant possibility of global holocaust, in which aggressors, victims, and bystanders are all likely to die, contributes to the belief that life is absurd. On the other hand, Viktor Frankl and Bruno Bettelheim both wrote of having meaningful and valued experiences while living under the most horrible of conditions in Nazi concentration camps. Facing disaster, then, does not necessarily produce nihilism. Could you find meaning while living in such a setting? Might your ability to live through such an experience depend upon finding meaning?

## ALIENATION AND PURPOSE

The famous 19th-century philosopher Nietzsche (1844–1900) once wrote "He who has a *why* to live can bear with almost any *how*." To this we would add that people who have no *why* to live will find alienation in any *how*. And suddenly we are only a short distance from the theme with which we began this book: "If you don't know where you're going, any road will take you there."

One of the most popular terms of the 1960s and early 1970s was *alienation*. An alien is variously defined as a stranger, a foreigner, an outsider, someone who is estranged from or unrelated to the community being discussed. From this root meaning the present use of the term *alienation* to describe a mental or emotional state evolved most understandably. Even though the concept is not so widely used now as it was a few years ago, we believe it is still a very useful one. One psychologist (Gold, 1969) has suggested that alienation has three interrelated meanings.

1. "One meaning of alienation is this: not part of those regulating systems, social or supernatural, which give structure and meaning to existence, which tame the passions, and which enable the human animal to realize his potential for humanity" (Gold, 1969, p. 122). As Rollo May (1967) suggests, people who look upon themselves as being insignificant and therefore powerless cease to feel responsibility and are no longer influenced by "the system."

2. The converse of "The system doesn't influence me" is "I don't influence the system," and this is a second meaning of alienation. When people feel that they lack power or influence, they experience frustration that may take the form of resignation or revolution. Resignation is expressed by May (1967) as "Why load yourself with responsibility if what you do doesn't matter anyway?" (p. 30). To illustrate, students of the 1960s who worked for civil rights or whose protests contributed to Lyndon Johnson's decision not to seek an additional

term as President believed that their actions made a difference. When social inequities and war continued, however, many of them came to feel that their impact was meaningless and that change was out of their hands. Whether they turned to apathy or to anger, they tended to see themselves as no longer part of the world they once knew.

3. The two previous definitions of alienation refer to individuals' estrangement from their social environment. The third meaning of the term concerns *self-estrangement*, in which people feel unrelated to themselves. It's very difficult to understand what this form of alienation is like unless you know through your own experience or intuition. Some of the expressions used to describe this phenomenon include "He lacks connectedness," "She isn't a whole person," "He isn't living an authentic life." Self-estrangement occurs when what people do isn't personally meaningful or is meaningful only in that it leads to some form of external reward. For example, Karl Marx talks about the alienation of workers whose work has meaning only in the income that it produces, not in itself. The same idea might be applied to students who aren't interested in the process of learning except insofar as it leads to a college degree that might be exchangeable for a job and subsequent material gain. Much of what these students do in school has little or no meaning for them in itself.

Erich Fromm (1941) once referred to this alienation from self as *moral aloneness*, which he rightfully claimed can be just as destructive as physical aloneness. Moral aloneness is not necessarily the outcome of living in isolation; a monk in his cell or a political prisoner may not be morally alone, whereas an individual "may live among people and yet be overcome with an utter feeling of isolation" (p. 19).

Another analysis of alienation is based upon the excellent novel by Albert Camus, *The Stranger*. The alienated person, the stranger, is described by Weisskopf-Joelson (1968) as: (1) indifferent, detached, aloof; (2) experiencing the world as unintelligible, beyond comprehension; (3) being unable to make spontaneous value judgments; (4) being indifferent to decisions that would be vital to others, such as whom to marry and what work to do; and (5) responding to negative motivation more than to positive motivation, being likely to answer "Why not?" when asked the reason for a particular decision. Obviously an alienated person cannot set personal goals. For the stranger, both the inner and the outer world have no substantial personal meaning; nothing matters.

If individuals are alienated only from the outer, objective world, they lose touch with external reality, and mental illness may result. Conversely, when people are alienated from their inner worlds but are in good contact with the objective world, they lack inner guidelines and are likely to conform like marionettes to the whims of their external environment. These people are often termed inauthentic, phony, unreal, plastic, or shallow, because they lack conviction and commitment (Weisskopf-Joelson, 1968).

In contrast to the alienated person, a whole or authentic person has both a rich inner life and a healthy awareness of objective reality, as well as the ability to keep the two in balance. A whole person is not a stranger but a part of society, at home in it. A whole person may or may not believe in a purpose of life. He or she may have learned to tolerate its absence while leaving the question open or decided that no such purpose exists and that it's possible to live with this decision. But it's unlikely that a whole person would lack all purpose *in* life.

These statements do not imply that authentic people accept the world as it is or never experience frustration, even immense frustration. Whole, integrated people can feel angry, unhappy, frustrated, resentful, and even powerless under certain circumstances. They may believe that some segments of society are ineffectual or even evil, and they may prefer to define themselves as functioning outside the "system." However, they can understand the social structure, know where they stand, and keep inner feelings and reality perceptions in balance. Being a whole person, then, requires neither acceptance of the status quo nor its rejection, nor any particular point between.

☐ The preceding paragraphs show our biases, which may not coincide with yours. Look into our biases, try to understand them, and determine whether they dovetail with your own views on alienation, wholeness, and authenticity. If they don't, how would you describe the stranger and the whole person? ☐

## THE INTERACTION OF VALUES AND BEHAVIOR

It should be evident by now that purpose is a concept that involves the interaction of values and behavior. But which comes first: the behavior or the value? That is, does your behavior tend to be consistent with previously developed values, or do you develop values in order to justify your behavior? The answer to these questions is undoubtedly: both. Behavior does tend to remain consistent with previously developed values, and values are developed to justify behavior. The two mechanisms operate together and affect each other. To illustrate, let's consider a few examples.

1. Your best friend has a habit of tossing soft-drink cans out the car window when you're driving together. You're very much upset by this behavior, but when you've mentioned it, she has only made fun of you. You know that you could get her to stop if you made an issue of it. However, you state that you value not interfering with the lives of

others. Which came first: your reluctance to talk firmly to your friend, or your value concerning non-interference?

2. You have strong feelings concerning the relatedness of all people, which you feel is probably the ultimate good. A close friend needs money badly to get out of a scrape, and the only way you can provide it is to sell your stereo. You do it, feeling that you *should*. But was it the value you place on caring for others or feelings of friendship that caused your decision? Would you have done the same for someone you weren't close to?

3. Under the Nazi regime, several million people were killed for no reason other than age, religion, physical health, emotional stability, or political views. The killings were committed by men and women, young and old, Nazi party members and nonmembers. After Germany lost the war, many of these persons claimed that they had acted only because of direct orders from those in power, but many survivors contended that they had shown little hesitancy about obeying these orders. To what extent were values underlying behavior? To what extent did behavior determine values?

Sometimes behavior initiates values; sometimes values initiate behavior. Your approach to the idea of the purpose of life is the outcome of your previous experiences and your present situation; part of your previous experiences and part of your present situation have resulted from your idea of the purpose of life. This value, like the other values you hold, is an intrinsic part of a dynamic, complex entity—*you*.

The same values may be reflected in quite different behavior. For example, a gentle and incorruptible policeman, a fire-and-brimstone preacher, and an eccentric painter might all be guided by the belief that the purpose of life is to serve God. By the same token, the same kind of behavior can result from very dissimilar views. Of two equally conscientious social workers, one might prize personal growth while the other believes in unselfish service to the community.

We've said that the notion of purpose is one of those concepts that incarnates your values in the world of behavior, and we've seen that the relationship of values to behavior is by no means a simple one. At this point you may well ask "If behavior and values determine each other, where is my input? Don't I choose my own values and decide on my own behavior?" These are good questions, and the next chapter is devoted to them.

## REFERENCES

Becker, E. *The denial of death*. New York: Free Press, 1973.
Carlyle, T. *Past and present*. London: Chapman and Hall, 1870.
Choron, J. *Modern man and mortality*. New York: Macmillan, 1964.

Cornford, F. *The republic of Plato*. New York: Oxford University Press, 1941.

Fromm, E. *Escape from freedom*. New York: Holt, Rinehart & Winston, 1941.

Fromm, E. *The art of loving*. New York: Harper, 1956.

Gold, M. Juvenile delinquency as a symptom of alienation. *Journal of Social Issues*, April 1969, *25*,121–135.

Greer, T. H. *A brief history of Western man*. New York: Harcourt, Brace, 1968.

Maddi, S. R. The search for meaning. *Nebraska symposium on motivation*, 1970, *18*,137–186.

Mann, H. *Commencement address*. Antioch College, 1859.

May, R. *Psychology and the human dilemma*. New York: Van Nostrand, 1967.

Osler, W. The master-word in medicine. Lecture, Toronto, October 1903.

Randall, J. H. *The making of the modern mind*. Boston: Houghton Mifflin, 1940.

Weisskopf-Joelson, E. Meaning as an integrating factor. In C. Buhler & F. Massarik (Eds.), *The course of human life*. New York: Springer, 1968.

# CHAPTER 2

## FREEDOM AND DETERMINISM

Are you free? Were you ever free?

The concepts of political, religious, and academic freedom are well known; the related but very different concept of individual freedom, freedom of the person, is much less discussed. Yet your ideas of right and wrong, of criminality, responsibility, and social welfare, all depend on the assumptions you make with regard to individual freedom.

Asked their position on freedom of choice, most people would probably say "I'm in favor—people should be free to choose." Then they might go on to expound the virtues of being able to travel without interference, attend the church of their choice, support political candidates without fear of punishment, or dress as they prefer. These political, social, and personal freedoms, which are part of human institutions and can be given or taken away, are all vitally important, but they are not at issue here. Our concern is with the psychological and philosophical issue of whether people are genuinely free to choose their own destinies or whether their lives are, in effect, designed for them by forces outside of their ability to influence in any meaningful fashion.

# FREE WILL AND DETERMINISM

The two basic points of view on the issue of personal freedom are usually referred to as *free will* and *determinism*, although other words are also used—predestination, fate, will, volition, and so forth. Those espousing free will normally claim that human beings are free to choose their destinies, that they can elect to behave as they will (at least within broad limits). In other words, the course of our lives is not totally controlled by fate, God, predestination, nature, heredity, or environment. To account for this personal freedom, some quality is believed to exist within each person such that the person is more than the sum of his or her bodily make-up and experiences in life. This quality is frequently called the *soul*, but it could also be called *the essential you* or *the true self*.

Some philosophers distinguish between humans considered as *Homo sapiens*, the human *animal*, and humans considered as human *beings*, or persons, on the basis of this quality. As *Homo sapiens*, humans can be expected to be driven by determining forces like any other animal, but as human beings they can choose, and in choosing realize their true natures. Some, especially those who accept the Judaeo-Christian picture of the world, see this quality as given by God, and indeed as the image of God in us. Others, such as Plato, come to this conclusion by studying the nature of humanity, by asking what makes us human.

There are two general versions of determinism, "hard" or Newtonian determinism and "soft" determinism. Hard determinism underlies the physics of Isaac Newton. To understand it, think of a ball on a pool table—say, the eight ball. We could predict exactly where the eight ball will go when it is hit by the cue ball if we knew enough about both balls. We'd have to know such things as how fast the cue ball was going, what its spin was, at what angle it hit the eight ball, and so on. But if we knew all those things, we could tell exactly where the eight ball would go. In fact, one essential skill in playing pool well is being able to make the right predictions.

The hard determinist maintains that all events, even human decisions, are like the rolling eight ball. If we knew enough about conditions before the event, we could predict the event exactly. If this position is correct, then everything you do, from waking up at 7:10 in the morning to having beer and pizza for dinner to going to bed after the 11:00 news, could be predicted by someone with enough information about you. Although this task might be too intricate and complicated for anyone to actually carry out, in principle it could be done if someone cared to—and had a big enough computer.

The soft determinist agrees with the hard determinist that some events are like the rolling eight balls but maintains that not all events are predictable in this way, even in principle. Consider the fertilization of an egg. There are millions of sperm in every ejaculation, so the chances of any given sperm being the one to fertilize the egg are vanishingly small; which one it will be seems to be a matter of chance. Of course, the hard determinist will respond that what seems to be a chance encounter only appears so because of the incredible complexity of prediction and that, in principle, this event is no less predictable (or determined) than the outcome of a pool shot.

If the soft determinist is right, there is room in human affairs for chance events. If the encounter of *this* sperm and *this* egg is random, then why not the encounter of this man and this woman? Or the event of being born in a given nation, at a given time, of a certain race? A soft determinist does not necessarily believe in free will but only that some events cannot be exactly predicted. Some soft determinists allow an element of choice in some of these unpredictable events, and some do not. Either way, soft determinism represents an intermediate position between free will and hard determinism.

Although physicists and other natural scientists tend to accept some form of determinism, determinism is not the exclusive property of science. Many theologians accept it too, with God as the Determiner. Such a view might allow for the possibility of miracles, or divine interventions that do not follow from the laws God has established to govern the universe. Hard determinists would find such apparent exceptions to natural law very strange and would expect to eventually find the laws from which they could have been predicted. Soft determinists might simply say that they were examples of unpredictable events. It all depends on how soft their determinism is.

## FATALISM AND PREDESTINATION

Fatalism and predestination should not be confused with determinism, although they are similar in certain respects. Fatalism assumes that our ultimate end has been determined in advance. If you're fated to be successful, or if you're fated to die without children, nothing you can do will change these outcomes. Fatalists do not necessarily assume that each specific act is determined, as long as the end result is the same. The following legend expresses this concept well:

> A merchant was spending a week in a strange city, when he came to feel uneasy. Turning around, he saw Death walking close behind him, and he was horrified to notice a strange look upon Death's face. He quickly returned to his lodging, took his belongings, leaped upon his horse, and fled back to his home city. As the merchant fled, Death turned to his companion: "That's odd—I didn't expect to see him here—I had an appointment with him tomorrow at his home."

Not every step of the merchant's life was preordained, but the time and place of his death were indeed predestined. Fatalism in the form of predestination has been part of the philosophies of St. Augustine, Martin Luther, and John Calvin. It is expressed by the Spanish *Que sera, sera* ("What will be, will be") and by the Japanese *Ikata ganai* ("It cannot be helped").

Although one can believe in predestination without believing in God, predestination is easiest to understand in theistic terms. Imagine that you're playing in an orchestra and that God has written the symphony. In this particular symphony you are free to play any note you wish, but, as you play, God so alters the music that it always comes out as intended. You have free will concerning the individual notes, but God has already figured out how the symphony will progress and ensures that it does so.

Compare this kind of fatalism with the position of the hard determinist. According to hard determinism, every event is predictable if we have enough information about prior events. Since every event is determined by preceding events, we are powerless to alter not only our ultimate fates but also every event between now and then. This is fatalism with a vengeance!

□ Some people have argued that a commitment to the truth of any future-tensed propositions, such as "It will rain tomorrow," involves a commitment to fatalism. If this argument interests you, think about why someone would think it valid, and try to argue against it. □

The issue of free will and determinism is a complex one. Philosophers, theologians, scientists, and just plain folks have debated it and been perplexed by it since ancient times. We will not resolve the issue in this book, of course, but we do invite you to consider how basic an issue it is. Before examining some of its philosophical and psychological implications, however, let's look at some of the attempts philosophers have made to understand and resolve this question of free will versus determinism.

# PHILOSOPHICAL ATTEMPTS TO RESOLVE THE ISSUE OF FREE WILL AND DETERMINISM

The principle of causality—that is, the principle that every event has a cause—is presumed by most forms of determinism. The Dutch philosopher Benedict de Spinoza (1632–1677) devised an interesting solution to the problem of how to reconcile this principle with the notion of free will. Spinoza believed that whether or not we have free will depends entirely on one's point of view. Consider your decision about what to eat for breakfast this morning. You probably weighed such factors as flavor, ease of preparation, how much time you had, and so on, making up your mind all on your own. From your point of view, it was a free choice. According to Spinoza, however, everything that happens in the universe follows necessary laws that are implicit in the nature of God. Being omniscient, God knows quite explicitly what effects these laws will bring about. In particular, God knew before you made your decision what it was going to be and what factors would cause you to make up your mind as you did. From God's point of view, then, our actions are *not* free; from our point of view, they are.

We can illustrate Spinoza's idea with the following fantasy. Imagine having built a computer that has a subjective awareness of its actions. You've built your computer well, and you know that, if you tell it to add 7 and 5, it must come up with 12. From your point of view the computer has no choice. But now imagine the same event from the computer's point of view: "Well, let's see. I've got these two numbers, 7 and 5, and I have a notion to add them. What will the sum be? I could pick almost any number. Oh, I don't know; I think I'll pick 12." It appears to the computer that its decision was free. Was it? It depends on your point of view.

Although the principle of causality may seem obviously sound, the Scottish philosopher David Hume (1711–1776) questioned how we *know* that one event causes another. Let's look at what we actually see happening. In the case of the eight ball, what do we observe? The cue ball approaches the eight ball with a certain velocity and spin; the balls collide; the balls roll away from each other. What we see, Hume noticed, is simply a succession of events. This event happens, and then that one, and then another. We do *not* see one event causing another at all! So how do we know about causes? Indeed, what reason is there for thinking that the principle of causality is true? At this point Hume went away muttering something about its being a "habit of thought" that one event causes another.

□ If Hume's answer sounds a little silly to you, ask yourself just how you do *know* (not merely come to *believe*) that the cue ball's hitting the eight ball *causes* the eight ball to roll away. Notice that you can't appeal to causality here. It won't do to say, for instance, "Well, nothing else could cause the ball to roll." Whether events *must* have causes is just the question at issue. But if the principle of causality is suspect, how can we ever make sure inferences from the past to the future? We can *expect* events in the future to be like those of the past, but can we have any certain ground for *knowing* they will be? If not, what is the basis for the inductive reasoning on which science depends? □

The German philosopher Immanuel Kant (1724–1804) read Hume's work and took up the puzzle himself. His reflections culminated in one of the most influential books in the Western philosophical tradition, *The Critique of Pure Reason*. Without attempting to do justice to the complexity and subtlety of Kant's thought, let's look at the main features of his response to Hume.

Kant begins by asking how any human knowledge is possible. What is necessary in order for us to be beings that *know*? Kant argued that a number of conditions must be met in order for us to have the coherent perceptions of the world that we in fact have. For example, he claimed that it is necessary for us to put things in a spatial order and in some kind of time order. Similarly, the coherence of our experience depends on our putting events into a causal order. So, according to Kant, the necessity of ordering events causally is an inseparable part of the human mind. This does not mean that all minds (such as those of angels or Martians) must order things causally; that is something we cannot know. But we *can* know that, for a mind to be a *human* mind, it must order events causally. Thus, we don't establish the principle of causality by looking at its operation in the world. Rather, we can look at and know things in the world because causality is a fundamental principle of the operation of the human mind. Our experience doesn't *demonstrate* that the principle of causality is true; it *presupposes* it.

There is a difficulty with this solution, however. If the principle of causality holds universally in our experience, what happens to moral responsibility? Kant noticed that, to be morally responsible for our actions, we must be free to make our own choices. But our actions are also events in the world. If they all must be understood in terms of laws of causality, then we have no choice in what we do and cannot be held responsible for our behavior. For example, suppose that your action in taking this course follows from the laws of causality. Then you have no choice and no control; it is inevitable that you take this course, just as it is inevitable that you pass or fail it. But if you have no choice or control, how can you be held responsible? When confronted, your obvious response is "Don't blame me; I had no choice."

Kant tried to solve this difficulty by separating the moral realm from the physical realm. In another important book, *The Critique of Practical Reason*, he tried to discover and analyze how we, as human beings, operate morally. Just as our experience of the physical world depends on certain fundamental principles of the human mind, so also our experience of the moral world depends on fundamental moral principles that are equally a part of the human mind. One of these principles is that the will is free. Without this principle, no moral order would be possible.

Kant thus tried to have both hard determinism and free will by separating the two. Both principles are so fundamental to the human mind that it is impossible to conceive of human beings without them. But they operate in different realms of our thought. Because of this separation, any contradiction between them is only apparent and can be removed by a careful understanding of the distinction between the moral realm and the physical realm.

A very different approach to the problem was taken by the American philosopher and psychologist William James (1842–1910). James was a leading figure in the movement called *pragmatism*. For James, the function of ideas is to make sense of the world; an idea is true for you to the extent that it serves this function. If an idea doesn't *work*—that is, if it doesn't help you make a coherent whole out of the world—then it isn't true for you. Notice that, for this viewpoint, an idea is true or false *for you* and not simply true or false.

In an essay entitled "What Pragmatism Is," James (1966) likened ideas to the rooms of an apartment house or a hotel. People come in, look at the apartments, and move into those that they find comfortable. One of these apartments is labeled "Free Will," another is labeled "Soft Determinism," and a third is labeled "Hard Determinism." There is no ultimate answer to the conflict between these ideas; the only answers are the ones that individual people find useful.

This sampling of answers presented by Western philosophers to the free will/determinism issue should give you some idea of the immense complexity of the problem and the difficulty of arriving at a satisfactory solution. Even without explicitly thinking about the issue, however, we all make assumptions about the origins of human behavior, assumptions that are based, at least in part, on our (usually unconscious) stand on this huge philosophical problem. And the stand we take has widespread implications for issues of everyday life.

# IMPLICATIONS OF FREE WILL AND DETERMINISM

Very few people assume that we are completely free; many more take the hard-determinist position. Your views needn't fall at either extreme in order to influence your behavior, your values, and your responses to others. Nor do you ever need to come out and say directly that you have a particular belief about free will or determinism. Your behavior reflects implicit, as well as explicit, philosophical assumptions. In this section we outline how your views on free will and determinism might affect your judgments concerning mental illness, criminal behavior, and social welfare.

# MENTAL ILLNESS

There is a constant tension between determinism and free will in discussions of mental illness. On the one hand, there do appear to be determinants of illness. On the other hand, people can overcome these forces, and it often seems that part of overcoming them is having the belief that one can and will improve. This tension is well illustrated by the following account written by a teacher.

I received my last note from Steve about three weeks before his second suicide attempt was successful. When I had visited with him about eighteen months prior to that, he was deeply depressed and most eager to tell me how he felt. As he spoke, it was obvious that he had rehearsed this talk—indeed, I later learned that his wife had spent so many hours hearing him talk endlessly about why he was depressed that she was actively considering suicide herself, neither an unusual nor an incomprehensible response. As Steve talked, it became obvious that there was nothing in his immediate life situation to cause the depression. His job was challenging, and he was meeting the challenge; his children were basically healthy and offered him their unquestioning love; his wife, although nearly exhausted by his extreme dependence on her, was receiving enough satisfaction from her work and children to be supportive of Steve; his financial situation, a matter that concerned Steve more than most people, was not up to his expectations, but was advancing at a sufficiently rapid rate to make him a wealthy man by his early fifties. The world was not perfect for Steve, but it was pretty good. And he had no complaints about external conditions.

But he was depressed, deeply depressed. He had switched psycho-therapists twice within four months, without noticeable change or improvement. And he talked with irritating glibness about his early life, a succession of foster home placements with sporadic visits to his own mother, an alcoholic, or his own father, remarried and not even slightly interested; he discussed these early dynamics with objectivity and insight; he described the dynamics that led to his marriage and what kept it going, in spite of the tension; he talked fluently about the role of work, children, psychotherapy, and money in his life.

Perhaps I should have known better, or perhaps I was correct but with insufficient influence. The way Steve talked, I felt that he could *will* himself out of his situation. With his insight, his intelligence, his high degree of discomfort, it objectively seemed that all he needed was enough will and he could see how well things were going for him, shake off the depression, and return to his previously happy—at least moderately happy—life. His psychotherapists had failed with their attempts at providing insight and understanding; so I encouraged him to use his will to perform small tasks, believing that success with these tasks would permit him to build, until he was able to return to his regular functioning.

But he killed himself anyway. His early life was too powerful to overthrow—or perhaps the experts, the psychotherapists and physicians and friends and relatives, missed the key. It always seemed to me that all he needed was enough will, but I underestimated whatever other forces were operative. His life history was obviously more powerful than his attempts to exert his will.

If you take a position espousing considerable free will in human behavior, you may be inclined to believe that mentally ill persons, alcoholics, compulsive gamblers, heavy smokers, or obese persons can overcome their difficulties "if they really want to." As a therapist, a spouse, or a friend, you would probably focus your attempts to assist such persons on their will and volition.

If such a view of free will implies that the mentally ill, for example, have no one to blame but themselves and would snap out of it if only they decided to, then we think it is a rather naive and sometimes dangerous view. A good example of the danger is the attitude of the Spanish Inquisition during the late 15th and early 16th centuries.

At this time, the Catholic leaders of Spain were so persuaded of their own righteous goals that they unmercifully tortured and killed their opponents, particularly Jews and Muslims. Among those who felt their anger, however, were people we would now call mentally ill. The leaders of the Inquisition took the position that people whose behavior was bizarre or disordered behaved as they did because they had, of their own free wills, made agreements with the Devil. Burning them in a religious ritual was thought to be merely an appropriate and necessary method of cleansing them of the infesting Devil.

Although the tactics of the Inquisition were uncommonly cruel, the belief that people are totally responsible for their conditions was generally held in Europe until the late 19th century. Thus there was no reason to provide the mentally ill with care and treatment, since they could get better themselves "if they really wanted to." The objective was rather to prevent them from harming others by segregating them from society, at the cost of letting innocent people rot in prisons or die slowly of starvation and exposure while begging. Of course, at the time these people were not seen as *innocent*; rather, they were thought to be guilty of consorting with the Devil or of willful and malicious behavior.

It is easy to believe that the mentally ill could rid themselves of their symptoms if only they would will themselves to get better. ("The trouble with the mentally ill is that they won't face reality.") But the fact of the matter seems to be that very often people cannot heal themselves alone no matter how much they want to. It may be that a decision to "get better" is necessary; the question is the extent to which people can make this decision and adhere to it by themselves, without help and without changes in their physical and social environments.

Perhaps mental illness is largely determined, and free will has little to do with it. If so, then we can try to influence the determinants of mental illness in order to prevent or cure it. For example, suppose a particular form of mental illness is caused by inadequate parenting in the early years. We might then attempt to reduce the occurrence of the disorder by preventing poor parenting through education and other means. For people who are already mature, we might try to reverse the illness by helping them understand the role of their parents, obtain and learn to accept substitutes for the deprivations they have experienced, and feel more adequate as persons.

If mental illness is *wholly* determined, so that the mentally ill have no choice at all, then we can (at least in principle) impose effective treatment on them whether they will it or not. We don't need to worry about their will to improve or their courage to maintain their improvement.

Most people today take it for granted that mental illness is at least partially determined. Nevertheless, there is considerable disagreement over how much control the mentally ill can exercise over their own behavior. Clearly, your assumptions about free will have significant implications for your view of mental illness.

□ If mental illness is wholly determined, an interesting and important question is whether we have the right to force treatment on people with behavioral disorders. What do you think? If people are not free to will themselves to become healthy (or sick), does it matter whether they consent to their treatment?

The notion of mental illness as determined raises other provocative and difficult questions. For example: If the mentally ill are not to be held responsible because their condition and behavior are determined, what about people who aren't mentally ill? If they are determined by positive factors to be "sane," are they any more responsible than the mentally ill for what they do? Is behavior determined only when it is bizarre and free only when it is acceptable? If so, acceptable to whom? If you believe that people are basically responsible for what they do, do you think that people who exhibit behavioral disorders should be punished rather than treated? If not, do you see any inconsistency in your position? □

## ILLEGAL BEHAVIOR

Another important issue that is affected by the free will/determinism controversy is that of individual responsibility versus collective guilt in the context of criminal behavior. Over the centuries, the most common position has been that the individual lawbreaker, and no one else, is responsible for the criminal act and should be appropriately punished. But consider this classic problem, immortalized in Victor Hugo's novel *Les Miserables*. A parent cannot find work, not because of laziness or lack of effort, but because there simply aren't enough jobs to go around. The children are hungry, ill, and inadequately clothed. In desperation, the parent turns to crime.

Is the parent, having free will, responsible for the crime? Is society responsible because it has failed to provide adequately for all its members? Some would take the position that, even though society bears the major share of responsibility for the crime, the parent must be punished because society cannot function unless individuals are held legally responsible for their acts. But is it fair to punish a person whom we absolve of moral guilt?

It's important to distinguish here between *legal* responsibility and *moral* responsibility. We are *legally* responsible for whatever actions fall under the law, whether or not these actions, in themselves, have any moral implications. For example, we are legally accountable for which side of the street we drive down, but the bare action of driving down the left side of a street has no moral force at all (though its consequences certainly might). At the same time, we might well bring *moral* blame on ourselves for actions the law totally ignores. For example, in some societies, including our own not so long ago, the law has allowed some people to own others and force them to do almost anything. But surely this is not morally acceptable.

□ In the context of the free will/determinism problem, then, there are two sets of difficulties: those that grow out of morally unacceptable behavior and those that grow out of legally unacceptable behavior. In this section we are primarily addressing the question of legal responsibility, but we invite you to apply the discussion to moral responsibility as well. □

In the musical *West Side Story*, some of the members of the Jets gang sing to Officer Kruppke "My sister has a moustache, my father wears a dress . . . No wonder I'm a mess." The Jets blame, or at least pretend to blame, social conditions for their illegal behavior. In the context of the show, the Jets are obviously using their guilt-denying device to manipulate the legal authorities. However, the fact that they know they're playing a game by blaming society for their unacceptable behavior doesn't necessarily mean that their claim is false.

This issue of the motive for using a certain argument comes up frequently in discussions of criminal responsibility. Consider the following example. John Q. Criminal comes from a broken home, was forced to leave school to help support younger siblings, and was cheated out of his job by a larcenous employer. John Q. turns to burglary as a means of support. Arrested and convicted for breaking and entering, he begs the judge for leniency because of his stressful life history, and the judge puts him on probation. Later John Q. snickers over the way he outwitted the judge with his story of being forced into a life of crime. All that John Q.'s insincerity implies is that he accepts the notions of free will and individual responsibility, whereas the judge is more of a determinist. John Q.'s attitude undoubtedly has implications for his later behavior, but it does not establish that the judge was wrong in surmising that his early life, over which he had no control, partially determined his criminal behavior. Nor does it entail that John Q. was wrong in thinking that his plea was just a story. What it implies is that the judge and John Q. have different views.

In 1843 a British murder case led to the establishment in England of the so-called M'Naghten rules in cases involving pleas of insanity. The rules state that people are not responsible for a crime if, because of a "defect of reason" or "disease of the mind," they are unaware when committing the crime that the action is wrong. A common rule of thumb has been the policeman-at-the-elbow approach. Would the person have committed the crime if there had been a policeman observing? If not, then presumably the person knew the action was illegal, and he or she cannot be excused by reason of insanity.

Notice that the M'Naghten rules assume that people who are not mentally ill can, of their free will, resist any criminal impulses. This assumption has led to considerable criticism of the rules by mental-health professionals and others, who argue that it implies a very naive view of human behavior. All of us sometimes do things we know are wrong, because we feel powerless to hold back. For example, suppose you know that a particular mannerism of yours, such as cracking your knuckles, drives your spouse to distraction. On the one hand, you know that cracking your knuckles seriously irritates someone else; on the other hand, you just can't seem to keep yourself from doing it. If you can generalize from this kind of incident to the performance of criminal acts, you may be able to see why the M'Naghten rules have been widely criticized. Of course, the question remains whether the inability to control one's behavior in a particular case is a sufficient reason to be absolved of responsibility for a crime. That is the real problem.

In theory, at least, extreme determinists would have to maintain that no individual is responsible for criminal behavior, since that behavior results necessarily from determining factors such as the will of God or the person's background or genetic make-up. If people are not personally responsible for their actions, then it is as unfair to punish them for crimes as it would be to punish a computer for coming up with the wrong answers, when it is the programmer who has made the mistake.

Advocates of complete free will, on the other hand, must claim that people do things because they decide to, and, in particular, that criminals commit crimes because they decide to. Some of those who believe in free will argue that swift, severe, and fair punishment should be a part of law because it influences people's wills against committing crimes. Others who question whether punishment deters nevertheless argue in favor of punishment on the grounds that the very act of committing a crime makes a person both legally and morally guilty. Consequently, society has a right, and perhaps even a duty, to punish the criminal.

Free-will advocates are more likely to stress persuading criminals to obey the law than changing society so that it does not produce criminals. Determinists, in contrast, usually concentrate on what they perceive as the underlying causes of crime and would attempt to rehabilitate criminals by optimizing whatever factors cause acceptable behavior. Since studies show that negative reinforcement (punishment for unacceptable behavior) is less effective than positive reinforcement (reward for acceptable behavior), determinists often do not think much of punishment as a deterrent but do sometimes accept it as one tool to be used in rehabilitation efforts.

Despite their differences, advocates of both positions will sometimes recommend the same approach for dealing with criminals, though for different reasons. Those who accept free will, for example, might encourage undereducated criminals to complete their education, reasoning that further education might lead them to understand the full impact of their actions and help persuade them to refrain from crime. Determinists might try the same tactic, reasoning that a lack of education is one part of a constellation of causes that can ultimately lead to criminal behavior. The identity of approach should not obscure the difference in the attitudes of the two groups toward the criminal.

Both positions, of course, can be stretched to the point of irrationality. On the free-will side, people sometimes say that, no matter what kind of treatment criminals receive, they have no cause for complaint. "They've asked for whatever they get and have no one to blame but themselves." On the determinist side, some people condone the practice of forcing lawbreakers to undergo intense programs of behavior modification.

☐ Clearly we are dealing in this section with some critical issues. How ought we to treat criminals, and why? If crime is a matter of free will, is punishment appropriate? Even capital punishment? How could we successfully appeal to criminals' wills so that they would be more likely to obey the law? And wouldn't that really be sneaking determinism in the back door by trying to alter people's wills? Is criminality akin to mental illness? Have we the right to "treat" it without the consent of the criminal?

And what of the connection between moral and legal obligations? Is a legal obligation automatically also a moral obligation? If so, what are we to do with a law that requires us to act immorally? How can civil disobedience be justified? How closely should the law mirror a moral code? Whose code? □

## SOCIAL WELFARE

Persons receiving payments from social welfare are presumably unable to earn a sufficient income. These people include children in disadvantaged families and their mothers, as well as elderly people who are unable to support themselves adequately because they have retired from one career and are unable to obtain work, or because they lack marketable skills, or because they have lost some of their capabilities through accident, illness, or the aging process. In addition, the physically or mentally disabled and the unemployed also receive social welfare.

At first blush, it might appear that free-will advocates would say that these people had freedom of choice and therefore chose the paths that led them to where they are now. "It's too bad, but you made your bed; now lie in it." A more sophisticated free-will position, however, would take into account that some of these people, such as children, the handicapped, and the incapacitated elderly, couldn't possibly have chosen their situation. Since we as a society are able to provide the care these people need, free-will advocates may argue that we have a duty to do so.

In addition, even those who contend that people freely choose their destinies might agree that human beings do not all start in the same place, with the same choices open to them. They might also agree that human beings are not always insightful, wise, or intelligent enough to make nothing but correct choices. Thus, when people make choices that lead to trouble, whether these choices are the best ones available or tragic mistakes, free-will advocates may allow that they are still worthy of help.

Consider, for example, a teacher who has given an arithmetic assignment. Not every student will make all the right choices, and it would be silly of the teacher to say "Gee, Johnny, it's a shame that you chose all the wrong answers, but you did it, not me. You'll just have to live with not knowing the right answers." Instead, any sensible teacher will help Johnny, so that he can learn to make the right choices.

Just so, people who adhere to a free-will position may accept the contention that people inevitably botch things up occasionally and need help when they do. They might argue, however, that such help should be limited to assisting people to correct their mistakes and carry on from there. Consequently, welfare should be a temporary measure, aimed at putting people back on their feet and sending them on their way.

Determinists usually advocate some form of social welfare, arguing that, as in everything else, people are at the mercy of heredity, past and present environment, and all the other causes that impel them to action. If people are dealt a short hand, they're not to blame, and it's only humane to help them out. The help determinists advocate, however, usually is much more extensive and permanent than that envisioned by free-will adherents. Determinists are likely to argue that "putting people back on their feet" entails changing the factors that cause their behavior.

As with crime and punishment, both parties might sometimes do some of the same things, but with very different attitudes and very different ends in view. These basic attitudes and goals are of the highest importance, because they govern how we perceive and treat other people.

□ Many questions could be raised here that would be similar to those we've asked in previous sections of this chapter. Instead of repeating ourselves, we'd like to make a suggestion: Go back over your positions on the issues raised in the preceding sections, and try to understand whether free will or determinism is implicit in those positions. Have you been consistently on one side of the free will/determinism issue? Or are there inconsistencies in your beliefs? □

## DETERMINISM AND THE SCIENCES

We noted earlier that most scientists tend to accept some form of determinism. A half-century ago most physical scientists could have been characterized as hard determinists, but the determinism of scientists is getting softer all the time. One impetus to a soft version of determinism came in the 1930s from some revolutionary discoveries in the branch of physics called *quantum mechanics*. We cannot describe these discoveries in detail here, but essentially they call into question whether every event in the physical world can be exactly predicted, even in principle. In addition to this development, there has been a revolution in the philosophical understanding of science that also serves to soften the determinism of those affected by it. Since much of this book is concerned with the science of psychology, we'd like to give a brief sketch of this philosophical revolution.

Until recently, it was thought that the laws of nature were objective realities, built into the very foundations of the universe and utterly unaffected by our knowledge of them. It was left to human beings to discover them if they could. This attitude, however, is increasingly being called into question.

Ask yourself what reason there is for thinking that there are unchanging, objective laws built into the basic order of things. How could we know either that such laws existed or that they did not? To borrow a page from Hume, all we ever experience is a succession of events, and that would be true whether or not there were fundamental laws underlying them.

Think of the stars, and ask whether some constellations exist objectively, while others are just fanciful imaginings projected onto the stars to make order out of the chaos of the sky. The answer should be clear: no constellation is "real"; they are all human artifacts. Now, consider the stars as analogous to events in the world. It has been plausibly suggested that the laws of nature, like the constellations, are projected by humans onto events to provide order where otherwise there would be chaos. If this is correct, then any body of laws we devise is acceptable as long as it is coherent and fits events as we encounter them.

There is thus a great deal of disagreement among scientists and philosophers concerning how hard a determinism is needed to explain events. Most contemporary physicists and chemists, impressed with quantum physics, reject the rigid determinism of Newtonian thought. But the import of quantum physics is controversial. Some, like Einstein, have argued that a strict determinism is still possible. Others accept the view that some events are inherently unpredictable and thus not wholly determined. Still others are trying to rethink the notions of causality and determinism in a way that will be compatible with quantum physics.

Disagreement on this issue also appears in biology, where some think that biological phenomena can all be explained in terms of physics and chemistry, while others believe that there is more to life than an incredibly complicated chemical reaction. And disagreement also appears in psychology. Roughly, there are two camps, distinguished by the strength of the deterministic principles accepted within them. The harder determinists include those physiological psychologists who attempt to understand human affairs in terms of the underlying biology and chemistry, as well as the behaviorists who attempt to understand human affairs strictly in terms of overt behavior. The softer determinists include humanistic, Gestalt, and existential psychologists, all of whom postulate something behind biology and overt behavior (although they differ considerably when it comes to just what this something is).

If it appears to you that the current state of the free will/determinism controversy is complicated and uncertain, welcome to the club. We think it is, too. But it's also exciting. We're looking at the cutting edge of human thought, and a full-scale explosion is going on.

## REFERENCES

Hume, D. *A treatise of human nature* (L. A. Selby-Bigge & P. H. Nidditch, Eds.). New York: Oxford University Press, 1978.

James, W. *What pragmatism is*. In J. B. Hartman (Ed.), *Philosophy of recent times*, Vol. I. New York: McGraw-Hill, 1966.

Kant, I. *Critique of pure reason* (Norman Kemp Smith, trans.). New York: St. Martin's Press, 1925.

Spinoza, B. de. *The ethics* (R. H. M. Elwes, trans.). In *Chief works of Benedict de Spinoza*, Vol. II. New York: Dover, 1951.

Zilboorg, G. *A history of medical psychology*. New York: Norton, 1941.

# CHAPTER 3

## FREE WILL, DETERMINISM, AND SELF-CONCEPT

In the preceding chapter, we discussed how our assumptions regarding freedom and determinism affect our beliefs about such social concerns as mental illness, criminality, and social welfare. Although these concerns are certainly important, for most people they are one step removed from the more demanding issue: What does all this have to do with *me*? How does this discussion relate to my personal feelings, behavior, and day-to-day reactions to people and events?

One answer to these questions is that your beliefs about free will and determinism affect your feelings about yourself no less profoundly than they affect your attitudes toward others. Your feelings about your personal adequacy and your ability to determine the course of your life are closely related to your assumptions about free will.

A further answer is that psychological notions about self-concept and personal development are also entangled with free-will questions. To grapple with the issues of your own adequacy and power, you need to know something about basic concepts of personal psychology. How you incorporate these concepts into your belief structure and how important you believe them to be will depend, in part, on your beliefs about free will and determinism.

# THE PSYCHODYNAMIC SELF-CONCEPT

Behavioral scientists often refer to "static" and "dynamic" conditions and concepts. The word *static* comes from a Greek word that means "standing," and the word *dynamic* comes from a Greek word that means "to be able." Something is referred to as "static" if it leaves everything else standing pretty much as it was. For example, if you decide to part your hair on the right instead of the left, you will have made a change. But, since it doesn't affect much else that you do, the change is static.

Something is referred to as "dynamic" if it is able to affect behavior and ideas beyond its immediate circumstances. For example, our self-concepts are dynamic, since they influence and interact with many parts of our personalities and behavior. To illustrate, let's take an imaginary person, Matilda. Matilda has a certain way of perceiving herself, a certain picture of the person she is. This is her self-concept. The self-concept Matilda has at any given time is influenced by all that she has experienced to that point in her life. The ways her parents and other loved ones have treated her, the reactions of her peers and teachers, her successes and failures, her body and her beliefs about it, all play a part in making her self-concept what it is. And Matilda's concept of herself, in turn, affects how she behaves and how she treats her parents, friends, teachers, body, and so on.

Since a person's self-concept and environment impinge on each other, the former will usually change as the latter changes. For example, suppose people have always treated Matilda as if she were physically attractive but suddenly start treating her as if she were not. The part of Matilda's self-concept that deals with her body is likely to change. However, it appears that not every change in the environment sets off a corresponding change in the self-concept. Again for example, suppose Matilda is a child who has been attending a school with open classrooms. If she has learned very easily in these classrooms, an important component in her self-concept may well be that she is intelligent. Now, let her move into a school with more traditional classrooms. If she still learns well, her self-concept may not be affected in spite of the new environment.

Opponents of determinism cite this apparent lack of a necessary connection between changes in environment and self-concept as evidence that the environment *influences*, but does not *determine*, our perceptions and behavior. Defenders of determinism caution patience, pointing out that a failure to understand what is going on doesn't mean that nothing is going on.

The question remains, then, whether our self-concepts are the necessary products of a naturalistically determined environment. Most people would probably agree that our self-concepts are formed through social interactions with others, a fact that seems to point to a deterministic frame of reference. However, individuals sometimes disregard the weight of social opinion and develop self-concepts that run contrary to what they have learned in most of their previous social interactions. For example, one of the authors was given the message throughout his childhood that he possessed an analytic mind and had the makings of an excellent physical scientist. The message was sufficiently strong that he began his college education as a physics major. Somewhere along the line, however, he began to recognize that his mind also had a strong holistic bent, a characteristic that led him first to philosophy and subsequently to the ministry.

It should be obvious that the self-concept and the self constantly interact. If Matilda believes that she can study harder any time she wishes, then, given the proper set of circumstances, she might alter those conditions within her that prevent her from studying. On the other hand, if she fails to change her study habits, she may abandon the idea that it's in her power to do so. Similarly, if Matilda is socially aggressive but thinks of herself as shy, she may modify her self-concept to coincide more with her behavior, or she may alter her behavior to coincide more with her self-concept.

By saying that the self and self-concept interact, we don't mean they are two distinct phenomena; rather, they are highly interrelated aspects of the whole entity that is *a person*. Although our language forces us to discuss them as if they were separate, self and self-concept are merely somewhat different ways of looking at the same thing.

☐ And now we have to come back to free will and determinism. If the self-concept is dynamic in the way we have described, a crucial question is whether or not it can be changed at will. If so, what other part of the whole person initiates such a change? And what would motivate that part to desire a change? Wouldn't it have to be some interaction with the environment? Then why not suppose that the interaction is directly between the environment and the self-concept? If the self-concept cannot be changed at will, are we at the mercy of our behavioral environment? Are we little more than sophisticated robots? How is it that we can appear on occasion to resist changes in our environment? ☐

# SELF-CONCEPT AND THE UNCONSCIOUS

The emphasis that Sigmund Freud placed upon unconscious motivation was undoubtedly one of his major contributions to psychology and psychiatry. Today, most psychologists and many other students of human behavior agree that we are unaware of many of the motives that underlie our behavior. For example, suppose Matilda finds herself in a situation in which she feels a threat to her stability or her feelings of adequacy. Let's say she is asked by her employer to administer clerical tests to job applicants—a task that many people find easy but that she finds extremely difficult. She may develop a defense against the psychological threat and act accordingly, perhaps by "discovering" that her existing duties are taking more of her time, making it impossible for her to take on this additional responsibility. Her motivation, of course, is defense, but, since she is unaware of it, it is an unconscious motivation.

Some people initially react very negatively to the claim that they do not grasp all the meanings of their own behavior, taking it as an accusation that they are not in full control of themselves. Others insist that people are rational beings who cannot act against their own enlightened self-interest. And still others complain that the notion of the unconscious negates free will, arguing that awareness is necessary for free decisions.

Despite these objections, most people can be convinced by taking a brief look into themselves that unconscious motivation does lead to at least some of their behavior. Have you ever met a person and decided instantly whether or not you liked him or her? Since you knew nothing about the person, what motivated your decision? Have you ever "forgotten" an appointment that was so important you couldn't possibly have just forgotten it? Have you ever experienced a total block in trying to recall a friend's name? Have you ever blamed someone else for initiating some trouble but had the lingering feeling that it was really your doing? You can undoubtedly add your own examples.

In addition to motivations, feelings can also be unconscious. While still very young, we are taught to be uncomfortable at the thought of having certain kinds of feelings: anger, the desire to destroy or attack, sexual desires, resentment of parents. When we do develop such feelings, they are often so unacceptable to the self-concept that we are not explicitly aware of having them.

Of course, some previously unconscious feelings and motives may become at least partially conscious. Perhaps you've had the experience of suddenly gaining the insight that you really hated someone whom you had always thought of as kind but whom you now regard as punitive and manipulative. Or perhaps you've discovered that you worked so hard to succeed, not to satisfy yourself, but to compete with a brilliant sibling.

□ What are the implications of the unconscious for the free will/determinism problem? Grant for a moment that the unconscious is real and does motivate behavior and feelings in some of the ways we have outlined. Is this consistent with free will? Why or why not? Is it consistent with determinism? Why or why not? Could it be that the conscious self is determined, but the unconscious is free—and one of the determiners of the conscious self? Or do you believe that the unconscious is determined, too? Is a belief in free will sufficient reason to reject the idea of the unconscious? How could these questions be resolved? □

# THE DEVELOPMENT
# OF DEFENSE MECHANISMS

As we've seen in the case of Matilda, when something happens to threaten our self-concept, we may ward off the threat without consciously realizing the true significance of our behavior. If our conscious processes were to become aware of the threat, it would become real and would have to be dealt with directly. The unconscious strategies we use to keep this from happening are called *defense mechanisms*.

Defense mechanisms have been studied and classified. Although different authors use different terms, you may be familiar with the concepts of *rationalization, projection, repression, identification, regression*, and *reaction formation*. Each of these terms refers to a behavioral device that protects the self-concept from attack. Let's consider each one briefly.

*Rationalization* describes the process of explaining some behavior in a way that makes it seem sensible and appropriate, whereas in fact the motivation for the behavior is something entirely different. An example of rationalization is the claim of the fox, after several unsuccessful attempts to reach the grapes, that he really didn't want them anyhow. We use rationalizations to defend our self-concepts against the notion that our feelings or actions have been inappropriate, unacceptable, foolish, inadequate, and so forth. When we rationalize, we are basically defending ourselves against ourselves while consciously remaining unaware of what we're up to.

*Projection* is the act of attributing our own thoughts, feelings, or actions to others, in much the same way slides are projected onto a screen. "So what if I steal? *I'm* getting ripped off all the time!" is one example; another is "It's not that I avoid talking to students—they avoid talking to me."

*Repression* is the inability to recall, feel, or perceive something because of a psychological need to avoid recalling, feeling, or perceiving it. We may repress feelings, anger, hostility, sexual and aggressive desires, or memories that are inconsistent with our self-concepts or otherwise too painful to recognize.

*Identification* refers to the process of associating or affiliating with a person or group, especially by taking on attributes, values, mannerisms, and so forth, in order to meet some need. For example, we may identify with a political party and associate ourselves with its values in order to gain the strength of the party. Or we might identify ourselves with an army and thus relieve ourselves of guilt for killing. Or we may identify with a movie star, a religious figure, or a close relative, so that we experience things as we imagine that person experiences them. Identification is not always a defense mechanism, since it is not always unconscious.

*Regression* is the act of returning to outgrown forms of behavior in response to stress. The newly toilet-trained child who loses control is regressing; so is the middle-aged person who goes through endless supplies of cosmetics and vitamins in a vain attempt to recapture lost youth.

*Reaction formation* is the act of leaning over backwards in order to deny to yourself your own views, feelings, or behavior. A common example is the self-proclaimed censor who denies his or her own sexual or aggressive interests by taking an extreme stand on certain books or films: "I don't have those impulses myself; why, I've spent my life fighting pornography."

To see how defense mechanisms operate in practice, consider a student who has the following talk with himself.

Good Lord, where has the time gone? It feels as if I sat down for the first lecture just yesterday, but already the quarter is half over. I should probably go to a school that's on the semester system; it's impossible to get any work done during a quarter! I wonder why they switched anyway. Probably a bunch of administrators wanted to make things tough for students.

That's not the only trouble with those damned administrators, either. I'd go right in and tell Dean Jay just what I think of that new exam requirement, but he's probably so busy he wouldn't even make an appointment. That's the way it is . . . most administrators and professors won't take the time to talk with us lowly students; there's no point in even *trying* to make an appointment. It isn't that I don't like them—they're all right in their own way, I guess—but most of them don't like *us*, which is why they're always doing research or going off to meetings somewhere.

I wish I *could* talk to them honestly. I mean, it isn't my fault I got behind this quarter. Why did Norm tell me to take old Zed's Math 100 anyhow? It was easy enough for him—a snap he said—but he forgot to tell me that Zed's grad student makes up all the exams and does all the grading. And I don't have the same guy Norm did. Without that course, this quarter would be smooth sailing . . . except for that damned Physiological Psych. That one wouldn't be so bad if they hadn't given me a section where half the students are Jews or Orientals. Those kids study so hard they break the curve for the rest of us. I guess their parents bring them up to really crack the books. They don't have as much fun in school, but they can't help it. It isn't their fault that they have to be like that.

This whole monologue is filled with defense mechanisms: rationalization, projection, repression, identification, and a few we haven't even talked about, such as displacement and stereotyping. In some cases, a thought might be described in terms of more than one defense mechanism.

As you read the monologue, it probably made a certain amount of sense. It isn't, after all, the statement of someone who is emotionally disturbed. Defense mechanisms are common processes, used by all of us at various times to explain away actions, feelings, and desires that don't fit our self-concepts. Defense mechanisms are usually more obvious when used by the mentally ill, since the distortion is much more extreme and sometimes even bizarre.

Notice how often a deterministic view enters the flow of this student's thoughts, almost as if it, too, can be a defense mechanism. Untoward events are often attributed to forces beyond his control or influence. You get the feeling that the speaker will finish school in the bottom half of the class, believing all the while that things would have been better if only he'd gotten the breaks.

Are defense mechanisms good, bad, or indifferent? How should we deal with them? If we agree that there are unconscious defense mechanisms, does this mean that many of our choices are not free—that we can't help acting in certain ways?

The hard determinist will say that our use of certain defense mechanisms is determined by forces outside of our control. All we can do is notice that we use them and accept the fact quietly. The extreme free-will advocate will say that we use defense mechanisms because, at some level, we choose to; if we wanted to, we could choose not to use them. It's up to us.

Most people would reject both extreme positions and say that we must decide when and how to face our own defense mechanisms. True, to the extent that our defense mechanisms are determined by conditions out of our control, we're stuck with them. But what is that extent? How much of this unconscious protection is inevitable, and how much are we free to modify? To what extent can we accept responsibility for our actions and consciously face challenges to our self-concepts? The answers to these questions are as individual as each self reading this book.

## SELF-DETERMINATION

At one time it was common to applaud those who "lifted themselves up by their bootstraps." The implication was clearly that they had succeeded in doing something very difficult through hard work and will power, without much outside help. Some years ago, when the federal government established a program to assist persons in getting formal education and job skills, the program was called "Operation Bootstrap."

Notice the subtle but extremely revealing shift. The government program was clearly an effort on the parts of those who were already "up" to help others get "up." Whereas it had once been commonly accepted that people could find the strength and ability within themselves to climb "up," now people commonly made the assumption that an outside force was needed to provide the necessary motivation or help.

Which of these views you accept says something about your self-concept and how you feel about the world. If you believe that people climb up primarily when they have the will within them, you will tend to look upon your successes and failures as largely due to the unique person that is you. If, on the other hand, you feel that environmental forces are most often required to change a person, then you are likely to feel relatively helpless and, perhaps, to seek some sort of outside support in your endeavors.

The deterministic point of view is more comforting when you're unable to do something or be something that you wish; it indicates that forces beyond your control keep you from attaining your goal. On the other hand, free will is more satisfying when you have accomplished something; it enables you to feel that you have the capability within yourself. This suggests, of course, that people may swing back and forth between determinism and free will, depending upon how they fare on a particular task. Indeed, that is exactly what people often do. You can certainly think of numerous examples.

◻ When this approach is applied to other people, the meaning often shifts slightly. Thus, you may assume that particular people are unable to climb up because of pressures against women, or Blacks, or Native Americans—that is, you become deterministic. If these persons do succeed, do you then continue to assume that their success is due to deterministic factors? Or do you take the position that they had something within them that enabled them to overcome outside pressures? When we remove, through determinism, the stigma of failure from a person or group, we are in danger of simultaneously removing the satisfaction of success. ◻

Behavioral scientists and other students of human behavior are trying to gain a greater understanding of how our assumptions about the nature of humanity interrelate with our personality dynamics to influence our behavior. Inevitably the social environment will play a role in the psycho-philosophic position an individual takes, although even this influence can be affected by personality needs. In any event, responses to individual events, persons, and circumstances—often reflecting inconsistent basic values—are surely in some kind of dynamic balance with the personality.

# CHAPTER 4

## HUMANITY: GOOD, EVIL, OR NEUTRAL?

Are we basically good? Are we born that way? Or are we basically bad? And are we born that way? Or would you say that we *tend* to be good or *tend* to be bad? The answers you give to these questions reflect fundamental attitudes about human beings that greatly influence many of your values.

Perhaps you take the *tabula rasa* (blank tablet) position that the newly born person is without tendencies to be either good or bad but is completely controlled by the environment. You might go even further and maintain that the very ideas *good* and *bad* are relative to individual societies or even individual persons. If so, you would probably reject the question of innate goodness or badness as meaningless or improper. Regardless of what position you support intellectually, however, you've probably been brought up in a society in which the concepts of original sin and the depravity of human nature still have some influence. Let's examine some of the history of these ideas, as well as their implications for your views on other issues. Then we'll take a look at a couple of alternative positions—that people are innately good and that people are innately neither good nor evil.

# THE CONCEPT OF ORIGINAL SIN AND THE INNATE DEPRAVITY OF HUMANITY

Adam was created good, but he was endowed with free will and chose to sin. Since his time, all people have been born in original sin and must be saved through the grace and love of God. Without grace, humanity is essentially depraved and sinful.

These are the views of St. Augustine (354–430) and John Calvin (1509–1564), as well as of many other Christians throughout the centuries; a similar position was taken by the Confucian philosopher Hsün Tzŭ (c. 300–235 B.C.).

Augustine and Calvin both insist that God's forgiveness and grace, which are accorded only to some people who have faith, are necessary to overcome human depravity. Hsün Tzŭ, in contrast, believed that our bad nature could be overcome by proper training:

> Crooked wood needs to undergo steaming and bending to conform to the carpenter's rule; then only is it straight. Blunt metal needs to undergo grinding and whetting; then only is it sharp. The original nature of man is evil, so he needs to undergo the instruction of teachers and laws; then only will he be upright.

Thus, although all three thinkers insisted that human nature is evil, they differed with respect to the proper remedy. Whereas the two Christian thinkers demanded faith in God, the Confucian required education and understanding. What kind of educational tradition do you suppose each of these thinkers would espouse?

Prior to Hsün Tzŭ, Confucius (c. 551–479 B.C.) and his follower Mencius (c. 370–289 B.C.) emphatically maintained that humanity, by nature, is good. Mencius wrote "The tendency of man's nature to good is like the tendency of water to flow downwards. There are none but have this tendency to good, just as water flows downwards." Confucianism was thus built upon the concept that humanity is innately good (with Hsün Tzŭ representing an unorthodox position); Christianity, both Catholic and Protestant, has been heavily influenced by the ideas of original sin and the intrinsic evilness of human nature.

## SOME CONSEQUENCES OF THE CONCEPT OF ORIGINAL SIN

The story of Adam and Eve can be interpreted literally. It can also be looked at symbolically, however, with the snake symbolizing the temptation of sin. The sin may be one of pride, of setting oneself up as capable of making decisions regardless of God's admonitions. The sin may also represent the attainment of knowledge in general or of the knowledge of good and evil in particular, with a consequent loss of innocence. It may even represent sexuality. In whatever way you interpret the story, surely one of its meanings is that human beings do have freedom of choice. But this freedom is bought at a very high price, for because of it we can sin.

This meaning has been an important part of the orthodox Judaeo-Christian interpretation of the story of Adam and Eve. Not only are we capable of sinning, but we all inevitably do sin. Since our propensity to sin is a basic, almost defining, trait of human nature, it is passed to us from our parents at birth (or conception). (It might be interesting to speculate about the connection between this view of how original sin gets passed along and Western attitudes about sex.)

The belief in human sinfulness has led to certain ways of preventing people from committing immoral actions, particularly through the instilling of guilt. If you believe that you were "conceived and born in sin," then your birth is an act that led to guilt, and you should feel guilty right from the start. Some form of divine intervention (grace) is needed for absolution. People who doubt their faith may feel that they have rejected God's offer of grace and consequently lack worth in some way. Indeed, even those who keep the faith and live upright lives can never be fully assured of their worth until after death, when they come to God for an accounting. Thus the belief in original sin is more than enough to produce vague but powerful feelings of uncertainty, confusion, and anxiety.

Belief in the innate depravity of human nature also influences child-rearing methods. If children are thought to be innately good, they can be permitted to mature without restrictions. Unless the environment and social institutions destroy their goodness, it will triumph over temptations. But if children are perceived as innately bad, then they must be carefully watched, frequently punished, and subjected to numerous restrictions on their behavior.

In this discussion, we have used the expression "innate depravity" because of its historical importance. Relatively few people today would even contemplate the notion that a child is innately "depraved." Nevertheless, many people believe that children will naturally "fall into evil ways" unless prevented from doing so by firm adult guidance, strong disciplinary measures, and alert legal action.

One of the most eloquent recent expressions of this idea is found in Aleksandr I. Solzhenitsyn's account of the Soviet penal system, *The Gulag Archipelago*. In a chapter entitled "The Bluecaps," Solzhenitsyn (1973) asks two questions. First, how could the torture and murder of innocent people have been committed? Even if we grant that the system may have been commanded by moral monsters, what kind of people carried out the day-to-day brutality of the camps? His answer: just ordinary people. Second, if just ordinary people actually ran the camps, doesn't that mean that even Solzhenitsyn himself—and all of the rest of us—could have committed the same atrocities?

At first, Solzhenitsyn recoils from the suggestion that he could have been as inhuman as the worst of the guards. But then he examines his life. Why should he think that he is any better than they? Has he really acted any better, even when he was a prisoner? His answer:

> If only it were all so simple! If only there were evil people somewhere insidiously committing evil deeds, and it were necessary only to separate them from the rest of us and destroy them. But the line dividing good and evil cuts through the heart of every human being. And who is willing to destroy a piece of his own heart?
>
> During the life of any heart this line keeps changing place; sometimes it is squeezed one way by exuberant evil and sometimes it shifts to allow enough space for good to flourish. One and the same human being is, at various ages under various circumstances, a totally different human being. At times he is close to being a devil, at times to sainthood. But his name doesn't change, and to that name we ascribe the whole lot, good and evil [p. 163].[1]

Solzhenitsyn concludes that he—or any of us—put in the shoes of those ordinary Russian citizens, would have acted just as they did. Left to ourselves, we will sin. As Solzhenitsyn writes elsewhere in the same book, "Pride grows in the human heart like lard on a pig" (p. 168).

At least in theory, prison life should differ depending on whether a society assumes that human nature is good or that it is innately evil. If we are basically good, criminal behavior must result from forces that are too strong for our goodness to withstand. Consequently, prisons should permit lawbreakers to regain a sense of personal integrity; instead of being highly punitive, they should offer the opportunity to change. In a society that believes in the innate goodness of humanity, then, we would expect a rehabilitative penal system rather than a retributive one.

Unfortunately, practice does not always keep step with theory. The Quakers in colonial Pennsylvania were among the first to try to establish a rehabilitative penal system. They reasoned that prisoners needed only to have time by themselves to contemplate the enormity of their offenses. Although this approach did improve the previously inhuman treatment of prisoners, it also led to the isolation of prisoners from one another so that they might consider their sins and repent. From the good intentions came tiny cells and solitary confinement.

---

[1]From *The Gulag Archipelago*, Volume 1, by A. Solzhenitsyn. Copyright © 1973 by Harper and Row, Inc. Reprinted by permission.

Where people are thought to be innately evil, a punitive penal system will probably be established. Much of our present system of punishment was set up in the belief that human nature is basically evil. Prison was therefore seen not as a means of reform but merely as a means of punishing criminals and keeping them out of society's way. The fact that our penal system has not diminished the incidence of crime may be seen as further evidence for people's innate tendency to behave in evil ways *or* as evidence for the failure of the system to learn how to reach the goodness within every person. The same statistics can easily be interpreted by people of diametrically opposed views to support the positions with which they began.

Your view of the proper function of prisons is one result of your assumptions about human nature. Another is your philosophy of education. A. S. Neil, founder of Summerhill, a famous British school, assumed that children are born good and that the social controls operative in today's schools tend to damage children's potential. In particular, children, with considerable intrinsic goodness, will want to learn if they are free to learn. Students at Summerhill are therefore allowed as much freedom as possible, both in academic and social life. Learning is not forced upon them, because doing so is thought to be an exercise in futility. Not only is forced learning often quickly forgotten, but the learning process may cause children emotional pain that can be destructive both to the self and to the self-concept.[2]

The traditional school systems of England and North America make no official assumptions about the nature of children, but teachers, administrators, school boards, and parents do have implicit (and sometimes explicit) philosophies. To judge by the way many schools are operated and many classes taught, these implicit values seem to be strongly influenced by the belief that children, like all people, are potentially sinful, that they should be punished when evil begins to appear, that they need to be coerced to learn if they don't learn quickly on their own, and that the profit to be gained by forced learning is considerably greater than any emotional cost involved. Indeed, painful learning is often believed to have a purifying and cleansing effect, so that its value is greater than the value of unforced, enjoyable learning. Although most parents, teachers, and school administrators might deny that these beliefs are still widely held, we think that the lingering influence of these views remains more pervasive than is generally realized.[3]

---

[2]The philosophy of Summerhill is considerably more sophisticated than this brief account can convey. If you're interested in learning more about it, consult the book *Summerhill* (Neil, 1960).

[3]There is a growing revolt against this kind of education, however. Two good and easily read books depicting this revolt are *How Children Fail* (Holt, 1964) and *Teaching As a Subversive Activity* (Postman & Weingartner, 1969). If education interests you, we recommend these books.

Do our personal experiences determine the kinds of assumptions we make about the innate goodness or sinfulness of human nature, or do our assumptions determine the kinds of experiences we have? The answer seems to be that sometimes our experiences are primary and sometimes our preconceptions are primary. Consider a woman who, as a result of a difficult home life, a brutal mother and father, and a frightening series of early sexual experiences with an older cousin, develops a very bitter attitude toward people. Although she was not brought up to believe in original sin, she comes to accept the idea that people are innately depraved. Her neighbor is a man who was reared in a warm, happy home in rural Nebraska. Almost everyone he knew, however, tacitly accepted the Calvinistic doctrine of original sin. Despite a natural friendliness, he remains fundamentally suspicious of other people and cautious in his dealings with them. His behavior is the direct outcome of the values he was taught. You might speculate about what, if anything, would get these people to reverse their positions.

□ Do you think people are innately evil? If so, then how do you account for the fact that even little children occasionally do things that seem to have no other motive than that it is good to act this way? If not, then how do you account for the fact that people do evil things? If we are not innately evil, how could the Holocaust, for example, possibly happen? Take a look at what you believe about education, the treatment of criminals, welfare, and so on. What assumptions about human nature are implicit in these beliefs? □

## AN ALTERNATIVE TO ORIGINAL SIN: PEOPLE ARE INNATELY GOOD

During the Renaissance, a revival of the spirit of humanism powerfully influenced traditional Christian thinking about the nature of people. Like any group of writers, the Renaissance humanists were not all saying exactly the same thing, but they did tend to share certain beliefs. First, although by and large they did not reject Christianity or God, they saw religion as serving humanity, not vice versa. They believed that our main concern should be for ourselves and our fellow human beings during our life on earth, rather than for God and our life after death. We should be free and proud; humility is less important than ability. Instead of self-denial and a monastic discipline, people should value the development of their capacities for self-expression and their ability to feel joy.

Second, the Renaissance humanists put at least as much stock in feeling as they did in thinking. Although some of them—Erasmus, for example—were among the West's most influential scholars, the humanists generally sought to balance intellect and feeling.

Third, the humanists totally denied that human nature is innately depraved. In place of supernatural revelation and original sin, they substituted "natural religion" and the innate goodness of humanity. They believed that religion is consistent with human nature and can be understood through our natural capacities. They also rejected predestination, believing that our lives develop through a natural course of events that is within our power to influence. (It's ironic that the revival of humanistic thought ushered in the age of science, which ultimately led to the hard determinism we discussed earlier.)

## *ROUSSEAU AND THE "NATURAL MAN"*

As often happens, the ideas of the Renaissance thinkers did not come to full fruition until many years later. Indeed, three centuries passed before Jean Jacques Rousseau (1712–1778) proclaimed his famous doctrine of the "natural man."[4] Rousseau's basic message was simple: The individual is fundamentally good, but organized in society and corrupted by culture, people become evil.

Culture consists of the customs and rules according to which people live together. For Rousseau, culture is an artificial overlay that masks the real relations among people and produces an unnatural uniformity of behavior. The natural man is free from such restraints and responds to reality, not to appearances. However, as culture becomes stronger, real human relationships are pushed more and more into the background, and people become increasingly alienated from themselves and from one another.

Culture thus destroys the basis of morality, which, for Rousseau, lies in genuine human relationships and the ability of people to treat one another in terms of reality. Whereas the natural man is able to lead a healthy moral life, the cultured man is not. In the natural state we have a healthy self-love (*amour de soi*). This self-love expresses the essence of human (as opposed to animal) existence. At the level of instincts, self-love takes the form of the natural tendency toward self-preservation. Combined with reason, it allows us to experience one another as human and not simply as objects to be manipulated like so many pieces of furniture. The natural man, able to live according to the dictates of self-love, is happy.

Unfortunately, culture imposes a facade of behavior on us and prevents us from behaving freely according to our own perceptions. It turns self-love into an artificial pride (*amour propre*), and it replaces natural relations with artificial ones. Culture thus prevents us from

---

[4]For historical reasons, we will use Rousseau's phrase "natural man" in this discussion, in spite of the implied exclusion of women. No such exclusion is intended.

perceiving one another—and, ultimately, ourselves—as human. By imposing uniformity of action on us, it takes away our freedom; and, as Rousseau wrote in *The Social Contract*, "To give up freedom is to give up one's human quality; to remove freedom from one's will is to remove all morality from one's actions." Civilized man, being less than human, is unhappy, and the imposition of culture represents a fall. (In this way Rousseau gives a sophisticated turn to the idea of original sin, with "natural man" as his Adam. Few basic ideas are fully rejected. More often, they slip from view for a time and then reappear in slightly different dress.)

To understand Rousseau's thought, it is important to understand the distinction he draws between *culture* and *society*. As we have seen, culture is an imposed uniformity of behavior. Society, however, is merely a group of people living together. Far from being a corrupting influence, society is necessary for our full human development.

For Rousseau, being fully human requires attaining an understanding not only of the self but also of the self in relation to others. We need to experience other people as human, and to do so we must have a healthy self-love, a healthy intellect, and society. It is only in society that our human freedom comes into full flower, since it is only in society that we can experience the kinds of choices our freedom requires. Hence, in *Emile* Rousseau wrote "All true education must eventually be for society."

The problem with this argument is obvious. It is hard to imagine a society without culture, yet culture would be busily undoing everything that society is intended to achieve. Suppose that, as "natural man," we freely enter into society. How do we prevent culture from destroying the very freedom that brought society into being? This question led Rousseau to an impassioned defense of democracy. He envisioned a society in which "each one uniting with all obeys . . . only himself and remains free as before . . . . Each one giving himself to all gives himself to nobody."

Does this line of thought sound familiar? Think of those two rallying cries of the '60s and '70s, "Power to the people!" and "Do your own thing!" They could almost have been coined by a latter-day Rousseau. And just as these slogans were considered radical in the 20th century, so Rousseau was considered radical in the 18th century. But his thinking was never completely ignored. Just 12 years after his death, the French monarchy was overthrown in the first of many revolutions that have been influenced by Rousseau's thought. His ideas can also be found in the writings of Karl Marx and the Socialist reformers of the 19th century. And, as we pointed out, his voice is still echoing.

We have discussed Rousseau at some length because this 18th-century writer gave voice to many of the issues that continue to arise in our contemporary social disruption. His dislike of social institutions, his belief that we are inherently good but corrupted by our evil environment, and his trust in the wisdom of the majority all mark him as a predecessor of what has been termed "the youth culture." It is, perhaps, not quite so youthful as we sometimes think.

□ We in the United States pride ourselves on believing many of the things Rousseau believed, yet many of our Founding Fathers found themselves in disagreement with him. John Adams, for example, distrusted the masses. Others, like Thomas Jefferson, did agree with Rousseau and espoused what many now would consider dangerously radical ideas—for example, that an occasional revolution is necessary for the health of a democracy. In your view, was Rousseau's thought radical or moderate? Suppose he was right; what implications would that have for contemporary American society? □

# A THIRD ALTERNATIVE: PEOPLE ARE BORN NEUTRAL

The belief that the mind is a blank tablet at birth, a *tabula rasa* to be written upon by experience, can be traced at least as far back as ancient Greece. Nearly 2000 years later, the English philosopher John Locke (1632–1704) made this idea the touchstone of his psychological theory. In direct opposition to René Descartes (1596–1650) and other European rationalists, who believed that some concepts are innate in the human mind, Locke insisted that all knowledge and all ideas come from experience.

Locke's stance has had an important influence on many of today's behavioral scientists, especially those who lean toward a naturalistic determinism. Many of these behavioral scientists not only agree with Locke that all knowledge comes from learning but readily extend this idea to include personality characteristics as well. Thus, we can learn all that is necessary to learn about human behavior by studying the environment, the individual, and the interaction between them.

This is not to say that contemporary scientists reject the possibility that intellectual capacity or certain temperamental tendencies might be genetically determined, although many behavioral scientists either ignore or downgrade this possibility. The source and development of genetically determined characteristics could still be studied scientifically. But a characteristic that could not be explained in terms of some combination of genetic inheritance, environment, and experience would be one that behavioral scientists could not hope to understand. For this reason, original sin or innate goodness are far less congenial notions for behavioral scientists than the *tabula rasa*, which is ready-made for their kind of theorizing.

If the *tabula rasa* approach is correct, then everything we know comes somehow from the environment. But among the things we know is that some actions are praiseworthy, others are morally neutral, and still others are immoral. How do we come to know this?

Reflection on this question has led many thinkers, especially contemporary ones, to conclude that we are not born either sinful or good, but morally neutral. From this point of view, moral qualities are rather like colors: they are not an essential quality of humans. Thus, to judge something to be human is not to make a moral judgment, as it would be if humans were essentially evil or essentially good. We humans become good or evil because we engage in good or evil actions, not because we are human. It may be that an action can be good or evil for us because we are human, but that doesn't make us good or evil.

An analogy may help here. Think about wood. Something is wood whether or not it is yellow. The color of the thing is totally beside the point of its being wooden. It can become yellow because, being wooden, it can be painted. But oxygen cannot become yellow. Nothing can paint it. The color of a thing does not determine what it is made of, though what it is made of does determine whether it can be colored. On a similar view of human nature, this is what moral qualities are like. The fact that we are human makes it possible for actions to be good, neutral, or evil, but being human does not itself make us good or evil, any more than being wooden makes something yellow.

□ There is a great deal that is attractive about this view, though it does have difficulties. If moral qualities adhere primarily to actions and not to people, how do we humans recognize that, for example, killing is immoral? Is there something inherent in certain actions—for example, the property of causing pain—that makes them immoral? Or is the judgment that some actions are immoral basically an agreement among members of a society, as is the judgment that certain actions are illegal? Do we perhaps have a moral sense that allows us to apprehend or intuit moral qualities directly? □

# THE PERFECTIBILITY OF HUMANITY

Are human beings moving toward perfection? Are we a little better, on the whole, every generation or century?

The view that we are perfectible, which is sometimes called "ameliorism," has been somewhat less popular in the 20th century, under the influence of such moral disasters as the Holocaust and Stalinism. Yet even the 20th century has its utopians. Some, like B. F. Skinner (1960), envision "ideal" societies in which behavior is carefully programmed so that everyone has optimum satisfaction and security. Delgado (1968) suggests the feasibility of increasing people's happiness by electrically influencing their brains, although he himself would not necessarily favor such a program. One objection to such schemes is that the definition of "perfection" would eventually be determined by those controlling the programming, whose motives may be unenlightened or even pernicious. (Skinner tries to get around this objection by insisting that the program should be planned for the good of all.)

Of course, not all utopians pin their hopes for a better world on technological advances. Part of the humanist spirit has been the idea that people are becoming more rational, more sensible, more enlightened. This view took root in the 18th century and was nurtured by the democratic revolutions in America and France. Since then, reformers have often advanced their ideas for change in the explicit hope that their reforms would enable people or society to move another step toward perfection.

Many younger people today—and not a few older ones—have been met with deep cynicism when they have presented enthusiastic views of a bright future for all people, to be gained through spiritualism, improved human encounters, ethnic integration, innovative educational programs, and other means. True, many people do continue to believe that humanity can move toward perfection without resorting to technological manipulations. They, like their 19th-century predecessors, commonly point to education as the primary tool of reform. Others, however, have too often seen similar enthusiasm wane in the face of global war, the establishment of totalitarian governments, and double-edged advances in science and technology that have spawned new and baffling moral questions.

☐ What is your view? Do we have within us the potential for approaching perfection? Are we prevented from doing so only by a corrupt environment? Or must we be in awe of some authority, divine or human, before we will function harmoniously? ☐

# FREEDOM AND NATURALISM

In this chapter we have presented three basic points of view on human nature: that we are innately sinful, innately good, and innately neutral. On the basis of our presentation, you might have found one of these views more comfortable or appealing than the others, but that, of course, doesn't make the view *true*. As you consider some of the implications of these viewpoints, keep in mind that the truth of a proposition in no way depends on its appeal to our feelings.

Whichever account of human nature is correct, is it *good* for people to live according to their nature? For example, if it is "natural" to seek stimulation or self-actualization, is it also *good* to do so? Does it lead to what you would define as success? Or should some natural inclinations be suppressed? What if your desire for stimulation or self-actualization interferes with the rights of others or runs contrary to the teachings of your faith?

Obviously, those who believe that human nature is inherently sinful do not subscribe to the idea that we should accept our nature and live accordingly. On the contrary: they insist that we should do everything possible to divest ourselves of our "natural" sinfulness. In contrast, those who believe that human nature is basically good are likely to encourage people to live according to this nature. This notion is easily extended; if, as Rousseau claims, our nature is basically good, then whatever is consistent with this nature must also be good. Thus, if the direct expression of strong sexual feelings is natural, then it is also appropriate, and perhaps even necessary.

You may have found humanism the most congenial of the three viewpoints we've discussed. Yet it's easy to see how humanism might carry implications that would conflict not only with the laws and customs of many religions and states but with other views you might hold. For example, present-day proponents of liberalized pornography laws often base their case on the assumption that the kind of sexual behavior exhibited is "normal" and that hiding it from either adults or children is actually unhealthy. But where should the line be drawn? Aggressive and even violent behavior also seems "natural." Should there be total freedom to view or exhibit such behavior? If we do draw some distinction between what is "natural" and what is "good," what are the bases of those distinctions? Who is to draw them?

Is there virtue in learning to curb your appetites? Do you admire people who exhibit moderation in all things, from working to making love? Who seem to keep everything in perspective? Or do you enjoy more those who freely do what they feel like doing? Presumably, it would be natural to eat until satisfied, but what about people who undereat in order to remain trim? They aren't acting in accordance with their "nature." Or are they? It seems that the more deeply we probe into these questions, the more complex they become.

# HUMAN NATURE AND PERSONAL FREEDOM

Supporters of various points of view concerning the innate goodness or badness of humanity might all claim that their theories allow for the greatest human freedom, although they might define "freedom" differently. It is not our intent to debate whether greater freedom, in the ultimate sense, is gained through traditional Judaeo-Christian creeds, through some form of humanism within the Judaeo-Christian tradition, or through a humanistic philosophy that falls outside traditional faiths. If, however, we define personal freedom as freedom from the possibility of being controlled by interventions, either divine or human, then some form of humanism seems most conducive to a belief in personal freedom.

Those who follow Augustine or Calvin are not only likely to assume predestination but also to require divine intervention as a means of overcoming humanity's innate sinfulness. Those who follow Locke and the naturalistic determinists emphasize the effects of environment upon all thought processes, including those involved in choice-making. Humanists, in contrast, are more likely to see us as capable of resisting external influences and of using our own resources to make the most of our capabilities.

The more your philosophy permits you to assume that you have personal freedom, the more it requires you to accept personal responsibility. Freedom and responsibility are, after all, correlative notions, whatever your view of the moral quality of human nature. That sounds fine when we think about praiseworthy actions, but it does make people squirm when we start thinking about immoral actions. Complete freedom means total responsibility, and limited responsibility means curtailing freedom. And so we close this section with one of the great questions of ethics: How free, and therefore how responsible, are we?

## REFERENCES

Delgado, J. M. R. Recent advances in brain control. In Baskin, W., & Powers, G., (Eds.), *New outlooks in psychology*. New York: Philosophical Library, 1968.

Holt, J. *How children fail*. New York: Delta, 1964.

Neil, A. S. *Summerhill: A radical approach to child-rearing*. New York: Hart, 1960.

Postman, N., & Weingartner, C. *Teaching as a subversive activity*. New York: Delacorte, 1969.

Skinner, B. F. *Walden Two*. New York: Macmillan, 1960.

Solzhenitsyn, A. I. *The Gulag archipelago*, Vol. I (Thomas Whitney, trans.). New York: Harper & Row, 1973.

# PART TWO
## KNOWLEDGE AND THE SELF

# CHAPTER 5

## KNOWING AS A WAY OF VALUING

Historically, philosophers have considered three primary values: the good, the true, and the beautiful. All discussions of values get subsumed somehow under these. So far our discussion has concentrated primarily on the moral and the immoral and related topics such as free will and determinism. All of these fall under the good and arise from a serious consideration of the question "What is good, and how is it realized in our lives?" We would like now to turn our attention to the second of the primary values. Here our questions will be "What is truth, and how do we discover it?" Just as much of the discussion of the good centered on ethics, much of this discussion will center on knowledge, since knowledge is an apprehension of truth.

The fact that we split values into categories does not mean that the good and the true, for example, have little to do with each other. On the contrary, many questions bridge any apparent gap between them. For example, how do we know what is good? *Can* we know what is good? Is it always good to possess knowledge? Any knowledge? Is the price we would have to pay for some knowledge just too expensive or beyond our moral right to pay? As you read, you might keep an eye out for connections among the categories of values.

# SOURCES OF KNOWLEDGE

Where does knowledge come from? How do we know what we know? Do we ever really know anything for certain? If we don't know something for certain, do we know it at all? Three basic sources of our knowledge and understanding of the world are most frequently recognized: experience (including sensation and perception), authority (the views of experts or the consensus views of the community), and reason (including the use of logic). But are these sources sufficient to guarantee our knowledge of the world? Do they exhaust all the possibilities? What about feelings, intuition, or Carl Jung's idea of a collective unconscious?

Everyone uses various sources of knowledge at various times, but the extent to which each source is trusted differs from individual to individual. Some people place more trust in what they actually perceive, while others rely more on feelings and intuition; some are more likely to fall back on authority, while others must be convinced by their own logic and reason. Unfortunately, these sources of purported knowledge are not always in agreement. Your experience may conflict with your reason; for example, your reason might tell you that there is no basis for the belief that vitamin C cures colds, but your experience might be that it works. Or your experience may disagree with authority; for example, the New York *Times* report of a meeting you attended might not match your recollection of it.

There can also be conflict within one kind of knowledge source. Your experience may contradict that of others; the authorities you respect most may disagree with one another; your reasoning or intuition and those of a friend may bring you to totally different conclusions.

Philosophers, taking note of these and other problems, have raised fundamental questions about what we really know and how we know it. These questions belong to the realm of philosophy called *epistemology*, from the Greek words *episteme* (knowledge) and *logos* (systematic account or explanation).

Clearly, questions about how we know anything at all go to the root of any beliefs we may have about the world, even those we take most for granted. For instance, much of our daily life assumes that the world is predictable. When you strike the "a" key on your typewriter, you need to assume that the "a" will appear on the sheet of paper in front of you, or else the typewriter is useless. When you arrive home in the evening, you need to assume that your living room—not a watch-repair shop or an elevator shaft—will be there behind the door. Nevertheless, our belief in the predictability of the world is not conclusively supported by our *knowledge* of the world. We can't always predict how the world will be, what will happen. Events do run counter to experience, authority, science, and sometimes even reason itself. How, then, do we know anything?

# "STRONG" AND "WEAK" KNOWLEDGE

Before considering various sources of knowledge in detail, we need to point out an important ambiguity in the word *to know*. Sometimes our use of this word implies that what we claim to know must be true, or else we're mistaken in saying we "know" it. If you claim to know that Napoleon was born at Crater Lake, it would be quite appropriate to point out that, since he was born on Corsica, you "know" no such thing. On the other hand, we sometimes use *to know* in the sense of "to believe something very strongly, whether it's true or not," as in "All children know that their parents are infallible." These two senses of *to know* are sometimes called the *philosophical* or *strong* sense and the *psychological* or *weak* sense.

This distinction is clearly an important one. Consider a court of law, for example. Let's assume that you're on a jury trying a capital case. With the life of the defendant at stake, it wouldn't do to base your verdict on something known in the weak sense, because you would have no assurance that your verdict was based on truth. You'd want to base your verdict on facts that were "known" in the strong sense. Or consider a person who "knows," through prayer, that God exists. In which sense does this person know? How can we decide?

As you can see, the application of the distinction between strong and weak knowledge can lead to puzzles. What tests can we use to distinguish between the strong sense of *to know* and the weak one? Are we *ever* entitled to say that we *know* in the strong sense? These are among the most enduring and puzzling problems in all of philosophy.

# KNOWLEDGE AND EXPERIENCE

We often claim to know something on the basis of experience. Obviously, experience is quite adequate as a basis for knowledge in the weak sense, since all that is required for this kind of knowing is that we be convinced. And we may find any number of things convincing, our experience included. But is experience ever an adequate basis for knowing something in the strong sense?

As you might expect, there is a continuum of possible answers to this question. At one extreme is skepticism, the view that strong knowledge can never be adequately based on experience. It would be possible, perhaps, to base strong knowledge on experience if we *knew* that the future must resemble the past. As Hume discovered, however, the only reason we have for expecting the future to be like the past is—experience! And with that observation, Hume neatly encloses us in a vicious circle.

The other extreme is naive empiricism, according to which *all* experience brings knowledge: "Seeing is believing." After all, what better defense could I give of my knowledge than that I've experienced what I claim to know?

□ The second of these extremes, naive empiricism, has never been very popular. Can you see why? What difficulties arise if we assume that *all* perceptions and experiences are a basis for knowledge in the strong sense? Skepticism, on the other hand, although it might initially seem rather unattractive, always seems to find adherents. How would you answer the skeptic's challenge? Do you think you could show that we do have strong knowledge from experience? How? □

Many philosophers essentially ignore the skeptic's challenge and assume that we do know at least some things in the strong sense. For these thinkers, the task is to distinguish strong from weak knowledge. This approach usually leads people to some middle point on the continuum between skepticism and naive empiricism. Two of these points are *rationalism* and *empiricism*.

For the rationalist, experience leads to strong knowledge only with the help of knowledge that is somehow grounded in, or verified by, reason alone. Descartes, for example, argued that even the most apparently certain truths based on experience were subject to doubt. Through reason alone, however, an unshakable foundation of knowledge could be established. Later, Kant claimed that human beings must perceive things in a causal order for experience to be possible. It is not through experience, but through reason, that we discover the necessity of the law of causality. Such claims that we can have some knowledge about the real world that is not based on experience are typical of rationalists.

Empiricists turn up their noses at such claims, arguing that we can't discover anything at all about the real world sitting back in our armchairs thinking about it. We have to experience the world in order to find out what it's like. If our knowledge depends on certain basic principles, such as the law of causality, then either the skeptics are right or we can discover these principles experientially. Instead of trying to reason their way to unshakable principles, empiricists try to distinguish the strong from the weak sense of knowing on the basis of the kind of evidence presented and the relation between the evidence and the claim being made.

The empiricist's task would be an easier one if it were not for one embarrassing and annoying difficulty: not everyone perceives the same reality. Most of us, seeing a group of people talking quietly in a corner, would perceive simply a group of friends in innocent conversation. But someone who is paranoid might see a group of enemies plotting. How do we establish which perception is the correct one? They are incompatible, yet both are "experienced." In order to distinguish between strong and weak knowing, we must be able to pick out which perception of reality is correct without begging the question by appealing to the correctness of *our* perception. We cannot appeal to perception at all, since all perceptions are equally suspect until we've established which ones are correct. And how on earth can we do that? (Does this sound like Hume's problem all over again? There's a reason for that. It is!)

If reality impinged on our senses with labels clearly marking the objective features and the subjective ones, then the problem would be solved. Unfortunately it doesn't. There is not a simple one-to-one relation between our perceptions and reality, or even between our perceptions and sensory inputs. Perceptions are *interpretations* of stimuli and are open to alteration in all sorts of ways. Consider the following classical study, conducted nearly three decades ago. It was found that social pressure could alter people's perceptions of which one of three lines drawn on a chart was the same length as a fourth line drawn on an adjacent chart. Without any group pressure, virtually no one erred. When others in the group purposely called out the wrong line, however, the experimental subjects often did also. In later interviews, some of these subjects continued to maintain that their perceptions were accurate, although there could be no doubt that they were in error (Asch, 1951).

It is not only our perceptions that can be distorted. Our memories can also be affected by the social environment, by group pressures, and by our values and beliefs. Nearly forty years ago, an ingenious investigator presented a drawing to a large group of students. The students were instructed to study the drawing for a period of time so that they would be able to describe it when it was removed. Among several persons depicted in the drawing was a well-dressed Black man talking with a White man. The White man was shown holding an open barber's razor in his hand. It so happens that at the time, one of the stereotypes of Black people was that they used such razors for acts of violence. When asked to describe the picture, a substantial number of the students stated that it was the Black man who was carrying the razor (Allport & Postman, 1947).

In spite of these very real difficulties with empiricism, difficulties that have never been adequately resolved, empiricism is more popular than rationalism among contemporary philosophers and scientists. We suspect that part of the reason for the popularity of empiricism is the apparent success of modern scientists, most of whom have been empiricists. However, difficulties arising in such arcane fields as quantum mechanics seem to require principles of investigation that are more easily reconciled with rationalist ideas. Indeed, rationalism may be making something of a comeback.

□ If knowledge implies truth, do we ever get any knowledge from experience? If it doesn't imply truth, how is it different from mere belief? If we don't get *knowledge* from experience, why should we be inclined to believe science any more than anything else? Or, to put it all in a single question, What reason is there for thinking that science and scientific method tell us more about the experiential world than any other method? □

# KNOWLEDGE AND AUTHORITY

Whatever the true role of experience may be in establishing our knowledge of the world, we surely do not rely exclusively on our own experience for all of our knowledge. In the first place, propositions in pure logic and mathematics are established without reference to experience. The fact that all squares have certain properties is not established on the basis of experiments but on the basis of pure reason. Indeed, our ability to construct such propositions is surely one of our most human characteristics. In the second place, we usually have neither the time nor the inclination to reproduce the experiences of other people. For much of our information we accept the authority of others.

Although accepting the testimony of others might seem both inevitable and reasonable, there are enormous problems with authority as a basis for knowledge. Do anyone's credentials guarantee the *truth* of what they say? Some people maintain that strong knowledge can *never* be based on authority. But if this is so, we may end up closer to skepticism than you might think. Consider for a moment how much of what you know is based either directly or in part on the testimony of some expert. Except for authority, most of us could not claim to know that there are koala bears in Australia—or even that there is an Australia! If authority cannot be a basis for strong knowledge, then much of the knowledge we take for granted is "knowledge" only in the weak sense. And somehow that seems wrong.

Nevertheless, there are several difficulties in basing knowledge on authority. First, most, if not all, authorities are fallible. How do we choose which experts to trust, without a circular appeal to their authority? Is there always an ultimate authority on any matter? Or are there ultimate authorities on some matters but not on others? And how are we to proceed when conflicting sources, such as the Bible and the Koran, are put forward as ultimate authorities?

Second, what are we to do when an expert tells us one thing and our experience tells us another? Sometimes, surely, our experience is wrong. One of us, a few years ago, began waking up early in the morning with severe foot pains. His experience told him that something was clearly wrong with the foot. He dutifully took himself off to a doctor, who made a very thorough examination and then told him there was nothing physically wrong with the foot. Despite the evidence of experience, the doctor proved to be correct, because the pains stopped. On the other hand, you probably know of cases in which doctors have authoritatively denied that people's symptoms were significant or even real—and been proven wrong. If authority always took precedence over experience, there would be no such thing as a malpractice suit. So how do we figure out when to believe the authority and when to believe our experience?

Third, there are times when the word of an authority cannot be directly verified. Sometimes this happens because the claim is not one that could be checked directly, even in principle; life after death is an example. And sometimes it happens because direct verification is beyond our power; for example, to check a historian's word directly, we would need a time machine. What do we do in these cases? Do we simply rule out the possibility of strong knowledge?

## AUTHORITY AND AUTHORITARIANISM

It is important to distinguish between *authority* and *authoritarianism*. As we are using the term, *authority* refers to some source that is in a privileged position with respect to certain kinds of claims. Because the source is an authority, it is especially likely to be correct. Thus, a physicist would be an authority on physical theory, and a Datsun repair manual would be an authority on Datsun repairs. *Authoritarianism* is the doctrine that authorities should be given unquestioned obedience, especially in political, religious, or moral matters. As an epistemological doctrine, authoritarianism hasn't much to recommend it, unless you can figure out which authority is unfailingly correct and can do so without having to be unfailingly correct yourself. Arguments are sometimes made for the infallibility of some authorities in religion and morals, but these are always extremely difficult arguments to make out without begging the question.

Authoritarianism rarely exists as a pure type, but it can be used to describe a pattern of behaviors and attitudes that individuals exhibit in varying degrees. As such, it is an excellent example of the relationships that can exist among an individual's beliefs, behavior, and personality dynamics.

Some people accept the word of an authority rather easily. As a result, they tend to have high respect for the authority of the community or of powerful individuals and to believe in abiding by "the authorities," whether they are legal, religious, or some other kind. At the same time, they expect to be obeyed when they are in authority.

Other people accept an authority only when they are forced to or when the authority is demonstrably likely to be correct. These people tend to view anyone in positions of command with suspicion and to expect authorities to back up their opinions with evidence and reason. When they are in authority, they don't expect others to simply take their word for things.

The more individuals shy away from authority, the more they must depend on other sources, especially their own experience and reason, for knowledge. This suggests that less authoritarian personalities would tend to be more secure, more tolerant of ambiguity, and less dogmatic, and there is some research evidence to confirm this supposition. In contrast, more authoritarian personalities, not as tolerant of ambiguity and uncertainty, want to *know* in no uncertain terms. They tend to see issues as black and white, with clear-cut right and wrong, correct and incorrect sides. They resent the physician who admits that a diagnosis is subject to error, or the minister who is unwilling to tell them exactly what they must do to gain immortality, or the counselor who is unable to guarantee the outcome of therapy. They like to know who the "good guys" are and who the "bad guys" are. In politics, they maintain heavily ideological views, whether these views are radical, reactionary, or middle of the road. In religion, they seek dogma, although the nature of the dogma may be fundamentalist, atheistic, or any point in between (Rokeach, 1960).

## KNOWLEDGE AND REASON

We have so far seen significant difficulties with the claims that strong knowledge can be based on experience or authority. These difficulties have led some thinkers to look to reason as the primary basis for strong knowledge. As you might expect, there are problems with this alternative as well.

As usual, we have to draw some rather fine lines. Sometimes philosophers may seem obsessed with drawing such lines, but there's a reason for it. You've probably had the experience of looking at a movie that was not quite in focus. You could put up with it, but you'd know that you were missing important details and perhaps even misconstruing what was going on. Then, when the projectionist woke up and focused the projector properly, it was a huge relief. You could see what was actually there. Similarly, we can put up with our minds being slightly out of focus and not bother to distinguish among similar concepts, but we run the risk of not understanding clearly just what's going on. When we focus our minds as sharply as we can, we often experience the relief of knowing what is actually there.

This time we need to distinguish between *logic* and what we'll call *rationality* or *reason*. By *logic* we mean arguments of a certain kind—namely, those that guarantee that the conclusion is true if the premises are all true. Such arguments are called *valid*. By *rationality* or *reason* we mean the attempt by humans to use logic in gaining knowledge.

As we have defined it, logic is infallible. Whenever we start with true premises and proceed logically, we are absolutely guaranteed to end up with true conclusions. We can't go wrong. So logic ought to be the Yellow Brick Road to knowledge, right? Wrong! First, even though *logic* is infallible, *reason* is not. Since reason involves the human use of logic, it is always open to human error. *If* we always applied logic correctly and always began with premises we knew to be true, *then* reason would indeed always pass from knowledge to knowledge. But we don't always use logic correctly. Needs, values, attitudes, expectancies, social pressures, and simple ignorance all lead us to make mistakes. To illustrate, several decades ago a psychologist cooked up some syllogisms, some of which were invalid but fed people's biases. To illustrate, consider the following syllogism:

> Some women are less intelligent than the average man.
>     Some bases of intelligence are biological.
> Therefore, women are biologically inferior to men.

The syllogism is invalid, but people who believe the conclusion are more likely to believe that the argument is valid.

A second difficulty is that logic has nothing to say about whether the premises of an argument are, in fact, true. If we know the premises and pass by means of a valid argument to the conclusion, then we know the conclusion. But how do we know the premises? If we have derived them from other valid arguments, then we face the same question. How did we know the premises of these prior arguments? Either we will continue this way forever (an infinite regress), or we'll reach a point at which we must fall back on some source of knowledge other than logic.

In spite of these difficulties, many philosophers have been deeply impressed both with logic's promise of an infallible route to knowledge and with reason. There is a persistent hope that this method, used with scrupulous care, will show the way to a kind of knowledge that is independent of the senses. As Plato wrote in *Phaedo*:

> And he attains to the purest knowledge ... who goes to each with the mind alone, not introducing or intruding in the act of thought, sight, or any other sense together with reason, but with the very light of the mind in her own clearness searches into the very truth of each; he who has got rid, as far as he can, of eyes and ears and, so to speak, of the whole body, these being in his opinion distracting elements [*Dialogues of Plato*, 1952, p. 224].

## *REASON AND SCIENCE*

We have seen that logic has nothing to say about whether the premises we start with are true. Another difficulty with logic is that the conclusion of a valid argument never contains more information than is contained in the premises. Logic simply exhibits the implications of a set of statements. In other words, logic gives us a somewhat different way to look at what we already know; it cannot introduce anything truly novel.

Logic is a perfectly delightful tool in a subject such as mathematics, in which we're concerned only with uncovering whatever is implied in our premises. In science, however, we're interested in taking specific observations and discovering the laws or principles that explain them. Such principles are more general, and thus contain more information, than the observations themselves. Logic, in the sense of the term we've been using, is useless for this purpose. It doesn't provide us with a way of discovering a general law of gravity from the observation that apples fall from trees instead of rising into the air. This kind of *inductive* reasoning requires a different guarantee of truth. Easily the most perplexing and critical epistemological problem in understanding science is the problem of how we pass from individual experiences to general principles, from observations to laws.

True, once we have such laws, we can use them as premises and move on by means of logic. On the basis of a law and certain "given" experiences, a new experience is deduced, or predicted. We then see whether or not the prediction is correct.

For example, from the law $F = MA$ (force equals the product of mass and acceleration), we deduce that, if we apply a force of 10 newtons to a 1-kilogram mass, it will accelerate 10 meters per second per second. Sure enough, when we perform an experiment, the mass accelerates just as predicted. If it hadn't, we could have concluded that, supposing our measurements were accurate, the "law" was not correct. The law is therefore a premise in a logical argument. But how do we come to know the law to begin with? If we could answer this question satisfactorily, then we could attack the basic question about the origin of knowledge. Unfortunately, no one has yet been able to give a completely satisfactory answer.

# OTHER SOURCES OF KNOWLEDGE

## *INTUITION*

It begins to appear that experience and reason cannot be all there is to knowledge. Whether we take these individually or together (as in science), we ultimately get backed up against a wall and have to turn elsewhere to find a basis for knowledge. Some philosophers, especially contemporary ones, have insisted that there is nowhere else to turn. The problems must be solved within the framework produced by experience, reason, and science (authority isn't even in the running). Others see that task as hopeless and propose other possible sources of knowledge. One of these sources is intuition.

Intuition is a difficult concept to pin down, but the etymology of the word helps. *Intuition* comes from the Latin word *tueri*, "to look at" or "to watch," and this, in turn, comes from an Indo-European word meaning "to pay attention to." Intuition is sometimes defined as *unmediated* or *direct* knowledge, knowledge we haven't arrived at through some process of reasoning. It is not simply that we are *unaware* of having deduced a particular bit of knowledge. Intuition means that we haven't deduced it at all. When we know simply and directly without any intervening process, then we know intuitively. Carl Jung (1923) writes that intuition is "neither sensation, nor feeling, nor intellectual conclusion, although it may appear in any of these forms. Through intuition any one content is presented as a complete whole, without our being able to explain or discover in what way this content has been arrived at" (p. 567). (Mystics depend on intuitive knowledge rather heavily. We discuss this use of intuition in the next chapter.)

Obviously, intuition is a very difficult notion to make sense of, let alone defend. Nevertheless, we believe that virtually everyone has experienced intuitive knowledge. For example, surely you've met someone and known immediately that you would get on well with that person ("We hit it off right away"). That's intuition. Or perhaps something has occurred to you "out of the clear blue sky." That's intuition, too (and an extremely good description at that). Moreover, it's difficult to understand how we could come to know some of the things we do know, except by intuition. For example, think of someone who loves you. How do you know that person loves you? You can point to all sorts of little clues—a tone of voice, a certain look, a way of acting toward you—but given all these things it still makes sense to ask "But how do you know that you are *loved*?" The great Bengali poet Rabindranath Tagore (1861–1941) answers:

> Love remains a secret even when spoken
> for only a lover truly knows that he is loved.

The notion of intuitive knowledge is not free of serious difficulties. Surely you've had intuitions that were simply wrong. How do you pick out the correct ones? And often people have incompatible intuitions. Surely our intuitions are no better than your intuitions, but what happens when they don't jibe? This begins to raise some familiar questions. The difficulties with authorities often apply here, as do those with experience.

## INHERITED KNOWLEDGE

Another source of knowledge that has been suggested, both on its own merits and in an attempt to explain intuition, is heredity. The suggestion is that certain ideas, or at least a predisposition to think along certain lines, are part of our make-up.

As you recall, Locke believed that at birth our minds are completely without any "innate ideas." Followers of Locke have had the task of explaining how we recognize some statements as certainly true when experience does not yield this kind of certainty. For example, how do we know with certainty that the angles of a triangle *must* sum to 180 degrees? Descartes, on the other hand, took a different tack. He believed that we all have a mental faculty, the *sensus communis*, that allows us to apprehend the truth of certain basic ideas "clearly and distinctly" (to use his phrase) when these ideas present themselves.

Jung presented a view somewhat like Descartes', although in a more subtle form. Jung pointed to the fact that myths and legends, developed in different parts of the world at different times, express similar themes. Together with other evidence, this observation suggested to Jung that some deep memories are not acquired through individual experience; rather, they are part of us as members of the human race. Whereas our conscious memories are of specific events, such as last night's dinner, the contents of this "collective unconscious" appear as predispositions to think about the world and to construct perceptions in certain ways.

According to Jung, events that are familiar and repeated come to represent experiences of the entire human race. For example, everyone was born of a mother. We are nurtured by our mothers in utero, and we were part of and totally dependent on our mothers until birth. Similarly, we are part of and totally dependent on the Earth until our death. And the Earth has been worshipped and regarded as a mother throughout the world.

In recent years, there has been renewed interest in many of Jung's ideas, including the collective unconscious. Perhaps this interest reflects a wish to see all people as part of a cosmological unity, as sharing a common humanity. The idea of the collective unconscious might fulfill this wish by suggesting that we share not only a common bodily structure but also common tendencies to respond to experience in particular ways.

A possible consequence of this view, however, is that changes in our common tendencies might require changes in the collective experience, rather than changes in individual persons. It could be argued, for example, that the past experience of our species with war and violence makes it difficult for people to avoid responding to aggression with further aggression, or that the dominance of the male will take many generations to eradicate because it has been so deeply programmed into our collective experience. On the other hand, since the reactions arising from the collective unconscious only *predispose* people to behave in certain ways, other kinds of learning or pressures might be able to overcome these tendencies. Either way, the notion of the collective unconscious does suggest that there is more to learning and action than individual experience and structural limitations or advantages.

## "UNCOMMON" SOURCES OF KNOWLEDGE

A third alternative source of knowledge is sometimes suggested, and it is the most controversial of all. This source encompasses the whole range of paranormal perception or experiences such as clairvoyance and telepathy. (Actually, we dislike the term *paranormal*, which to some people suggests "abnormality," thus predisposing them to reject these phenomena. Perhaps we should use the term *uncommon perception*.) Our aim in this section is not to persuade you one way or the other on this issue but to invite you to think carefully about it without prejudice in either direction. Since the idea of uncommon sources of knowledge can seem implausible or even bizarre, let's consider a possible case that can be made for it.

Common sense seems to tell us that reality is fully external to us and independent of our experience of it. The qualities of reality are objectively there, as we perceive them. Although we can make mistakes, for the most part our various senses tell us what reality is like. In this way we come to know certain fundamental facts about reality—for instance, that it is spatial and temporal. Let us call this reality *common reality*, since it is the world that is shared by most of us most of the time.

But now let's think about common reality a little more carefully. Consider colors, for example. Look at a red apple. You and a friend normally have no difficulty in agreeing that the apple is red. According to common reality, the apple really is red, just as you see it. Suppose, however, that the red apple is next to a green one and that your friend is color-blind and can't tell one from the other. Common reality has it that the colors are in the apples, that they are objectively different. But this is not the reality your friend experiences. Naturally, you assume that *your* perception is correct. But how do you know? All you *know* is that your friend's perceptions are different from most people's. And even if you can show that common reality is, in some sense, "correct," surely your friend's perceptions are as real to your friend as your perceptions are to you.

To take another example, think of seeing a mirage as you drive across the desert. You might say that you know that what you see is a mirage, but the important point is that you really do see it. Your perception of it is as real to you as your perception of the red color of an apple.

Now suppose your friend claims to see a new color that you can't see and that is not part of common reality. If that sounds absurd, consider the following experience of one of the authors. At a particularly intense moment during a group session he attended one evening, he noticed one participant blink several times and appear astounded, although she didn't say anything. Later she explained that she had seen colored auras surrounding the three people who had been involved in a dramatic interchange; each person had been bathed in a different color that seemed to outline him or her. No one else in the group had seen these colored auras. Were these colors really there, or did the woman imagine them? (Two other alternatives—that she was emotionally disturbed or that she was lying—we will discard, although these explanations have frequently been used to discredit such experiences.) If they were "really" there, why didn't the other people see them? If they weren't "really" there, what did the woman actually see? These questions are important, and we could speculate on possible answers to them; but our goal here is to emphasize that the colored auras *were* really there *for this one person*. They were part of what we will call her *individual reality*.

Individual reality, then, seems to be in the eye of the beholder. What about common reality? Consider the table our apples are resting on. Common reality says that the table is solid matter at rest. Contemporary physics tells us that the table is mostly empty space, and that what matter there is consists of tiny particles in constant motion. Which table is the real one, the table of common reality or the table of scientific reality? There seems to be more than one reality, or, if you prefer, more than one level of reality. Perhaps each has its own validity, possibly a single facet of a deeper reality that we cannot reach directly.

If we admit the possibility of different realities or levels of reality, then uncommon perception does not appear quite so improbable. Perhaps there is a level of reality in which we can indeed be clairvoyant or telepathic. If you refuse to accept any reality beyond common reality and scientific reality, then of course you'll reject this suggestion out of hand. But stop and think a moment about what that rejection involves. Surely the existence of individual reality must be acknowledged. The perceptions of your color-blind friend are, as perceptions, just as real as your own. Can we say that individual reality is in some way less real than common reality?

Let's go back to our apples. How do you construct your perceptions of them? In some way the apples impinge on your sensory apparatus. At that point an electrochemical impulse that bears no intrinsic likeness to an apple is sent to your brain. There the impulse is *interpreted*, along with a whole series of neural firings that are also quite unlike apples. It appears that common reality is nothing more than the generally agreed-upon way of interpreting these impulses and neural firings. What is the relationship between this interpretation and "reality"? Is there any guarantee that it is correct, or even probably correct? How could we ever know whether or not it is correct? Is there any reason for our preference for common reality other than habit and the necessity to have a common ground of communication?

These questions are quite difficult, and we don't propose to answer them. But we do want to indicate how "uncommon" experiences might be thought possible. If you want to reject this possibility, then you must find a way of selecting out some reality as having a preferred status, so that any "reality" that is at odds with it can be rejected. To do this, you must find some way of comparing realities that doesn't require still another "preferred" reality. If you want to accept the possibility of uncommon perception, then you need to argue that there is evidence for a psychic reality that is co-equal with common reality, individual reality, and scientific reality. Neither of these tasks is an easy one, so we must caution you against taking a position on this question too hastily.

□ You might speculate on the problems that arise if the existence of psychic reality is accepted. Consider, for example, precognition, or knowledge of future events. One sure way to dehumanize people is to strip them of the use of their own minds and initiative. When we do this, we turn people into the human robots of Aldous Huxley's *Brave New World*, people who are taken care of and who are unable to make their own decisions. It is for this reason that many people maintain that, even if they could tell other people what the future would be like, they wouldn't do it. It would be a major step toward removing people's ability to plan and cope with uncertainty. And that ability is a major spur to our minds. If you had no uncertainty about the future, what would you have to think about and plan for? How would you be different from a very sophisticated cow or dog? □

# TWO APPROACHES TO REALITY

Although experience seems to be an indispensable source of knowledge, our perceptions and memories aren't necessarily complete and accurate representations of reality. At the very least, we can question whether common reality is all there is to know. It is in the light of this questioning that we should consider the claims of people who say they have certain perceptions or sources of knowledge that do not accord with those of others. Confronted with such claims, we can do one of two things. If we assume that there is an objective reality against which perceptions can be evaluated, we can look for the needs, values, and prior experiences that explain why some people would have distorted perceptions. Our strategy would be to try to understand the dynamics underlying uncommon perceptions and memories. Alternatively, we can assume that some reality different from common reality lies behind these claims and try to understand, and even accept, this other reality. The first alternative assumes that all truth is objective; the second countenances some nonobjective truth.

One of the authors leans toward the first approach, feeling more comfortable with the picture of the universe and of humanity that it implies; the other leans toward the second approach for the same kinds of reasons. Neither of us, however, believes that he has *the* answer to these questions. You may opt for one or the other approach or for some third view. Or you may be totally bewildered and not know what to think. Wherever you end up, though, our hope is that you get there thoughtfully.

By now you've probably noticed that two themes have played with and against each other in our discussion—the primacy of experience and the primacy of the mind. We will come upon the interplay of these alternative themes again and again in this book, because it recurs separately in many facets of human endeavor. As you read this book, and indeed as you live through your life, be alert to it and to its subtleties.

# REFERENCES

Allport, G. W., & Postman, L. J. The basic psychology of rumor. In T. M. Newcomb & E. L. Hartley (Eds.), *Readings in social psychology*. New York: Holt, 1947.

Asch, S. E. Effects of group pressure upon the modification and distortion of judgment. In H. S. Guetzkow (Ed.), *Groups, leadership, and men*. Pittsburgh: Carnegie Press, 1951.

*Dialogues of Plato* (B. Jowett, trans.). In *Great Books of the Western World*, Vol. 7. Encyclopaedia Britannica, 1952.

Jung, C. G. *Psychological types*. London: Routledge & Kegan Paul, 1923.

Lefford, A. The influence of emotional subject matter on logical reasoning. *Journal of General Psychology*, 1946, *34*, 127–151.

Rokeach, M. *The open and closed mind*. New York: Basic Books, 1960.

Tagore, R. *Fireflies*. New York: Collier Books, 1976. (Originally published, 1928.)

# CHAPTER 6

## INTO THE SELF AND BEYOND

*On Beyond Z* wrote Dr. Seuss, author and illustrator of a seemingly endless series of children's books. And beyond Z were new and delightful letters with exotic sounds, for use in naming equally new, exotic, and delightful creatures. As you read this book to children, you begin to wonder why not—why not on beyond Z? What might lie beyond Z? You suspend your normal, reality-bound belief system for a few moments and contemplate what would happen if only you could press a little beyond the limits of the real world. You recall wandering with Dorothy through Oz; seeing Mary Poppins drifting in your window with her umbrella; conversing with Babar; following Alice in a long tumble into Wonderland.

Through books, films, and plays we can easily loosen our hold on reality for as long as we are immersed in the fiction; then we return to the world we know. Many religions also require that we forego our usual beliefs in order to accept the reality of miracles. The scriptures of most major religions demand that we incorporate into our belief systems innumerable occurrences that cannot be explained in naturalistic fashion. And such out-of-the-ordinary events as miraculous cures, the appearance of the stigmata, and religious visions have been experienced by persons who, before the event, would have scoffed at the possibility of encountering a miracle; some of these experiences have apparently been verified by independent observers.

How do you get beyond Z? Perhaps death is one way. Severe mental illness is another. Dreaming is a third. What other ways are there? Mysticism, extrasensory perception, certain kinds of meditation, and drugs—psychedelic, mood, and alcoholic. Finally, religious experiences of many kinds can put people in touch with some extraordinary realm of experience.

The possibility of such experiences brings us back to the basic question, Who are you? *What* are you? What is the real, ultimate existence of you? Is the you that *you* experience bound by time and by space? Do you exist only in the here and now? Are you identical with your body? Are you distinct from every other thing in the world? Many people look for ways to go beyond themselves, to transcend themselves in new forms of awareness. What do these experiences tell us about who we are?

## MOTIVES FOR EXPANSION OF SENSITIVITY BEYOND THE SELF

People wish to go beyond themselves for a variety of reasons. For some, the wish comes because the life they know is so stressful that they want to leave it temporarily. And if they experience being away as much more pleasant than being here, they're likely to get hooked on sensitivity expansion. Others are trying to expand the self rather than leave it. They wish to relate more effectively with people; they want to learn to love and be loved; they want to sleep better; they want to make more sales; they want to be Lauren Bacall or Humphrey Bogart.

The desires of another group are less concretely expressed. They talk about wanting to experience more vividly, to live more fully, to feel at one with humanity or the universe. If you try to pin them down, they become elusive; they may tell you that words won't explain what they mean but that others who have experienced it understand. And they appear to be correct in this surmise, although an outside observer may question whether various persons in this category have really experienced the same thing.

Undoubtedly, some people are motivated to go beyond themselves for reasons that might be termed neurotic or given some comparable label. Undoubtedly, for some people mysticism, extrasensory perception, meditation, or drugs become a way of life, a cause, a movement, a purpose in life, if not indeed a purpose of life. Whether these people are actually more numerous than those who find less obvious but equally neurotic outlets in other movements and causes we don't know. Perhaps they just stand out more because they are more likely to have unusual habits and values.

There are also those who, paradoxically, wish to expand beyond the self in order to find themselves. They feel they can best learn who they really are through experiences that remove the normal constraints of everyday life.

Expanding sensitivity beyond the self can be a solitary or a group experience, although people doing it alone often express a feeling of relatedness to others, while some who select group methods report feelings of being alone or of ultimate privacy.

# MYSTICISM

In Chapter 5, we discussed the topic of knowledge. Now we want to broach a subject that is all too often dismissed by Western philosophers and psychologists—what we will call *nonmaterial* knowledge. So far, we have spoken only of knowledge of things in this material world. Even intuition and knowledge gained by uncommon perception are concerned with this material reality, even if the *source* of the knowledge seems out of the ordinary. A critical question, however, is whether this reality is all there is to know. Do some modes of knowledge reach beyond our material world?

In Western thought, at least since Descartes, it has been taken for granted that material knowledge is indeed all there is, but in Eastern thought it is taken for granted that material knowledge is only one among many modes of knowing. In the East it is normally assumed that nonmaterial knowledge is just as valid and important as material knowledge. The Eastern thinker is likely to see the Western thinker as somewhat provincial, remarking with Tagore (1976):

> The dew-drop knows the sun
>  only within its own tiny orb.

We don't intend to cast our lot with either the East or the West, especially since we're not in complete agreement on this subject. But we do intend to consider as many aspects of human activity as possible, and to do so without passing our assumptions on to you (you can make your own assumptions). Our primary attention in this chapter will be given to mysticism and drug experiences, because these seem to be the most important candidates for the title of nonmaterial knowledge. It is easy for Westerners to throw up their hands at any talk of nonmaterial knowledge, but it's important to note that those who do are in a minority of the world's population. So we think the subject deserves your thoughtful attention.

## *THE MYSTICAL EXPERIENCE*

The obvious place to begin our discussion is to say just what mysticism is, and it is here that we run into our first problem. No one has yet been able to give a completely adequate definition of the word.

A large part of the difficulty is that it is impossible to capture the experience of the mystic in words. Since the ineffable experience of the mystic is critical to any understanding of mystical truth, the mystical *experience*, rather than mystical *knowledge*, is usually the focus of attention.

The contemporary philosopher W. T. Stace (1960) has described a core set of qualities that seem to be present in most, if not all, mystical experiences, and these constitute as good a characterization of the mystical experience as we know of. Note that this list is not a definition but a characterization. Thus, someone may well have a mystical experience that does not include all these characteristics. However, *most* mystical experiences include *most* of them. Here is the list:

1. The mystic feels a sense of the *ultimate reality* of what is experienced; the mystic usually describes this reality as transcending ordinary, material, spatiotemporal reality.
2. The mystic experiences a profound sense of peace or calmness. Very often this peace is carried beyond the mystical experience and stays with the mystic throughout life.
3. The mystic feels that he or she is in the presence of a pure or abstract being. Mystics who are religiously inclined usually describe this being as divine or holy; those who are not so inclined characterize it in some other way, but they usually point to some kind of presence or even to "being" itself.
4. When trying to describe the experience, the mystic will use paradoxical descriptions. For example, some mystics speak of losing themselves in the unity of being.
5. The mystic usually claims that the experience is ineffable, indescribable, so far beyond the power of ordinary words to reach that trying to capture it in language is like trying to hold a ray of sun in your hands.

Imagine that you're looking at a field of flowers. You see the yellow expanse of the flowers clearly against a background of green foliage. As you look, the flowers become more and more distinct, so that you begin to see them separately, as unique, individual entities. This kind of heightened perception is not uncommon. But now suppose that, as you look, the flowers become Alive, not just as biologically living things, but Vibrant with the power of existence, so that you are drawn into this power and experience your own vitality as one with the vitality of the flowers. Then you will have had what is called an *extrovertive* mystical experience—that is, one in which you are drawn out of yourself and made aware of a basic unity in all things. It was this kind of experience that led one mystic to exclaim "I am in all things, and all things are in me!"

Now imagine concentrating very hard on something, perhaps a problem or an engrossing book or TV program. In your concentration, you shut out awareness of everything else, so much so that, if someone were to speak to you, you wouldn't hear. This is the basic principle of prepared childbirth, in which the woman is taught to concentrate hard enough on certain breathing patterns that she can ignore the distress signals coming from her uterus. Again, this kind of heightened concentration is not uncommon. But now suppose that you manage to concentrate your attention even further, so that all sensory inputs other than the object of your concentration are completely blocked out. A fair number of people are able to do this, including one of your authors (Collier). Now imagine deepening your concentration even further, so that even the original object of thought is removed. What happens? A typical Western answer is that you would experience nothing at all, a complete lack of awareness. The "introvertive" mystic, however, answers that, far from experiencing nothing, you would experience "Pure Consciousness," "Absolute Selfhood," or perhaps what the theologian Paul Tillich called "the Ground of Being." This sinking inward to find the unity of being is the essence of the *introvertive* mystical experience.

In each of these two major modes of mystical experience, the mystic has an immediate experience of a fundamental kinship with all things. This kinship is so strong that the mystic may describe it as a joining of polar opposites or a unity of all things. In one mode, the mystic is drawn out to other things to the point of seeing through their differences to their fundamental unity (the extrovertive experience); in the other, the mystic sinks so deeply within his or her own consciousness that all separateness vanishes and all is Oneness, Unity, or God (the introvertive experience).

Let us illustrate this rather abstract description of the mystical state with two accounts of mystical experiences provided by the mystics themselves. The first recounts an extrovertive experience. It is quoted in Stace's book *Mysticism and Philosophy*. The mystic is a contemporary American whom Stace (1960) calls "N.M."

> The room in which I was standing looked out onto the back yards of a Negro tenement. The buildings were decrepit and ugly, the ground covered with boards, rags, and debris. Suddenly every object in my field of vision took on a curious and intense kind of existence of its own; that is, everything appeared to have an "inside"—to exist as I existed, having inwardness, a kind of individual life, and every object, seen under this aspect, appeared exceedingly beautiful. There was a cat out there, with its head lifted, effortlessly watching a wasp that moved without moving just above its head. Everything was *urgent* with life ... which was the same in the cat, the wasp, the broken bottles, and merely manifested itself differently in these individuals (which did not therefore cease to be individuals, however). All things seemed to glow with a light that came from within them.
>
> I experienced a complete certainty that at that moment I saw things

as they really were, and I was filled with grief at the realization of the real situation of human beings, living in the midst of all this without being aware of it [pp. 71–72].

The second is an introvertive experience described by a 19th-century man of letters, J. A. Symonds. This passage is quoted by William James (1936) in *The Varieties of Religious Experience.*

> Suddenly at church, or in company, or when I was reading . . . I felt the approach of the mood. Irresistibly it took possession of my mind and will, lasted what seemed an eternity and disappeared in a series of rapid sensations which resembled the awakening from an anaesthetic influence. One reason why I disliked this kind of trance was that I could not describe it to myself. I cannot even now find words to render it intelligible. It consisted in a gradual but swiftly progressive obliteration of space, time, sensation, and the multifarious factors of experience which seem to qualify what we are pleased to call our Self. In proportion as these conditions of ordinary consciousness were subtracted, the sense of an underlying or essential consciousness acquired intensity. At last nothing remained but a pure, absolute, abstract Self. The universe became without form and void of content. But Self persisted, formidable in its vivid keenness. . . . [p. 385].

## MYSTICISM AND OUR VIEW OF REALITY

Assuming that the mystics are neither lying nor suffering from some mental aberration (both very unlikely, given the agreement among mystics widely scattered in both space and time), there can be little doubt about the authenticity of mystical experiences. The mystics do experience something extraordinary that is indisputably part of their individual realities. The controversy has to do with whether they experience a reality that in any way goes beyond individual reality—whether they report intersubjective truths or individual observations.

What would we have to believe if we were to accept the mystics' claims about reality? It's very difficult to give a straightforward answer to this question, because mystics almost always are forced to express their reports in terms of a prevailing myth and way of speaking. St. Teresa of Avila makes her claims in the language of medieval Catholicism; Sri Ramakrishna makes his claims in the language of Hindu myth and metaphor. (Notice that we are *not* using the word *myth* in a belittling sense, as denoting a false or discredited story; we are using it in its original sense, as denoting a nonliteral expression of truth. Every religion and culture, including ours, uses myth.) In spite of this difficulty, we can indicate, in a rudimentary way, the claims that most mystics make.

First, mystics usually claim that common reality, with its insistence on the separateness and diversity of things, is not correct. Let us go back to our two apples. At the level of common reality, the apples are separate, solid, distinct entities. This way of perceiving, the mystic tells us, allows us to function in the material world, but is an illusion. At a more fundamental level, such distinctions between objects fall away to reveal a unitary reality in which there is neither separation nor diversity.

Second, mystics generally claim that the rule of logic is limited to common reality and does not apply to mystical reality. "True" and "false" are polar opposites, and all such opposites are swallowed up. Thus, mystics make claims such as "I am in all things, and all things are in me," an evident impossibility in common reality. This does not mean that mystical reality is chaotic. All it means is that it is not organized according to the dictates of logic.

Third, mystics usually claim that all things and beings are interrelated. At the level of common reality, mystics may see themselves as independent beings, but at the more fundamental level of mystical reality, they see that they are inseparable from the rest of the world.

There are other claims mystics generally make—for example, that space and time are features of common reality alone—but these three should suffice to show the kinds of radical changes we will have to make in our thinking about reality if we accept the vision of the mystics.

## MYSTICAL REALITY:
## A PERSONAL ASSESSMENT

So far we have described mystical reality, but we haven't asked why anyone might accept its existence. As we see it, there are essentially three reasons.

First, there is strong reason to believe that modern physics is being forced to accept ideas that are not only compatible with mysticism but actually parallel to it. We cannot draw this argument out in detail here; if you're interested, consult *The Tao of Physics*, by University of California physicist Fritjof Capra.

Second, as we pointed out earlier, the vast majority of cultures have accepted mystical reality. In the face of this acceptance, the burden of proof seems to be on the skeptics to show why there is no such thing. Those who accept mystical reality are not convinced that the skeptics have succeeded.

Stated briefly, the skeptics' argument amounts to this: If we take the mystics at their word, mystical "reality" is inherently paradoxical and contains outright contradictions, like N.M.'s "wasp that moved without moving." But that means that mystical "reality" is impossible and so not real at all.

This argument, however, begs the question. It assumes that all reality is like the skeptics' reality; that is, all reality fits into a logical order. If a central claim of mystics is that their reality *doesn't* fit that logical order, one of the issues to be decided is whether or not all reality must be logical. It won't do, then, to fault mystics for disagreeing with the skeptics. It's certainly true that they disagree, but that doesn't settle the issue; it just restates that there is an issue.

The third reason for accepting mystical reality is really the central one. We could argue at length about mystical reality, but, if we aren't mystics, we would be like blind people arguing about the existence of color. Unless they actually experienced color, their knowledge would at best be secondhand, conditional, indirect. People accept mystical reality for the same reason they accept color: because they experience it.

□ If you've had a mystical experience, how do you understand it? Does your experience convince you that mystical reality is as real as common reality? If not, what more evidence do you need? Is it possible to get that evidence? If you haven't had a mystical experience, are the claims of the mystics sufficient to convince you at secondhand? If not, what evidence do you need? If so, how do you answer the skeptics? □

# DRUG-INDUCED EXPERIENCES

Much of our discussion of mysticism carries over to drug-induced experiences. Here we have two basic questions: can drugs induce genuinely mystical experiences? If so, are these experiences as authentic and as valuable as those that are not induced by drugs? Clearly, not all drug experiences are mystical. Some drug experiences, however, are experientially indistinguishable from unquestionably mystical experiences. If this does not seem obvious, consider the following evidence borrowed from a contemporary philosopher, Huston Smith (1964). Here are two experiences, one a drug experience, one not. See whether you can tell which is which.

> I. Suddenly I burst into a vast, new, indescribably wonderful universe. Although I am writing this over a year later, the thrill of the surprise and amazement, the awesomeness of the revelation, the engulfment in an overwhelming feeling-wave of gratitude and blessed wonderment, are as fresh, and the memory of the experience is as vivid, as if it had happened five minutes ago. And yet to concoct anything by way of description that would even hint at the magnitude, the sense of ultimate reality . . . this seems such an impossible task. The knowledge which has infused and affected every aspect of my life came instantaneously and with such complete force of certainty that it was impossible, then or since, to doubt its validity.

II. All at once, without warning of any kind, I found myself wrapped in a flame-colored cloud. For an instant I thought of fire ... the next, I knew that the fire was within myself. Directly afterward there came upon me a sense of exultation, of immense joyousness accompanied or immediately followed by an intellectual illumination impossible to describe. Among other things, I did not merely come to believe, but I saw that the universe is not composed of dead matter, but is, on the contrary, a living Presence; I became conscious in myself of eternal life.... I saw that all men are immortal: that the cosmic order is such that without any preadventure all things work together for the good of each and all; that the foundation principle of the world ... is what we call love, and that the happiness of each and all is in the long run absolutely certain [p. 522].[1]

Smith remarks that, when he invited 69 students to take this test, twice as many answered wrong as answered right. (The correct answer is given in a footnote at the end of this chapter.)

Even those who grant that a drug experience can be experientially the same as a mystical experience may argue that the need for the drug makes the experience less genuine or valuable than a true mystical experience. One extremely important feature of mystical experiences seems to be that they can sometimes reshape a person's entire life. Consider the Buddha. When he received his enlightenment, he was sitting under a tree in deep meditation. The traditional story is that the Evil One, Mara, realizing the significance of what was happening, came to destroy the young Buddha. Mara knew that it was fruitless to sway the Buddha from his emerging enlightenment, so he tempted him instead. Pointing to the bliss of Nirvana and the difficulty of life on Earth, he told the Buddha that he should not sully himself with the material world but remain in Nirvana throughout eternity. But the Buddha, who knew that giving in to this temptation would be a denial of his enlightenment, roused himself from his meditation and returned to spend the remaining 50 years of his life using that enlightenment in the world. (Interestingly, similar stories are told of both Jesus and Mohammed.)

Now it may be argued that drug-induced experiences, unlike the Buddha's enlightenment, are likely to become ends in themselves and thus differ from "genuine" mystical experiences. Religion or mysticism should involve something more than extraordinary experiences. Thus we find Smith (1964) saying in the context of a religious understanding of mysticism:

If the religion of religious experience is a snare and a delusion, it follows that no religion that fixes its faith primarily in substances that

[1]From "Do Drugs Have Religious Import?" by H. Smith, *Journal of Philosophy*, 1964, *61*, 517–530. Reprinted by permission.

induce religious experience can be expected to come to a good end. What promised to be a shortcut will prove to be a short circuit; what began as a religion will end up as a religion surrogate. Whether chemical substances can be a helpful *adjunct* to faith is another question [p. 529].

□ What is *your* answer to Smith's question? Can chemical substances be an adjunct, an aid, to faith? Can we gain important insight into other realms of reality with drugs? Are there other realms at all, or is their existence just another delusion? If it is a delusion, how do you answer the arguments of those who believe in it? □

# MEDITATION

Meditation is an ancient method of developing a receptive attitude. It is practice in the skill of being quiet and paying attention (Maupin, 1969). In Christianity, meditation is thoughtful reflection on a particular theme, with the goal of improving spiritual insight and feelings. *Contemplation* refers to a similar state, one that is more difficult to attain; in contemplation, "the attempt is made to empty the mind of everything except the percept of the object in question" (Deikman, 1969, p. 27). However, contemporary interest in meditation and contemplation probably arises less from Christian tradition than from Eastern religions. Like many other newly popular forms of religious consciousness and expanded sensitivity, what is sometimes termed contemplative meditation is part of a trend away from the Western notion of the importance of action and change and toward the Eastern goal of looking within, of trying to attain spiritual rather than social or practical satisfaction.

This form of meditation has come under attack for at least three reasons. First, it can be carried too far, so that its practitioners lose the ability to cope with the real world that surrounds them. Second, it drains the energies of potentially productive people who might otherwise be using their energy to ameliorate social problems. Third, the alleged personal growth achieved through meditation may have little or no impact on other aspects of the individual's life.

Do the benefits of meditation outweigh these potential difficulties? Proponents of Transcendental Meditation argue that, according to research studies, TM leads to these positive outcomes: reduced use of tranquilizers, stimulants, and nonprescribed drugs; enhanced recall over both short-term and long-term periods; better perceptual and motor performance; reduced time lag for response; greater relaxation; and so forth (Transcendental Meditation Society, 1972). Moreover, subjects report experiencing very positive feelings both during the experience and afterwards.

The basic value of meditation can be debated, but there can be no doubt that meditation does produce both physiological and psychological changes in human beings that most probably differ from changes induced by hypnosis or self-hypnosis. Although the underlying mechanisms that enable meditation to produce these changes are not fully understood, the changes themselves have been documented. Wallace (1970) lists physiological changes in skin resistance, electroencephalographic patterns, and oxygen consumption, among others. The psychological changes are even more dramatic. One investigator had eight men, all in their thirties and forties, concentrate upon a vase with the goal of seeing it in its wholeness, as it exists, without associated ideas and without being aware of distracting occurrences or thoughts. The goal was to "experience the vase." Each person underwent 12 sessions of 15 to 20 minutes over a three-week period. Many effects were noted. For example, the color of the vase was perceived as becoming more vivid and intense, and the duration of the sessions often seemed very brief but was sometimes perceived as very long. All subjects agreed that the experience was extremely positive. Several of them described unique experiences involving altered perceptions and awareness (Deikman, 1969).

Meditation works without drugs, devices, hypnosis, or surrender of power to someone else. It has therefore received support both from persons involved in new religious (and nonreligious) consciousness and from those who adhere to the status quo. Although the excitement it initially generated has diminished, meditation is no longer considered exotic or peculiar; it seems to be here to stay.

## THE IMPORTANCE OF MYSTICISM

Mysticism is rarely discussed in the writings of behavioral scientists. When it is mentioned, it is usually in the context of aberrant behavior, unusual religious cults, or historical events. Nonetheless, a great many persons believe in the possibility of a direct and immediate knowledge of God or some other supernatural reality. Many others who have not established a definite position in their own thinking have had one or more personal experiences that they feel can best be interpreted in some mystical or supernatural fashion.

Why do behavioral scholars avoid the subject of mysticism? There are several reasons. They may feel that mystical experience is beyond their ability to probe. Their theories of the universe may require explanations that do not go beyond the bounds of what is normally assumed to be nature. They may avoid mysticism because a mystical experience cannot be empirically evaluated; that is, it is so personal to the individual experiencing it that others cannot share in the experience or perceive its occurrence. Some scientists may believe that a naturalistic explanation of mysticism will be forthcoming but that present methodologies are inadequate. Or it may simply be that the assumptions behavioral scientists make about the orderliness of the universe do not allow for divine or supernatural interventions.

Regardless of what behavioral scientists choose to study, mystical experience is very much a part of the lives of many people. To ignore it is to ignore an important kind of influence on human behavior, on ways of coping with stress, and on the individual realities of a large segment of the population. In a study conducted a few years ago, nearly half of 434 interviewees admitted to some form of encounter with a person already dead; although many of these encounters occurred in dreams, the returned dead person was perceived as much more real than a dream figure (Kalish & Reynolds, 1973). Many recent books have described experiences both with the dead and with a kind of temporary visit to death (see, for example, Moody, 1975, and Osis & Haraldsson, 1977).

Referring to a well-known study of the great mystics by the philosopher Henri Bergson (1935), who was not committed to the Christian faith, Becker (1971) states:

> He discovered, to his own surprise, that the mystics were individuals of great vitality and action and "from their increased vitality there radiated an extraordinary energy, daring, power of conception and realization" (Bergson, 1935, p. 216). So great is Bergson's estimation of the mystics that he sees in them the soaring embodiment of humanity's own possibilities which otherwise travel at a pedestrian level. It is the mystics who light up humanity and set an example of what men may become [p. 414].

Admittedly, Bergson's analysis was limited to the major figures of Christianity, and not all persons who have mystical experiences exhibit the vitality, energy, daring, and power that he describes. Nonetheless, many "ordinary" persons who have had these experiences describe the effects in glowing terms and feel that their lives subsequently changed, sometimes in remarkable ways.

Obviously, the subject of mysticism is a deep and involved one. There is wide disagreement (even between your authors) concerning how the claims made by mystics should be evaluated. We do agree on this, though: mysticism is a serious subject, and it deserves more serious attention than the rather cavalier treatment usually afforded it in the West.

We want to close this chapter by mentioning one other consideration. Our society is sometimes seen as losing some of its vitality, some of its vision of its own worth and place. Some have attributed this loss to a religious decline. Perhaps this explanation is correct, and perhaps it is not. But many mystics have argued that the mystical vision can be a source of renewed vitality. Smith (1964) speaks eloquently of the challenge of mysticism, again in a religious context:

The distinctive emotion and the one drugs unquestionably can occasion ... in a phrase, the phenomenon of religious awe, seems to be declining sharply. As Paul Tillich said in an address to the Hillel Society at Harvard several years ago:

The question our century puts before [us] is: Is it possible to regain the lost dimension, the encounter with the Holy, the dimension which cuts through the world of subjectivity and objectivity and goes down to that which is not world but is the mystery of the Ground of Being?

Tillich may be right; this may be the religious question of our century. For if ... religion cannot be equated with the religious experience, neither can it long survive its absence [p. 530].

# REFERENCES

Becker, R. J. Religion and psychological health. In M. P. Strommen (Ed.), *Research on religious development*. New York: Hawthorn, 1971.

Bergson, H. *The two sources of morality and religion*. (R. A. Audra & C. Brerenton, trans.) New York: Holt, 1935.

Capra, F. *The Tao of physics*. Boulder, Colorado: Shambala, 1975.

Deikman, A. J. Deautomaticsation and the mystic experience. In C. T. Tart (Ed.), *Altered states of consciousness*. New York: Wiley, 1969.

James, W. *The varieties of religious experience*. New York: Modern Library, 1936. (Originally published, 1902.)

Kalish, R. A., & Reynolds, D. K. Phenomenological reality and post-death contact. *Journal for the Scientific Study of Religion*, 1973, *12*, 209–221.

Maupin, E. W. On meditation. In C. T. Tart (Ed.), *Altered states of consciousness*. New York: Wiley, 1969.

Moody, R. A. *Life after life*. New York: Bantam, 1975.

Osis, K., & Haraldsson, E. *At the hour of death*. New York: Avon, 1977.

Smith, H. Do drugs have religious import? *Journal of Philosophy*, 1964, *61*, 517–530.

Stace, W. T. *Mysticism and philosophy*. Philadelphia: Lippincott, 1960.

Tagore, R. *Fireflies*. New York: Collier Books, 1976. (Originally published, 1928.)

Transcendental Meditation Society. *Scientific research on Transcendental Meditation*. Transcendental Meditation Society, 1972.

Wallace, R. K. The physiological effects of transcendental meditation. *Science*, 1970, *167*, 1751–1754.

Note: The first experience described by Smith is a drug experience; the second is a mystical experience.

# CHAPTER 7

## CULTURE AND MORALITY

Can values be absolute? For all persons and all times? Must they be relative? Limited to certain cultures? To certain eras? Can a value be so relative as to be valid only for you? Or so relative that it is valid only for you *today*?

In our own time the cultural relativity of values, including moral and ethical values, seems virtually to be taken for granted. Yet the issue of the absoluteness or relativity of values is a complicated one, and the answer may not be as straightforward as most people assume. The significance of this issue is that it impinges directly on the moral considerations underlying our day-to-day behavior, on what we think is right or wrong or, perhaps, beyond evaluation.

## ABSOLUTISM VERSUS RELATIVISM

One of the most basic questions we can ask about moral values is whether or not there is an absolute, or independent, basis for morality and moral behavior. Are there moral universals that stand outside how a person is taught and reared? Are there kinds of behavior that are right or wrong, now and forever, here and everywhere?

Notice that these questions have nothing to do with individuals' moral *judgments*. Most philosophers agree that the judgments we make are necessarily relative to our knowledge, our social situations, and many other factors. The argument has to do with the *basis* of morality itself. Regardless of whether or not you perceive an act as right or good, is there some absolute standard that makes it a good act?

Philosophers call those who believe that there is an independent basis for morality *deontologists* (from the Greek *deontos*, meaning "necessity"). Typical of their position is the claim that there is a moral reality not unlike physical reality. Just as the physical world is governed by physical laws that do not depend on us and our knowledge of them, the moral world is governed by moral laws that are independent of our knowledge. Our moral judgments reflect our imperfect understanding of these laws and must not be confused with them, just as our scientific formulas reflect our imperfect understanding of the physical world. How else, the deontologist asks, could we make mistakes in our moral judgments? Doesn't the possibility of being in error require that there be an independent standard of correctness? And wouldn't most of us agree that humans do make mistakes in their moral judgments?

Those who believe that there is no independent basis for morality are called *relativists*. They argue, typically, that what moral judgments reflect is not some independent moral reality but the feelings of some individual or group of individuals. Morality is essentially based on people's *feelings* about things, and translated into standards of action. But since our feelings, surely, are highly influenced by all kinds of things, from culture to climate, there are no moral absolutes. To say otherwise would require the silly claim that there are absolute feelings.

☐ Obviously this is a very complicated problem. Both sides seem equally right—and equally wrong! Think of your favorite good. Is it in any sense an absolute good? Or is it good because you or your society feel good about it and have developed it as a value? How can you decide? How would your beliefs and actions be affected if you were convinced that your "good" was a relative one? An absolute one? ☐

Absolutism can be demanding and restrictive; it may leave little room for individual differences in temperament, ability, or upbringing; it may require an acceptance of supernaturally revealed divine laws or a belief that human reason is strong enough to comprehend a universal, natural law of morality. Relativism can mean that people have no ultimate guidelines—that, whatever you do, the only moral error you can make is not being attentive enough to your own feelings.

# CULTURAL RELATIVISM:
# ITS EVOLUTIONARY ROOTS

When it was assumed that the world as people knew it was made by God in seven days and seven nights, and that the creation took place only some 6000 years ago, it was easier to believe that God, in creating the earth, had also put forth some universal values and morals, especially as interpreted in the Old and New Testaments. As more and more people questioned whether God had created the earth in the way described in the Old Testament and began to believe instead that the earth and its peoples had developed to their present status over many millions of years, the basis for unchanging God-given moral principles was undermined.

In 1830, a book by Charles Lyell, a British geologist, provided evidence that the world had not necessarily been created in 4004 B.C., as was generally assumed at the time, but rather had been formed millions, perhaps hundreds of millions, of years earlier. Moreover, Lyell insisted that the present form of the earth had resulted from gradual change over its entire history (Greer, 1968). If the earth's history was a long story of gradual change, produced by natural and observable (to some extent predictable) causes, rather than a brief story in which changes resulted only from divine intervention, then the origins of human life might similarly be traced backward in time. About 20 years later, the virtually simultaneous work of Charles Darwin and Alfred Russel Wallace made exactly this point. Just as Lyell had argued that the world's geological structure had evolved from earlier geological forms, Darwin and Wallace gave evidence that observed biological structures had evolved from earlier biological forms.

The concept of evolution encouraged the acceptance of cultural relativity by calling into question the very bases of contemporary theology and shifting the focus of scientists and philosophers. No longer did scientists assume that they could help discover some ultimate truth leading to an understanding of the purpose of the world or the cause of existence. Now they began to think of the *process* of change as much more important than the *object* of change. This shift in focus is one of the most profound revolutions in human thought. (See Capra [1975] for some of the implications of this revolution.) With this shift, the entire Judaeo-Christian concept of Creation and its purpose was called into question.

The Judaeo-Christian God was hardly eliminated by these writings, but His role in Creation was pushed far back in time. Purpose was put at the end of process instead of the beginning, and attention was put on process. Of course, many opposed—and some still oppose—the concept of evolution, explaining it as a trap established by

God to test the faith of the believer or attempting to throw doubt upon the adequacy of the evolutionists' scientific evidence and research methodologies. Nonetheless, although the precise origins of Homo sapiens remain somewhat obscure, and although the explanation for the appearance of new species is still not agreed upon, the general notion that biological forms change through an evolutionary process is reasonably well established and effectively incorporated into Christian teachings. Our present concern is with the influence of evolutionary thought upon personal and social values and resultant human behavior.

## INFLUENCES OF EVOLUTIONARY THOUGHT UPON BEHAVIOR AND VALUES

Evolution, a historian has written, "toppled Man from his exalted position as the end and purpose of creation, the crown of Nature, and the image of God, and classified him prosaically with the anthropoids" (Commager, 1950, p. 83). Yet, by leaving open the possibility that the evolution of Homo sapiens from its earliest organic beginnings to its present form could have been guided by the hand of God—operating more slowly than previously assumed and working through natural processes—Darwin enabled many of the devout to reconcile their religious views with the new concepts of evolution.

It was Herbert Spencer, a follower of Darwin, who coined the phrase "survival of the fittest" to describe what he perceived to be a major principle of evolutionary development. Spencer further insisted that the concept was applicable not only to plants and animals but also to human culture. Since the idea of the evolution of organic life found fairly rapid acceptance, Spencer's notion that customs and ideas might also go through a process of evolution likewise was reasonably well received, at least in some circles.

The implications of this line of thought were far-reaching. First, if institutions, customs, and ideas survive only if they are found congenial by the culture, then the notion of absolute moral and religious truth makes no sense. The ideas that we now hold are those that have survived, not necessarily those that are, in any absolute sense, true. (The Pragmatists of the late 19th and early 20th centuries did turn survival into a test of truth, however. This maneuver didn't rescue *absolute* truth, but it did make the important link between survival and truth and helped reintroduce the notion of truth to ethics and religion.) The social sciences of anthropology, psychology, and sociology had their modern origins during the years immediately following Darwin's major work, and some of their findings, especially anthropological descriptions of various cultures, added fuel to the argument that human customs and institutions are relevant only to certain times and certain places. This principle, that the values by which people live are time-bound and space-bound, remains controversial.

Second, if survival of the fittest is a law of nature, then there can be no circumventing it. We are all equally caught in its web, just as we are all forced to obey Newton's laws of motion. In earlier centuries, those who were successful viewed their success as the outcome of divine will, while those who failed were perceived as having been divinely designated for failure. Armed with Spencer's Law of Survival, the successful now saw themselves as vindicated not only by God but by natural selection, while the failures were condemned not only by divine plan but by natural necessity. Moreover, war, starvation, slavery, and financial exploitation were justified as expediting Nature's plan to do away with the weak and to establish the dominance of the strong. The survival of the fittest that was thought to occur in the jungle of trees and wild animals was generalized to the jungle of human civilization. John D. Rockefeller, Sr., compared his success in developing Standard Oil to the breeding of the American Beauty rose, insisting that both required the sacrifice of inferior buds, which is "merely the working-out of a law of nature and a law of God." The application of evolution to human life also buttressed the laissez-faire approach to economics (the theory that the market works best when it is left strictly alone), a theory that still influences Western thought.

Third, although evolution was perceived as moving in a "good" direction, toward its goal of universal harmony, acceptance of natural selection changed God from an active agent, able to intervene at will, to a guiding light who tended to follow the established principle of permitting the fittest to survive. Natural selection also reduced the potential of people to determine their own fates, since only the most fit were destined to survive. Americans, though, tended to ignore these latter implications, since their own history had made them, in Commager's words, "tinkerers, and experience had taught them that they could change anything" (Commager, 1950, p. 89).

Fourth, it was soon realized that cultural progress was not inevitable, that those persons most fit for survival might not be those who would provide an optimum future for the other residents of the planet. Therefore, in the long run, acceptance of evolution enhanced the demand for intelligent social planning and active interventions. One result was the development of eugenics, or scientific breeding; another was the encouragement of the social sciences as, to quote John Hermann Randall (1940), "detailed study of the specific causes that produce specific results, and an intensive manipulation of our social heritage to produce what seems *to us* good." (We have italicized two words in the previous sentence to emphasize the catch in all this social planning.)

The notion of evolution, then, coinciding with increased sophistication about life and values in various cultures, moved people to question the idea that their moral principles were laid down by God for time eternal. Consider the moral values and concerns of people who have continued to oppose the teaching of evolution in the schools: not only do these opponents of evolutionary thought adhere to traditional religious views and literal interpretations of the Old Testament, but they also have traditional moral values about such issues as sexual behavior and roles, authority, and child rearing.

□ Evolution, even the teaching of evolution in the schools, is still an issue. What are your beliefs on the validity of evolution as an explanation for the origins of the human race? Do you believe that moral guidelines are equally valid throughout the ages or that they are time-bound and place-bound, at least to some extent? What are the implications of your assumptions about evolution and morality? □

## CULTURAL VARIABILITY ACROSS TIME AND ACROSS SPACE

Assume for the moment that, through chance or through magic, two other people have been conceived whose genetic structure exactly duplicates yours. One of these duplicates was conceived 2000 years ago (or 20,000 years ago, if you prefer), wherever your parent's ancestors were at that time. The other duplicate was conceived at the very same moment as you by a man and woman living in the mountain country of Peru, a small city in Kenya, a rural commune in southern China, a ski resort in the Swiss Alps, or in whatever place you'd like to imagine.

Despite your genetic identity, by the time each of the three of you was born, some differences would already have occurred; by the time each of you reached the age of 2, considerable differences would be evident; by the age of 16 or 28 or 53, increasingly striking differences would be apparent. These differences, obviously, would have been produced by your respective environments, which in turn would largely be determined by your respective cultures and subcultures.

Definitions of *culture* abound in the behavioral literature, but—in spite of considerable differences in wording—the general meanings are similar. One definition that seems to integrate the various approaches states that culture is *socially shared and transmitted knowledge, represented through behavioral and material artifacts, concerning both what does exist and what ought to exist* (after Wilson, 1971).

The influence of your culture upon your behavior, your feelings, and your values is so immense and pervasive that grasping it is difficult. Let us cite just a few culturally influenced behavior patterns:

- the food you eat, the way it is prepared, the persons with whom you feel it is appropriate to eat, the utensils you eat with, and the kinds of food you consume at different times of the day or week or year;
- the persons eligible for you to make love to and to marry, the preludes to love-making and marriage, the physical conditions of love-making, the obligations implicit in sexual relationships, methods of avoiding pregnancy, your responsibilities as a parent in or out of wedlock;
- your formal education, the kind of person who serves as your teacher and the obligations you have toward this person, the established goals of your education, the physical conditions of your school;
- your views of how the world and the universe began, of the role of humanity in the universe, of the nature of a divine being (if any), of your ability to alter the direction of your own life, of whether death leads to total extinction or to some other form of existence;
- your interaction with machinery and technology, your understanding or ignorance of electricity and other forms of power, your grasp of the mechanics of machines and of how to utilize them to best advantage;
- your work arrangements and fiscal considerations, the jobs for which you consider yourself eligible, the relative status of your job, alternative ways of obtaining income and the relative status of these various ways, the worth of money and of what it will buy, job mobility.

This list of culturally influenced behavior patterns could be expanded almost indefinitely. Notice, however, that behavior and artifacts are the *products* of culture, not the culture itself. Culture is *not* the skeleton and accompanying pottery found in an Indian burial mound; nor is it a marijuana joint, a high divorce rate, or the habit of spending Sunday afternoons watching football games. Rather, culture is the knowledge of how to bury a person according to what is considered proper ritual, the values that determine whether marijuana is socially and legally acceptable, the customs that permit or encourage divorce, and the knowledge and values of rules and traditions concerning football. (Our use of the word *culture* is somewhat different from Rousseau's, but the two uses are related.)

Inevitably, not everyone in a given culture functions in exactly the same fashion. You bring to your culture your own unique genetic make-up and your own individual physical appearance, and these interact with the culture; you are also assigned several roles by the culture, depending upon your sex, age, education, family status, and so forth; and your own life experiences will differ from those of other persons who share your roles and your culture. Ultimately the interaction between what you bring to the world and what the world does to you will differentiate you from all other persons.

Also, larger cultures have crosscurrents occurring within them. Some of these crosscurrents develop from the multiplicity of subcultures—smaller groups of people with clearly identifiable values that exist *within* the geographical boundaries of a dominant culture.

Within the dominant culture of the United States there are ethnic, religious, and regional subcultures. In addition, individual and group deviations from cultural norms are always found within any given culture or subculture. Among middle-class male Whites of European ancestry, for example, will be found homosexuals, persons living on rural communes, militant advocates of Black supremacy, men who want to father children without marrying the mothers, men who wish to bake bread rather than buy it, men who refuse to eat meat, men who are in training to serve as guerilla fighters when the Communists take over the country, and men who are addicted to heroin. Moreover, the degree to which a culture will tolerate deviation and accept the conflicting values of its subcultures depends on the values of the culture. Vegetarians are more tolerated than homosexuals; workers on communes are more tolerated than advocates of violence.

You would differ not only from a contemporary duplicate reared in another culture, but from a duplicate reared in your own culture in another era or even in another generation. You probably are more sophisticated with regard to the differing values of other cultures and subcultures elsewhere in today's world than you are with respect to the differing values of your own culture just a few decades ago. No doubt you have no difficulty recognizing that a duplicate of you born 2000 years ago would differ from you because of cultural influences, but have you given real consideration to the dramatic changes in your culture since 1900?

Joe was born in Nebraska in 1902 to parents of Germanic extraction. As a child he had no telephone, movies, airplanes, automobiles, running water, or electricity. His country was not a world leader, had no race problem it was aware of, had no income tax or social security, and was not cognizant of having urban problems. He was reared on a family farm, later moving to a small town. Raised as a Protestant, Joe knew no Jews and few Catholics and never considered the possibility of a Black man as a peer.

After finishing ninth grade, Joe went to work. Shortly afterward he entered the armed forces just as World War I was ending. Mustered out of the service at 19, he reentered the work force, married, had children, bought insurance, and eventually voted for "a chicken in every pot." When he was 27, the stock market crash wiped out the investment money Joe had been speculating with, forced him to give up his insurance policies, and scared the daylights out of him.

At 31, Joe felt his world cave in. With a 3-year-old and an 8-year-old to take care of, he was jobless and standing in line at soup kitchens. With much persistence and good luck, he managed to land another job fairly quickly and was able to keep his family fed and clothed, although it was hand-to-mouth for a while.

In his early forties, Joe left his job for war industry and, for the first time, was covered by social security. However, in spite of a few good years, he was tossed back onto the job market by technological developments at the age of 44, without salable skills. His next job carried less status and paid less money, but he held on and retired in 1967 with a modest amount of social security, a small house with the mortgage nearly paid up, a married daughter, and a son whose starting salary on his first job nearly equalled the highest salary Joe had ever earned.

Now Joe hears talk of abortion on demand, affirmative action, negative income tax, and Supreme Court restrictions on local police. The entire value system he felt comfortable with seems distressingly challenged.

Joe's son, Matthew, had a much different life. He was still a child during the Depression, but he has some vivid images and remembers that his family had very little money to spend. He recalls being pushed to do well in school and go to college so that he could obtain a good job and never be unemployed. He went into the armed services just in time to catch the GI Bill, and he spent two years in college before dropping out to take a job in a large city teeming with people and automobiles. His life has been a series of steps up the economic ladder, and it seems logical to him that study and hard work should do for everyone what it did for him. After all, despite being poor and uneducated, his father had made the sacrifices necessary to do a good job of raising two kids. So Matthew works, achieves, purchases, buys on credit, improves his housing and his automobiles, and ultimately moves to a White suburb. He decides that his children will go to the best college possible and will move up even higher. He has worked hard to earn what he now enjoys, and although fleeting images of Depression days occasionally disturb him, he feels as secure as his credit payments and health permit. Although not a church-goer, he has internalized many of his father's traditional Protestant beliefs, and he expects his children to do so also [adapted from Kalish, 1969].

The third generation you already know. But, as we described Generations I and II, we might have been describing the backgrounds of two different social-class or ethnic groups, so different are the experiences of father and son. Today we are so alert to social-class and ethnic differences in values that it seems strikingly naive to ignore that age differences have a similar impact.

☐ What differences do you see between your parents and their parents in terms of the world they faced at the same age and the ways in which they met challenges? How do you differ from them? How do (or will) your children differ from you? ☐

# SOME MORAL ISSUES
# AND MORAL JUDGMENTS

So far in this chapter we've discussed the nature of moral and social issues and some cultural and historical influences on views of moral behavior. Now we would like to select some specific problems that we believe have particular importance and outline some thoughts on each one. The first four questions are *about* moral behavior and moral principles in general; the last three concern specific moral judgments.

These seven questions are not merely theoretical abstractions, and there is danger in seeing them as removed from the real world. We believe that they are highly contemporary and meaningful questions that you decide and act upon daily, either knowingly or innocently. It will be no surprise that we have no intention of giving our answers to these questions (we'd probably disagree with each other anyway). As individuals, we do have our own positions that we continually reevaluate, hopefully improving our understanding. We hope you will also get caught up in this reflective process.

First, are there any universally accepted standards of morality? In a general sense, the answer is yes. Some form of property rights exists in every known society; some family obligations are assumed in every known society; honor and reputation are important everywhere; truthfulness and keeping one's promises, at least within a particular group, are always encouraged; homicide and bodily violence to those within the group are condemned; mutual aid is advocated. However, the nature of property rights, family obligations, honor, and reputation differ from society to society. The conditions under which truthfulness, promises, and mutual aid must occur likewise vary. The conditions under which homicide and bodily violence are condemned are far from universally agreed upon. Therefore, although certain general areas are universally included in ethical standards, the specific prescriptions and proscriptions vary considerably. So how do we decide on the validity of these specifics?

Second, are there any moral principles that are so self-evident that they *should be* universalized? If you had the ability to enforce your will in an absolute way, are there any standards that you would insist on making universal? Avoiding homicide? If so, under what circumstances? Would you prohibit killing in self-defense, capital punishment, killing in wartime, and abortion? Or don't you consider all these forms of life destruction to be homicide? Mutual respect or brotherly love? These concepts are vague and need to be made specific—and the specifics are rarely self-evident. *Is* there such a thing as absolute right? If so, what is it and how would you know it?

Third, is an action made moral by its intention, its nature, or its consequences? Suppose that, in a fit of fury, a man goes out, gun in hand, to kill a neighbor for spreading rumors about him. He shoots but misses. The neighbor, frightened by the attack, evaluates his own life and thereafter lives in exemplary fashion. Here is a worthy consequence, but would you praise its cause? Why or why not? Or suppose that you're driving along a lonely road, and you see a man lying in a field. You stop and discover that he has been wounded. Knowing that medical help is at least an hour away, you put him in your car and drive him to the nearest hospital. As a result of the automobile trip, however, he is dead when you arrive. You are told that, had you left him in the field and merely gone for help, he could have survived. Here is an unfortunate end produced by a well-intentioned act. Was your action "moral"? How do you decide?

Fourth, who is capable—or who has adequate authority—to make moral decisions? Can you trust to your own intelligence and integrity, knowing what you do about the many influences that have socialized and molded you? Is there an authority to whom you can turn? Scriptures? A social movement? A teacher? A philosophy? Do you play it by ear, making decisions as life calls for them? Or do you attempt to establish guidelines for yourself, so that not every situation requires a fresh evaluation? What is the basis for your guidelines?

Fifth, which shows greater morality: to enhance greatly the life of one individual or to improve slightly the conditions of a whole society? Or turn the question around: is it ever moral to destroy an innocent person for the sake of society? To modify the classical question asked most eloquently by Dostoevski in *The Brothers Karamazov:* would you kill a randomly selected person in a faraway country, if his death would assure a century of peace? (Imagine that you personally must do the killing.) Is it moral to reduce health-care assistance for the poor, knowing that more people now will suffer as a result, if thereby the economy of the country can be improved, leading to a better standard of living in the long run for the majority?

Sixth, do you have the right to bring your influence to bear upon persons in another culture whose social values violate yours? Communities exist today in which the following behaviors are accepted: a man may have more than one wife; girls are sold by their parents into prostitution; children are commonly beaten for misbehaving; voting is permitted for one candidate only; animals are trained to fight and kill one another for the gambling sport of humans; new leaders are selected by old leaders, who in turn base their decisions on the influence of their fathers. If you believe that one or more of these customs is morally wrong, perhaps indefensible, do you have the moral right— or even the moral obligation—to try to get them changed? If so, what kinds of interventions would be moral? Can you morally use force? Violence? Manipulation? Deceit?

Seventh, is the failure to take a stand on some issue tantamount to taking a stand? By not voting for any candidate, by not using your influence in an argument, by not attending a meeting, do you absolve yourself of responsibility? Or is it true, as the activists of a decade ago claimed, that if you aren't part of the solution, you're part of the problem?

We certainly have posed many questions and answered very few. You may have definite opinions about cultural relativity and moral values, of course, especially since our society essentially seems to have adopted a strongly relativistic position. We have tried to show how even this position is the result of historical forces. Further, we've argued that all of us are constantly making moral decisions or acting on moral values, often in ways we take so much for granted that we do not even recognize the value system that underlies our own behavior.

# REFERENCES

Capra, F. *The Tao of physics*. Boulder, Colo.: Shambala, 1975.

Commager, H. S. *The American mind*. New Haven, Conn.: Yale University Press, 1950.

Geertz, C. The impact of the concept of culture on the concept of man. In J. R. Platt (Ed.), *New views of man*. Chicago: University of Chicago Press, 1965. Reprinted in Y. A. Cohen (Ed.), *Man in adaptation: The cultural present*. Chicago: Aldine, 1968.

Greer, T. H. *A brief history of Western man*. New York: Harcourt, Brace, & World, 1968.

Feshbach, S. Dynamics and morality of violence and aggression: Some psychological considerations. *American Psychologist*, 1971, *26*, 281–292.

Kalish, R. A. Of children and grandfathers: A speculative essay. In R. A. Kalish (Ed.), *The dependencies of old people*. Occasional Papers in Gerontology, #6. Institute of Gerontology, University of Michigan & Wayne State University, 1969.

Randall, J. H. *The making of the modern mind*. Boston: Houghton Mifflin, 1940.

Wilson, E. K. *Sociology: Rules, roles, and relationships* (rev. ed.). Homewood, Ill.: Dorsey Press, 1971.

# CHAPTER 8

## HUMANISTIC PSYCHOLOGY AND PERSONAL GROWTH

Ideas, like people, are dynamic; they are constantly changing as they interact with other ideas and as they are affected by technological, cultural, and political developments. Thus, about the middle of the 20th century, a new fruit began to develop from the seeds of humanistic thinking. It was eventually named *humanistic psychology,* and it shared some—but by no means all—of the views of the traditional humanistic philosophy.

Many supporters of humanistic psychology saw it as an alternative to the two prevailing views in psychology of the nature of humanity—the behavioristic view (probably held by the majority of behavioral scientists) and the psychoanalytic view (probably held by the majority of psychiatrists). Because humanistic psychologists differed from behaviorists and psychoanalytic thinkers in their view of the nature of humanity, they also differed in their views on the most effective methods of studying people and of intervening to produce change.

Since the concept of humanistic psychology is a broad one, its advocates do not agree on every question. Nevertheless, the most important currents in humanistic psychology can be delineated and contrasted with those of behavioristic and psychoanalytic thought.

# HUMANISTIC PSYCHOLOGY AND DETERMINISM

Humanistic psychologists tend to discount the kinds of determinism upheld by behaviorists and psychoanalytic thinkers. They discuss human behavior in terms of such notions as freedom, authenticity, choice, will, volition, and responsibility. By and large, they try to understand behavior as it occurs rather than in terms of its causes. Instead of attempting to reduce behavior to its smallest components or to a neurological or physiological base, they try to understand the person as a whole entity, all at once. Many humanistic psychologists discount the significance of statistics and quantitative measures in research; others even discount most kinds of research, preferring to depend on feelings and intuition while tending to reject generalizations about people.

The position of humanistic psychology is very appealing, since most of us *feel* that we are in control of our behavior; we *feel* that we are free to make many choices. Many people find humanistic psychology nearer to what they always assumed psychology to be, seeing traditional, research-oriented, deterministic psychology as mechanistic and sterile.

Of course, not all persons of a particular theoretical school agree on every issue. Similarly, adherents of different schools may find themselves in agreement on particular issues, although they may have arrived at their positions in different ways. Thus, humanistic psychologists, who are likely to accept Rousseau's view that human nature is basically good until it is corrupted by the social system, may agree with naturalistic determinists that the environment exerts a determining influence on criminals, the mentally ill, and others. Even though the humanistic psychologist emphasizes the need to accept responsibility and the determinist does not, they may both be avid in their support of services for those who are unable to care for themselves. While positing a great deal of freedom in the functioning of any given individual, humanistic psychologists recognize the untoward effects of restrictive environments. In order for human beings to be free, they may argue, certain basic needs must be satisfied. (Does this sound a bit like Rousseau?)

## PERSONAL GROWTH

"When I use a word, it means just what I choose it to mean," Humpty Dumpty told Alice; and indeed many words are so difficult to define that they can appear to mean almost anything. A case in point is the term *personal growth*.

For the purposes of this book, "personal growth" will mean just what you choose it to mean, within the following bounds. Personal growth is a process, not an event. It occurs as you become more capable of doing the things you wish to do, as you change in directions you wish to change in, as you become better able to be the sort of person you wish to be—whether or not this is the sort of person others wish you to be. And these things must occur with minimum cost in terms of maintaining defense mechanisms, engaging in self-defeating behavior, inflicting pain on yourself or others, or violating your integrity. For some, personal growth occurs through achievement and productivity, through moving up the ladder of an organization or gaining academic certificates. For others, it comes with greater ability to relate to others, to give and receive love, to participate in artistic creativity. To still others, personal growth means enjoying whatever one is presently doing, getting through each day with enjoyment of that day and without much concern about the next.

Humanistic psychologists place a great deal of emphasis upon the potential each individual has for personal growth. In essence, they tend to believe that self-actualization is inevitable if people are given the opportunity for personal growth. For Maslow (1970), there is a hierarchy of personal needs, culminating in self-actualization. The more basic needs require satisfaction first. Individuals who suffer hunger or thirst, who are fearful for their safety, who cannot love or be loved, or who lack self-esteem will find it difficult, perhaps impossible, to achieve full personal growth. Given reasonable satisfaction of these highly demanding basic needs, however, our very nature will motivate us to develop ourselves and improve our capabilities for personal growth and satisfaction.

This view of personal growth may seem obvious, but consider some alternative views. Both behaviorism and psychoanalytic thought describe behavior in terms of cause and effect; for this reason, we have grouped them together under the rubric of "naturalistic determinism." How do they differ from humanistic psychology on the question of personal growth?

Most of the psychologists we have grouped together as naturalistic determinists assume that human behavior is a little like a mechanical system in that it will continue to operate in the same way until something upsets the balance and changes it. Whatever upsets the balance will be perceived as a tension, and the person who feels the tension will act to reduce it and restore balance to the system. For example, why do we eat? Because our blood sugar falls below a certain level, and that is perceived as hunger—a tension. So we eat to raise our blood sugar—reduce the tension. Notice that tension can be purely physiological.

When these psychologists look for a motive for action, they look for some tension that the person is trying to reduce. If there is no tension, they maintain, there will be no motive and thus no action. So, in response to the contention that our nature causes us to seek personal growth, behaviorists ask what the evidence for this claim is, or they assert that sufficient knowledge of the social environment would explain why some people live up to their capabilities while others do not. The assumption that self-actualization is "natural" is, to the behaviorist, unverifiable, unobservable, and unscientific. Further, if someone insists that people have a purpose residing within them when they are born, the behaviorist responds that every person is born a tabula rasa. Environment, interaction with biological needs, causes some people to *learn* to want to self-actualize because it is pleasurable or to *learn* to wish for personal growth because many other needs are simultaneously satisfied. Behaviorists may not reject the notion of personal growth, but they do not believe it is programmed into our very "nature." Rather, their view of humanity assumes that a person must *learn* to want to do the things that lead to self-actualization.

Some psychologists have attempted to reconcile the humanistic and behavioristic approaches to this issue. R. W. White (1959) suggested that human beings are born with a drive he called *effectance*. This drive leads people to wish to have an impact upon the environment and to develop competence. Thus, rather than talk about human nature, this view assumes that people are motivated to satisfy their needs for competence just as they are motivated to satisfy their hunger and thirst needs, except that survival is not at stake. One difficulty with this view is that we can satisfy hunger and thirst needs temporarily, but it sometimes seems as though we never cease seeking to be increasingly competent. The more competence we achieve, the more we desire. Therefore, the tension produced by the need for effectance can never truly be reduced.

Among the motivating forces related to effectance are: activity, curiosity, manipulation, exploration, novelty, and affection. Interestingly, each of these needs can readily be observed in animals, which suggests that effectance is not a uniquely human need. Perhaps the best known experimental example is that in which young monkeys were shown to prefer a soft, terrycloth doll to a wire doll as a surrogate mother, even though they were fed by the wire doll by means of a bottle enmeshed in the wires (Harlow & Harlow, 1966). The hunger for physical affection thus seems to be as powerful as the hunger for food.

As with most compromises, this attempt doesn't sit well with either camp. Humanistic psychologists would undoubtedly complain that this listing of characteristics is not sufficient to explain the complexity of personal growth and the person's potential for integrated development. Some behaviorists reject the notion also, apparently in the belief that some of these motivating forces are unobservable.

Maslow (1970) does not claim that all motivation leads to personal growth. He differentiates *growth motives* from *deficiency motives*. Growth motives arise from the need to develop one's capabilities; deficiency motives arise from the need to correct some deficit, such as a lack of food. For example, eating to diminish one's hunger is a response to a deficiency motive; eating for the pleasure of eating or to improve one's competence as a gourmet is a response to a growth motive. Although this distinction may seem perfectly straightforward, in practice it can be difficult to apply. For example, suppose you find satisfaction in first staying away from food until you're very hungry, and then eating a great deal. Is your motive a growth or deficiency motive? Both? Neither? Or suppose your desire to improve your competence as a gourmet is based on a need to overcompensate for the feeling that you're clumsy and stupid. Can we still call this desire a growth motive? It is this kind of vagueness and ambiguity that rankles behaviorists. They complain that the humanistic view of humanity is difficult to pin down; the general idea seems clear, but the specifics are vague.

Psychoanalytic theory has some elements in common with both behavioristic and humanistic thought. Like behaviorism, psychoanalytic theory is a tension-reduction model; it presupposes that persons basically wish to come to rest, to attain homeostasis or equilibrium. Like humanism, it assumes that some differences among people are traceable to genetic factors. However, psychoanalytic theory differs from both other views concerning personal growth in one important regard. As Hall and Lindzey (1970) state, "Practically all the adult person's interests, preferences, tastes, habits, and attitudes represent the displacements of energy from original instinctual object-choice" (p. 38). Thus, the desire for personal growth is not "natural" and may not even be emotionally healthy; it occurs because some other, instinctual, drive is being rechanneled. For example, Freud postulated the existence of instinctual tendencies leading toward destructiveness and death, which he termed *thanatos*. Throwing oneself into work or humanitarian activities might be a way of unconsciously rechanneling these energies.

In summary, behaviorism and psychoanalysis both view the drive for personal growth as derived from some other need, either through association with biological needs or through redirection of instinctual drives. Humanistic psychologists believe that the move toward personal growth is natural, not learned, and that it exists in its own right, not as the by-product of anxiety, frustration, or some other state.

# INTENTIONALITY

Unlike behaviorism and psychoanalytic theory, humanistic psychology has readily accepted the existential notion that we have choice. Without dismissing the effects of social environment, the humanistic psychologist generally views persons as capable of growing and developing through the use of their free will. Indeed, they maintain that free will can sometimes be strong enough to overcome considerable environmental obstacles to the pursuit of personal growth, authenticity, or self-actualization.

Drawing upon his background as a minister and clinical psychologist, Rollo May has probed deeply into the concepts of will, love, meaning, significance, humanism, and existentialism. In *Love and Will*, May (1969) used the term *intentionality* to refer to a person's capacity to have intentions, to utilize his or her will to accomplish things. May pointed out that the word *intention* is closely related to *intent*, which brings us right back to meaning. (Both come from the Latin *intendere*, "to direct one's mind to.") When we talk about the "intent of the law," we refer both to the purpose of the law and the meaning of the law (May, 1969).

According to May, one's identity is bound up with the ability to have intent and will, to resolve to do something. " 'I' is the 'I' of 'I can.' " This ability entails acting instead of being acted upon, being active instead of being passive, being subject instead of being object.

What do behaviorists say about "will"? Not very much. The terms *will* and *intentionality* are part of the lexicon of humanistic and existential psychology, not behaviorism. A behaviorist who consented to use the terms (reluctantly, no doubt, since they seem to refer to something unobservable) would probably claim that a person *learns* to will or exercise intentionality. Since behaviorists view persons as impelled by forces in the environment, interacting with heredity, they presumably would replace the verb "will" with "is motivated to." Instead of "I will myself to succeed on this job," a behaviorist would say "I am motivated to succeed on this job." Notice the subtle shift from subjective to objective in these formulations and the differences in activity, intent, and responsibility. The humanistic statement is in the active voice; it indicates intent and an acceptance of responsibility for the outcome. The behavioristic statements are either passive ("I am motivated to succeed") or detached ("I have a need to succeed"). In either case the source of the motive for success lies outside the "I" of the statement. Both statements are one step removed from the intimacy and urgency of "I will."

B. F. Skinner (1971), a spokesman for many behaviorists, has written: "When a person changes his ... environment 'intentionally,' he plays two roles: one as controller, as the designer of a controlling culture, and another as the controlled, as the product of a culture" (p. 78). There is a chicken-or-egg problem here. If people are controlled by their cultures, then their efforts to control their cultures are themselves products of the controlling culture! Essentially, Skinner's is a social-deterministic approach, tempered by the recognition that people participate in the constellation of forces that determine their behavior.

Like the behaviorists, most psychoanalytic thinkers would probably find the terms "will" and "intentionality" difficult to utilize. According to the Freudian notion of biologically based instincts, people are basically dominated by inherited needs, represented by the *id*. The nearest thing to the "self" of the humanist is the *ego*, which "controls the gateways to action, selects the features of the environment to which it will respond, and decides what instincts will be satisfied and in what manner" (Hall & Lindzey, 1970, p. 34). This is a far cry from May's concept of intentionality.

# HOLISTIC STUDY OF THE PERSON

We have noted that humanistic psychology endeavors to be holistic; that is, humanistic psychologists see the individual as more than a collection of parts. Consequently, they attempt to study the whole person all at once, believing that the person can best be understood in this fashion. Behaviorists also want to understand the whole person, but they make just the opposite assumption and tend to study the person one part (or perhaps a few parts) at a time. They argue that the person is too complex to understand as a unit but that careful study of how each part works will eventually enable them to put the parts back into a meaningful whole. This approach seems to be based on the model of the physical sciences, although even physicists are coming to despair of ever finding the building blocks that will enable them to put the physical universe back together again.

Because the humanist wants to study the entire person at once, the methodologies developed by behaviorists are not relevant for humanistic psychology. As a result, many humanistic psychologists have avoided doing any quantitative or experimental research. They react strongly against categorizing people or applying numbers to them, no matter how much care has gone into the development of the categories or the verification of the numbers. Whereas quantification and replication are two basic premises of standard behavioristic research, humanistic psychologists' research methods often defy quantification, and their studies cannot easily be replicated.

In addition, humanistic psychologists are likely to place their trust in their own ability to understand others; they accept subjectivity in their research. Behaviorists make every effort to make their research objective, to eliminate as much as possible any bias brought to the study by the experimenter (even though many philosophers from Kant forward have maintained that this endeavor is futile).

Humanistic psychologists are likely to study the life histories of a small number of persons in order to ascertain trends and general relationships; behaviorists select a much larger number of respondents and measure specific characteristics with greater objectivity and precision, but without necessarily inquiring how these characteristics fit into the entirety that is a human being.

An understanding of the whole person depends on an understanding of the entire life cycle. Many psychologists, especially those of the psychoanalytic school, look only to the childhood years in their efforts to understand adult personality; others focus so completely upon the present that the person is seen as virtually without a history. Life-cycle psychology requires a knowledge both of trends within the lives of individuals and of similarities and differences among persons. For example, behaviorists might study changes in memory or changes in religious attitudes over a period of time. To do so, they would probably use a battery of memory tests or a series of questionnaires and interviews regarding religious beliefs. These tests would be developed with great care and administered by persons who were unlikely to know anything about the past lives of those taking the tests or to have any likes or dislikes for these people. If humanistic psychologists were performing the same studies, they would probably ignore tests; instead, they would try to spend a great deal of time with a very few people, to learn through actual circumstances what happens with memory changes or how religious views develop over a period of years.

Like all other views of human behavior, psychoanalysis has as its ultimate goal the understanding of the whole person. However, like behaviorism, it focuses upon the component parts rather than upon the entire person. (The word "to analyze" comes from an Indo-European word meaning "to divide.") Psychoanalysis does make use of constructs that are inferred rather than observed, but this is necessary in any conceptual scheme, including behaviorism. We do not see, hear, or smell memory or intelligence; rather, we observe the occurrence of certain behavior and infer that memory or intelligence lies behind it.

Behaviorists and psychoanalysts differ, however, in how they define their constructs. Behaviorists define memory or religious attitude functionally, in terms of a particular memory test or a particular attitude scale. Psychoanalytically oriented persons are more likely to trust their own perceptions and to be less concerned with translating concepts into quantitative measures or subjecting their results to independent verification. Their constructs are usually defined in terms of an abstract concept, which in turn is based on their assumptions about what they are observing.

As we have seen, much of humanistic psychology has developed partly in reaction to the behavioristic and psychoanalytic approaches, and humanistic research methodologies are no exception. Humanistic psychologists dislike the reductionistic approach of the behaviorists, believing that this method contributes very little to our understanding of *persons*, whatever it may contribute to our knowledge of Homo sapiens, the human *animal*. Worse, it communicates an image of the person that is so quantitative that it obscures the humanity of the individuals being studied. For its part, psychoanalytic research is seen as depending more upon theories than upon observations. To the humanistic psychologist, psychoanalytic thought is a closed system in which the investigator first hypothesizes something and subsequently finds what was hypothesized—not necessarily because it's there but because the researcher interprets the situation in the light of his or her preconceptions. Despite these objections, however, it is not yet known whether humanistic psychology will be any more successful than either of the other schools in providing useful insights and making meaningful predictions.

## THE HEALTHY PERSONALITY

Until recently, behavioral scientists have tended to study disturbed individuals rather than presumably healthy ones. When at last the spotlight shifted to the healthy personality, it turned out to be extremely difficult to define just what mental or emotional health is.

The healthy person has been variously described as mature, adjusted, capable, warm, achieving, self-confident, happy, content, self-actualizing, growing, becoming, and so forth. Different writers naturally select those characteristics that appeal to them, while rejecting those that do not. And each writer naturally develops a following of readers who resonate to a particular set of vibrations.

A more sophisticated look will show that the question of what is "healthy" is extremely complex. Presumably, "healthy" is a good thing to be; yet we might argue that, in terms of our favorite definition of personal growth, emotional and social health are undesirable. For example, if we define personal growth in terms of a high degree of achievement and productivity, we may have to admit that a person driven by neurotic anxiety can show more "personal growth" than someone who is stable and happy. We seem to have another case of "A word means just what I choose it to mean." You can define the healthy personality as you wish, but be forewarned that, once you depart from platitudes, you invite controversy.

Let's approach this issue in terms of four key words: *normality, adjustment, mental health,* and *self-actualization* (or *personal growth*). These four terms might be seen as four crudely defined points upon a continuum. One end of the continuum can be indicated by such words as *active* and responds to *internal control*; the other can be indicated by *passive*, responds to *external control*. You might wish to argue that behavioristic and humanistic psychology put individuals near opposite ends of the continuum. Similarly, social determinism and free will can also be interpreted as polar points on this continuum, although this is a matter of some debate.

## NORMALITY

At what point on the scale of stress and tension do we cease to be normal? The answer is exceedingly complex; in part it depends on our definition of normality. Let's try on a few for size (the list is adapted from Maslow, 1970):

- Normality is around the average of what most people do.
- Normality is what is traditional or conventional, whatever "people have always done."
- Normality is that which the scriptures or theology of one's church says it is.
- Normality is what I like, whatever I think is right and good and just.
- Normality is being adjusted, getting along well in whatever society one lives in.
- Normality is the absence of anything really wrong.
- Normality is behaving in accordance with one's own nature, so that one's potential can be fulfilled.

The last definition in the list is very likely to gain the most general acceptance. Maslow (1970) takes this definition one step farther, suggesting that normality may theoretically be equated with ideal social and emotional health, so that each of us can be considered normal to the degree that we fulfill the requirements of this definition. If we use the term *normality* in this way, its meaning will not only reflect the influence of humanistic psychology but make normality an ideal to be aimed at rather than a state most of us have achieved.

☐ When you say of someone that he or she is "normal," are you *describing* the person's behavior, or are you *evaluating* it? Do you detect a moral (judgmental) meaning in the word *normal*? Can you distinguish a sense of *normal* that does not involve a value judgment? ☐

## ADJUSTMENT

A highly authoritative reference (English & English, 1958, p. 13) gives two definitions of *adjustment*. The first is "a static equilibrium between an organism and its surroundings in which there is no stimulus change evoking a response, no need is unsatisfied, and all the continuative [ongoing] functions of the organism are proceeding normally." The second is "a condition of harmonious relation to the environment wherein one is able to obtain satisfaction for most of one's needs and to meet fairly well the demands, physical and social, put upon one." Both definitions are stated in terms of an ultimate abstraction that can never occur in real life but can only be approached on a relative basis.

The term *adjustment* is the psychological equivalent of the biological concept of adaptation, which Darwin related to a species' ability to survive. Organisms that adapted or adjusted to their environments survived and reproduced. The horse adapted, but the dinosaur did not. Human adjustment includes adjustment to both the social, or interpersonal, environment and the physical environment. Simply to exist a person must cope with social roles, structures, and institutions, with family, friends, power relationships, laws, churches, schools, and so forth. At the same time, the individual must satisfy basic biological demands for food, water, air, sleep, and temperature regulation.

Adjustment seems to be a behavioristic concept. It implies that the external demands upon the organism must be dealt with if the organism is to function normally. Even the use of the term *organism* suggests a philosophical bias, since no self-respecting humanistic psychologist would use that word in talking about a person. To many people, adjustment suggests a stable, somewhat static way of dealing with life; the adjusted person gets along, never depressed but also never exhilarated, content and satisfied but not fully happy.

How does an adjusted person respond to a disturbed world? Would an adjusted person write angry letters to a public official or demonstrate for lower taxes, higher pay, or an end to racism or communism? Given the connotation of the term *adjusted*, the answer is "probably not." Adjusted people may or may not be conformists, but the term suggests that they are in harmony with their environment. If the environment is itself unharmonious, a person might have to be rather confused in order to remain adjusted; some people claim that you have to be insane to be normal in a crazy world. Bühler and Marschak (1968) point out that many persons who could not adapt to life in Germany under the Nazis made an excellent adjustment elsewhere. The debate on this topic is lively and far from resolved.

Adjustment is an extremely useful concept; indeed, some think that the adjusted person is the ideal. The English philosopher Jeremy Bentham (1748–1832) once remarked that it is better to be a pig satisfied than a Socrates unsatisfied. We will show our bias, however, by suggesting that the term does not describe optimum functioning unless its meaning is significantly altered. In our view, good adjustment is neither necessary nor sufficient for personal growth. We acknowledge, though, that poor adjustment does make personal growth more difficult, since energy often must be invested in dealing with problems, leaving little left over to aid in growth.

## MENTAL HEALTH

As we discussed earlier, definitions of mental health vary with their sources. The term certainly encompasses adjustment in indicating the absence of important emotional or social pathology, but it also implies something positive. Being in good health means more than *not* being ill or disabled; it means having the capability to function at a better-than-adequate level, to withstand stress and illness, and to remain in this condition for an extended period.

## SELF-ACTUALIZATION/PERSONAL GROWTH

The process of self-actualization leads to personal growth, and many people assume that the capacity for personal growth is the major characteristic of a healthy personality. Self-actualization is dynamic; it involves moving ahead, rather than remaining in static adjustment. It is not just good health; it is good health becoming better. Maslow (1970) states that self-actualization is the tendency to become more and more what one is, to become everything that one is capable of becoming. Notice that self-actualization involves accepting one's own nature for what it is. Here we see vividly the assumption that by free will, by intentionality, we can "become." Similarly, Maslow assumes that each person has a "true nature," not one that results merely from social learning.

Each person self-actualizes in ways that suit that person. Some people might exercise their creativity through the arts, others through office work, cooking, gardening, or relating to other human beings. Unfortunately, although most writers who discuss self-actualization indicate that the process is highly idiosyncratic, many adherents have set up their own hierarchies of values. It may thus appear that a person who is painting a picture is more self-actualizing than someone who is developing a new sales technique. This type of elitism pervades almost all approaches to human nature when they are actually put into practice, and that is a serious problem.

Is self-actualization a useful concept? Is it a valid concept? Jourard (1968) answers without hesitation: "Healthy personality is growing personality. It is a way for a person to function in his world, a way that yields growth without placing other important values in jeopardy" (p. 45). Jourard further states that people with healthy personalities try to live up to individual values and, moreover, defend them when they are under threat. They find life meaningful and know who they are; they are neither alienated nor isolated. Such people are flexible enough to see the world as it is and, simultaneously, to see it as it might be. They are in touch with their unconscious; they notice themselves feeling and reacting in certain ways and are open to understanding why they feel and react as they do. And they are open to others as well. They do not have one self when alone and another self for display. They are "authentic"—a term borrowed from existentialism that Jourard and others use extensively; they behave honestly, spontaneously, and trustfully. Rogers (1961) says much the same thing in observing that "it does not help . . . to act as though I were something I am not. . . . I am more effective when I can listen acceptingly to myself, and can be myself. . . . I have found it of enormous value when I permit myself to understand another person" (p. 740).

In spite of the obvious appeal of self-actualization, many—perhaps most—behavioral scientists consider it an intriguing philosophical position rather than a valid psychological theory. It is elitist, they argue, since the self-actualizing person must already have satisfied basic needs, such as the needs for food and sex, as well as the needs for effectance, for safety and security, for love, and for esteem and self-esteem. Those who do not have the resources to take care of these needs cannot begin the process of self-actualizing. Similarly, many advocates of self-actualization would be most reluctant to admit that watching television, drinking beer, or bowling contribute as much to personal growth as watching ballet, drinking wine, or backpacking. Values that are related to a certain social class do seem to permeate the school.

The most important objection of those who dislike the notion of self-actualization is that it is a myth, harmless or otherwise, that interferes with our efforts to understand the true nature of humanity. Acceptance of this concept results from a psychological need to believe it, rather than from its foundation in reality. Some might claim that behavior seen as self-actualization in reality stems from learning and reinforcement. Others might contend that persons who are supposedly utilizing their capacities to self-actualize are in reality rechanneling unacknowledged fears, anxieties, sexual or aggressive impulses, and so on.

☐ If you find the notion of self-actualization attractive, how would you respond to the criticisms leveled against it? Are the values and social bias that are often associated with it a necessary part of the idea? If not, how could you eliminate them without plunging into a morass of value relativism ("Anything that turns you on is OK")? ☐

# GROWTH VERSUS RESPONSIBILITY

The recent emphasis on personal growth as a "good" is seldom questioned, but there are situations in which personal growth conflicts with other "goods." In these cases each individual must establish his or her own priorities. A particularly common conflict is that between personal growth and responsibility to others.

Some individuals achieve their greatest satisfaction and realize their maximum growth through relationships with others; for these persons, there may be no conflict between growth and responsibility. However, this is not true of everyone, and considerable self-centered behavior has been excused on the grounds that it was essential to the individual's personal growth. The classical example of this kind of reasoning appears in Dostoevsky's *Crime and Punishment*, in which Raskolnikov decides that it is appropriate for him to murder an elderly woman because her money is necessary to further his career and his life has greater value than hers.

It's doubtful that any of us would commit homicide to further our personal growth, but we might do things that are destructive to other people. Politicians who justify taking ethical shortcuts in order to achieve what they believe are laudable political goals rationalize that the end justifies the means ("If I don't take this illegal campaign contribution, I can't get elected and put into effect my worthwhile programs"). One can imagine such a politician reasoning along the following lines after being elected: "Now that I'm in a position of trust and responsibility, it's essential that I continue to grow personally so that I can better serve my constituents. In order to grow personally, I need to travel, have a quiet place in the mountains to think, entertain important people, and the like—and those things take money. As long as I don't hurt anyone too much, my having these niceties will, in the long run, help everyone by helping me. So I'm justified in taking money now and then from constituents who offer it to me."

Although the example of the politician may seem to present a clear case of rationalization, it is not that different from less obvious cases. Consider the father who has always wanted to pursue a second career in art but has never taken the time to do so. Although he has three school-age children, he devotes all his spare time to painting. His claim is that, even though he rarely sees his children, he would be a much less adequate parent if he were not painting. "I need the fulfillment that painting gives me. Although the *quantity* of time I spend with my kids isn't great, the *quality* of that time is much greater than before. If I couldn't paint, I would be sullen, irritable, and basically unhappy."

In summary, some individuals clearly exploit the notion of personal growth to justify simple selfishness in their allocation of time and money. Others grow most effectively through relating responsibly to other people. For still other persons, however, the issue of growth versus responsibility can be a very difficult one. Compelled to choose between what they see as personal growth and their apparent responsibility to others, they may deny that there was responsibility in the first place or claim that they would handle the responsibility poorly without the opportunity for growth.

☐ Even in our two examples, the issues are more complex than they might seem. What the painter and the politician are saying may indeed have merit. How do you balance what you owe to yourself and what you owe to others? Do you have a responsibility to be with your children a certain number of hours a week? What kind of time and attention do you owe your parents, when you can hardly find the time to do the things you absolutely need to do? Do you owe it to humanity to donate time, energy, and money to your church? To your favored political cause? To the elimination of heart disease or cancer? ☐

As the issue of responsibility to others shows, the price of personal growth can be high. Most of us would say that personal growth and responsible relatedness to others are both "goods." We might therefore want to include both of them in our conception of the healthy personality. On the other hand, can anything be "healthy" that leads to conflict, anxiety, harm to others, or self-deprivation? These are some of the difficult questions any attempt to define "personal growth" and "emotional health" must answer.

## REFERENCES

Bühler, C., & Marschak, M. Basic tendencies of human life. In C. Bühler & F. Massarik (Eds.), *The course of human life.* New York: Springer, 1968.
English, H. B., & English, A. C. *A comprehensive dictionary of psychological and psychoanalytical terms.* New York: Longmans, Green, 1958.
Hall, C. S., & Lindzey, G. *Theories of personality* (2nd ed.). Wiley, 1970.
Harlow, H. F., & Harlow, M. K. Learning to love. *American Scientist,* 1966, *54,* 244–272.
Jourard, S. M. *Disclosing man to himself.* New York: Van Nostrand, 1968.
Lazarus, R. S. *Patterns of adjustment and human effectiveness.* New York: McGraw-Hill, 1969.
Maslow, A. H. *Motivation and personality* (2nd ed.). New York: Harper & Row, 1970.
May, R. *Love & will.* New York: Norton, 1969.
Rogers, C. R. *On becoming a person.* Boston: Houghton Mifflin, 1961.
Skinner, B. F. *Beyond freedom and dignity.* New York: Knopf, 1971.
White, R. W. Motivation reconsidered: The concept of competence. *Psychological Review,* 1959, *66,* 297–333.

# PART THREE
# HUMAN BEHAVIOR AND DEVELOPMENT

# CHAPTER 9

## ISSUES IN
## INDIVIDUAL DIFFERENCES

Virtually all readers of this book would probably agree with the following statement: Human personality and behavior are largely determined by the interaction of heredity and environment. This statement, however, raises many questions. And there are few issues in behavioral science that are more intertwined with one's social and political values.

First, how much do children inherit from parents and how much do they learn from the environment? Second, what nonhereditary physiological factors affect personality and behavior? Third, what characteristics of human behavior can be altered by the learning process, and what characteristics can be changed through biological, biomedical, or biochemical processes?

Obviously, such physical characteristics as eye color, hair color, shape of head, resistance to certain diseases, and sex are controlled by heredity, although biochemical influences, especially during gestation, may produce some change. In this chapter, we are concerned with human characteristics that are less well understood—such as motivation, temperament, personality, learning and thinking, intelligence, talent, and creativity.

# HEREDITARY AND
# PHYSIOLOGICAL BASES OF BEHAVIOR

There is no doubt that physiology influences behavior. Anyone who has ever taken a tranquilizer or aspirin, smoked marijuana, consumed a couple of shots of bourbon or a bottle of beer, or become hungry or fatigued has experienced the effects of physiological/biochemical changes on behavior. All these effects reflect the impact of interference in body chemistry, but people respond differently to tranquilizers, drugs, alcohol, and fatigue, and it is difficult to determine whether their responses originate in hereditary, environmental, or acquired biological characteristics.

The consensus is that heredity plays an important, probably dominant, role in determining physiological traits. "Every person is endowed with a distinctive gastrointestinal tract, a distinctive endocrine system, a distinctive nervous system, and a morphologically distinctive brain; furthermore ... the differences ... are never trifling and often are enormous" (Williams, 1969, p. 311). And many of these differences are evident at birth. For example, "individuals start life with brains differing enormously in structure; unlike in number, size, and arrangement of neurons as well as in grosser features" (Lashley, 1947; quoted in Williams, 1969, p. 311). Biochemical and physiological changes also occur in the same individual as he or she ages. However, while many of the physiological differences in and among individuals are determined by heredity, we can safely assume that the environment also affects the development of differences in both cases.

What we do not know is the *extent* of genetic or environmental influence on physiological traits and behavior and the extent to which environment can modify genetically determined characteristics. We also do not understand how to relate a particular kind of brain structure to a particular behavior pattern; nor do we know much about how genes interact with each other and with biochemical structures and processes. Some information on these topics has been provided by recent research with DNA and RNA, as well as by research in the area of cellular biology (cytology), and theories on the extent of genetic and environmental influences on behavior have also been discussed by psychologists and philosophers. For example, the philosopher Ernest Nagel invites us to consider the implications of a hypothesized discovery of a relationship between authoritarianism in parents and neurosis in children. This would raise the possibility that a parent's authoritarian behavior and the child's neurotic behavior could be understood in terms of body chemistry. If this were so, then human relationships could be explained in terms of interacting biochemical systems. Obviously, no one knows yet whether or not this can be done. Even if the necessary theory could be constructed and verified, its laws might turn out to be so complex that practicing psychologists would not bother with them. But Nagel does raise a fascinating question: Are psychological phenomena, including intelligence, biochemically predetermined? And, if so, to what extent?

The probability is high that much new information on the development of human traits and behavior will come to light during the next few decades. Whether this knowledge will help us or hurt us is itself a matter worth more—much more—than a few moments of attention.

## AN EXAMPLE: MENTAL ILLNESS

Many psychologists and social workers (and some psychiatrists) think mental illness is caused by psychogenic and sociogenic factors (that is, factors of psychological and sociological origins); they give only token recognition to biogenic, especially hereditary, factors. Physicians, biochemists, and other psychiatrists, however, express the reverse. Where is the truth?

In considering the answer to this question, we must mention that mental illness is a broad, all-embracing concept that covers a multitude of specific kinds of behavior. For example, we might show something to be true of schizophrenia, but this fact may not be true of psychotic depression. Furthermore, there are many varieties of schizophrenia, and vast differences in the origins of the problem are readily shown. Indeed, some psychologists contend that the use of the term *schizophrenia* is misleading, because they feel that schizophrenia, as an entity, does not exist.

There are situations, however, in which heredity is fairly constant. A substantial number of studies of mental illness in twins were reviewed by Lindzey and others (Lindzey et al., 1971). These researchers concluded that, when one member of a pair of identical twins is diagnosed schizophrenic, the other member has a higher-than-average chance of being similarly diagnosed. Studies also show that the probability of both identical twins being schizophrenic is greater than with fraternal twins or with pairs of siblings of the same sex but different ages. Additional research on schizophrenics who had been adopted (Lindzey et al., 1971) found more schizophrenia and other mental disorders among the biological relatives of the schizophrenics than among the adoptive family members. All of this is strong, but not conclusive, evidence that heredity does play a role in at least one kind of mental illness—the great number of disorders lumped together as schizophrenia.

We must also consider that some of the initial studies that did show extremely high degrees of similarity in mental illness among identical twins have not been fully confirmed. Recent work suggests the similarity is much greater than chance but still well under half; for example, these studies show that, if one member of a pair of identical twins is schizophrenic, the odds are greater than average but less than fifty-fifty that the other member will also be diagnosed as schizophrenic. If heredity were an overwhelming factor in causing this disorder, we would expect that the odds would be much higher. Therefore, we may still assume that schizophrenia results in part from genetic predisposition, but we must also recognize the importance of the environment when we try to define the origin of schizophrenia. We should also mention that research on the origins of other kinds of mental illness has had less definitive results than the studies on schizophrenia.

Trying to understand the origins of mental illness has practical importance. If we assume that there are different levels of inherited predisposition to schizophrenia, we may hypothesize that some people will become schizophrenic as the result of almost any environmental stress, whereas other people will withstand vast amounts of stress and anxiety before becoming schizophrenic. Still others will never become schizophrenic but will become alcoholic or suicidal. The knowledge of whether or not a mental illness has a hereditary cause can determine the type of therapy a therapist chooses.

If, for example, a mental disorder is primarily psychogenic—perhaps the result of tense relationships with parents during childhood and a tense relationship with a spouse who has taken over the destructive role of the parent—then treatment must center around the client's psychological state. Although biochemical changes induced by drugs might temporarily relieve the symptoms, eventual elimination of the difficulties will probably come about only by altering the client's self-concept and improving his or her capacity for mature human relationships. If, however, the mental disorder occurs in a person who has an extremely high inherited predisposition to this form of disorder, altering the person's self-concept and social environment will probably produce only temporary change; in this instance the biological mechanisms that have produced the condition will have to be treated.

Most behaviorists and Freudians support the psychogenic interpretations of mental illness and aim their therapies at psychological change evolving out of the interaction between the therapist and the client. Humanistic psychologists might be neutral on this issue, or, more likely, claim that the entire issue is irrelevant; they see mental illness as the outcome of despair or of a futile search for meaning—a sense of alienation and isolation—and they do not foresee long-term alleviation of the symptoms of mental illness through biochemical means. Humanistic psychologists are reminiscent of Rousseau in that they believe mentally ill people have been prevented by a distorting, contorting environment from living according to their biological natures. For example, Maslow (1967) claims that certain values are "instinctoid"; that is, they are necessary in order to avoid illness (presumably mental illness) and to achieve full humanness or growth. Maslow seems to be saying that mental disorders arise from inadequate values that do not permit people to be truly human; people who deny their true or authentic selves are likely to become emotionally disturbed.

□ Think back to our discussion of the free will/determinism controversy. Some of the issues we discussed there should begin to sound important to you now. Also, consider these questions: In what ways are people responsible for their own mental illnesses? If schizophrenia is found to be preventable through, for example, an inoculation, should schools require that all children receive this inoculation? What if some children respond to the shot with extreme nausea? □

# HEREDITARY INFLUENCES ON PERSONALITY

Research results on personality and interest tests from the United States and Europe resemble the results of the studies on mental disorders. Test scores of identical twins show greater similarity than test scores of fraternal twins, who, in turn, show greater similarity on tests than siblings do. These results again suggest that heredity determines at least some aspects of personality.

On the other hand, even identical twins differ considerably, and this suggests the important role that environment has in determining personality. Aldous Huxley (1965) reminds us that mankind has not undergone any meaningful genetic change in the last thirty thousand years. Therefore, we might assume that the differences that exist between people today and people 300 centuries ago are primarily due to environmental change.

□ In what ways do you think humanity has changed in 30,000 years? In what ways do you think humanity is still the same? Which seem more striking to you—the similarities or the differences? Can the differences all be accounted for in terms of environmental influences? □

Research on genetic transmission of personality attributes is difficult, if not impossible, to carry out with human beings. A substantial amount of research, however, has shown "that selective breeding can alter the level of general activity, maze behavior, emotionality, and aggressiveness in laboratory rats" (Beach, 1955). You may also have read something about the selective breeding of dogs to develop certain characteristics such as hunting ability, ferocity, working capacity, and gentleness.

Is aggressive behavior genetically based? Is it environmentally modifiable? Can individuals and groups learn nonaggressive and nonviolent ways of coping with problems and frustrations, or must they inevitably act out of aggressive anger and greed? In order to answer these questions we need a better understanding of the genetic components of human aggression.

Territoriality may be an example of a genetic component of aggression. *Territoriality* refers to the tendency, apparently inherited, of some animals to "lay claim to" a particular area—territory—and to fight any intrusion into this area. For example, when dogs are moved from one home to another, they often urinate freely in their new home; they thereby leave their scent, which marks their claim to the new territory. This behavior is even more likely to occur if another dog has previously left its scent in the house.

Robert Ardrey (1966) has suggested that humans also exhibit— and, presumably, inherit—territoriality. He makes his case by showing how important "turf" is to people, how they will defend their own land with much more vigor than they will attack the land of another, and how much sacrifice people will undergo to own a small piece of land. The notion that humans have an innate need, drive, instinct, propensity, or passion to claim and maintain territory, however, is far from established. Where do you stand?

# VALUES AND COGNITIVE CAPACITY

*Cognitive behavior* refers to behavior relating to intellectual capacities—to perception and knowledge. *Affective behavior* refers to behavior relating to mood and feelings. The line between the two is often hazy, and much behavior can be understood only by looking at both cognitive and affective components. Remembering an earlier event, for example, is cognitive behavior; so is learning to make a moral judgment. Becoming angry is affective behavior; so is having feelings of love. Yet our moral judgments are obviously based not only on knowledge but on emotion; our moods of anger are based not only on emotion but on recognizing what is taking place. Although both these types of behavior may be influenced by heredity, consider how heredity affects cognitive capacity, which largely determines related behavior, and consider some of the sociological ramifications of intellectual differences.

## *THE SIGNIFICANCE OF INTELLECT*

What is the true measure of a person? What is it that causes a person to have worth, to have value? Your first answers to these questions are likely to be "every person has worth," or "God has given us worth," or "we all have equal worth in the eyes of God." If you probe a little further, however, into what people really believe, you will find that certain qualities are valued more than other qualities.

One quality that is highly valued by most people—certainly by most people who live in Western societies—is intelligence. However, definitions of intelligence vary considerably; here we refer to intelligence in terms of the capacity for abstract thought (with emphasis on verbal concepts), learning ability, and adaptability. A person who is highly capable in these ways is forgiven much, whereas a person who lacks these abilities is required by society to compensate by excelling in other ways.

There are many reasons for valuing the intellectually competent person. One reason is that every community values those human characteristics that advance the goals of the community. For example, communities that viewed farming, hunting, or fighting as important community concerns also honored the hard worker, the capable hunter, or the brave warrior. Present-day Western society defines its progress on the basis of technology, science, and language, and the concept of intelligence has developed to encompass technological, scientific, and linguistic skills. (How does this change in the criteria for intelligent behavior affect women differently from the way it affects men?)

If it is your feeling that technological or verbal skills are required to help you and your community reach your goals, you will value persons who show high intelligence in these areas.

Until very recently, higher education in America focused primarily on the development of capable, intellectual students (and, in some cases, still does). However, some educators now believe that the goals of the community are best attained by focusing more attention on children who do not exhibit much intellectual competence but who seem to have potential that is greater than their performance level. It is felt that children with high performance levels function at a higher level not because they have greater potential than children with low performance levels but because they have experienced more stimulating and supportive environments. Since, in the past, both schools and homes have given much attention to high-achieving children, the rationale is that schools should now attend more to low achievers; the high achievers will continue to learn as a result of the stimulation, encouragement, and goals provided for them at home. As you can see, achievement, in this case, is defined by the value system of the community in reference to the goals the community wishes to pursue. Thus, the teenager who takes care of the home while both parents work, who gets three younger brothers and sisters off to school on time each morning, and who also brings a few dollars home, will often not be seen as a high achiever if his or her schoolwork is poor.

The previous comments lead directly to the core of one of the most demanding and difficult social problems that exists today—the problem of prejudice. Because a highly disproportionate percentage of academically low-achieving students come from Black, Mexican-American, Puerto Rican, and Native American homes, there is a potential for conflict not only between the parents of high achievers and the parents of low achievers, or between educators who emphasize abstract and verbal learning skills and educators who emphasize manual or motor skills, but also between educators and parents on the basis of old racial prejudices, stereotypes, fears, and angers.

## INDIVIDUAL AND GROUP DIFFERENCES IN INTELLIGENCE

There are two basic questions to ask regarding individual and group differences in intelligence. The first question is whether cognitive differences exist among *individuals* as the result of heredity. In other words, if everyone's environment were the same, would you have the same intelligence, skills, talents, learning capacity, and so forth, as everyone else?

The second question is whether cognitive differences exist between *groups* as the result of heredity. If everyone's environment were the same, would all groups have the same average intelligence, skills, talents, and learning capacity? (The term *group* here refers to any classification of people according to race, ethnic background, sex, social class, nationality, and so forth.)

If all individuals have the same genetic make-up, then it follows that all groups have the same genetic make-up. If you believe that all individuals are the same, then you must believe that any differences that exist among groups are the result of environmental factors.

On the other hand, your assumption that groups—on the average—are genetically the same in this regard does not imply that all individuals are the same. And if you believe that groups differ, you must assume that some individuals also differ. However, you do not need to assume that *all* individuals in Group A have greater or less intelligence than *all* individuals in Group B. You could assume that the two groups are moderately alike, with the average of Group A being noticeably higher than the average of Group B—for example, 60% of Group A might be higher than the average of Group B.

Since there is a great deal of controversy about whether or not differences in intelligence do exist among groups, we have reserved an entire chapter to examine some aspects of the controversy. At this point, we will concentrate on individual differences.

Evidence for the connection of heredity and individual intelligence is supplied by studies similar to the studies mentioned in the section on heredity and mental illness and in the section on heredity and aptitude and interest. These studies show substantially closer relationships between the intelligence scores of identical twins than between the intelligence scores of fraternal twins or siblings. Research also shows substantial correlation between the intelligence scores of children and their parents and among the intelligence scores of siblings. These studies, however, do not prove that heredity alone determines intelligence, since the similarities shown could be the result of similarities in the environment.

The study of mental retardation has also supplied evidence for the connection of heredity and intelligence, since it has been fairly conclusively established that certain kinds of mental retardation are inherited. For example, some inherited metabolic disorders (PKU disease) and some congenital defects (hydrocephalus) may result in low intelligence quotients. It must also be pointed out, however, that intelligence in these cases is not necessarily fixed. If treatment of certain metabolic and congenital disorders (such as our two examples) is introduced early in life, the afflicted individual will not suffer from mental retardation as a result. Indeed, some investigators have made the front pages by claiming that such biomedical/biochemical intervention, or treatment, could raise the intelligence of everyone.

□ The suggestion of universal "treatment" raises some intriguing questions. For example: What would be the outer limit of intelligence? Would this limit be the same for everyone, or would the limit vary according to each person's level of intelligence before biochemical intervention? Who would control the distribution of and the dosage of the medication? How would increased intelligence affect work roles? You can easily think of other questions. □

The limit of intelligence is commonly believed to be determined by heredity; whether or not this limit is reached is determined by the interaction of heredity and environment (this is a sophisticated version of the fixed-intelligence theory). It is also possible, however, that there are no limits to cognitive capacities and that, as humanistic psychologists believe, we can transcend those limits we have arbitrarily established for ourselves. In fact, we are just beginning to explore ways of breaking through what have always been assumed to be the limits of cognitive development. Intensive special-education programs, for example, have made remarkable improvements in cognitive functioning in countless cases, especially in those cases when behavior that appeared retarded was actually the outcome of emotional crisis or the result of a sensory deficit. As an example of the first type of case, one young boy in a foster home was believed by his foster parents to be retarded, because he had not talked since he had entered the home—his parents had been killed in an automobile accident. It was only when he was overheard talking to other children that his foster parents realized he wasn't retarded. As an example of the second type of case, a baby experienced an accidental head injury at the age of three weeks and subsequently was thought to be retarded until, as a teenager, he had a hearing test that showed substantial hearing loss. After the problem was corrected, the young man went on to graduate from a well-known university.

Our opinion is that the inherited elements of cognitive capacity are as individually distinctive as facial structure. As Hirsch explains: "Since mitosis [the formation of two cell nuclei, during cell division, each of which has the same number of chromosomes as the parent nucleus] projects our unique genotype into the nucleus, or executive, of every cell in our bodies, the individuality that is so obvious in the human faces ... must also characterize the unseen components" (Hirsch, 1970, p. 96). However, we also believe that the influence of the environment can lead to variation in the ability to *use* cognitive capacity. Lack of stimulation, inadequate nutrition, or faulty upbringing may produce a situation in which a person never realizes more than a small proportion of his or her intellectual potential.

## EUGENICS

If certain individual characteristics are indeed genetically transmitted, and if some of these characteristics are useful to the individual or to the community, we might want to consider the possibility of increasing the portion of the population born with many useful characteristics and decreasing the proportion of the population born with few useful characteristics. Not only does the eugenics movement believe that this is possible, but eugenicists are already attempting to bring about the social reforms required to permit their programs to become reality.

For example, we know that some forms of diabetes are inherited. Until recently, many children suffering from diabetes died before they reached child-bearing age, and thus diabetes did not increase in the population. Now, however, diabetics can have normal life spans and can reproduce, so the number of people in the world who are diabetic will increase. Some eugenicists might go so far as to find some way to keep diabetic persons from having children. Genetic counseling is probably the optimum approach for accomplishing this goal, but other methods might be considered: legal action, abortion, sterilization, money payments, social pressure, and so forth. Similar consideration may be given to other genetic conditions, such as hemophilia.

In his *Republic*, Plato supported the improvement of society through a type of eugenics program. Much later, Francis Galton (1822–1911), a famous British biologist, established eugenics as a respectable applied science. Some people, however, have used this new science to enact personal hates and prejudices. For example, Hitler basically used a few racist publications on eugenics to support his belief in the superiority of the Germanic race, and he initiated a program that destroyed Jews, Blacks, Gypsies and other minority groups and that permitted only the "superior" Germanic types to reproduce.

□ Many questions arise regarding the use of eugenic principles to eradicate genetically based disease. Assuming that a eugenics program could be instituted, would it work? For example, the eugenic elimination of one disease might cause the increase of another disease, or a program might take centuries before the incidence of an anomaly was significantly reduced. Under what circumstances do we permit one individual or group to determine who may and who may not have offspring? And how should that determination be made? Does the potential benefit of a particular program justify giving certain persons the legal, medical, or social power to influence or control such intimate events as conceiving and bearing children? To go a step farther, is there *any* possible benefit that is important enough to justify taking away from prospective parents the right to make their own decisions concerning conceiving and bearing (or *not* conceiving or bearing) children? □

The problem becomes still more complex when we consider a eugenics program to eliminate mental illness. Should we develop a eugenics program to reduce human aggression and violence? Such a program would initially require enough understanding of mental illness, aggression, and violence to know whether there was, indeed, a biological or genetic base to such behavior. If geneticists are able to establish beyond a reasonable doubt that this genetic base exists, *do* we wish to eliminate mental illness, aggressiveness, and the potential for violence in our society? Perhaps a degree of aggressivity is useful, for example, because people who are docile might soon be conquered by those who are not, and thus the only way to keep a society strong is to allow a certain amount of aggressivity to remain in spite of the problems it can create. But if a degree of aggression is useful, how do we decide how much?

Another point to consider when discussing the usefulness of eugenic programs is that the characteristics we want to strengthen or eradicate are designated positive or negative by our society's value system. What one group of people currently perceives as good may later be perceived as bad by another group. The amount of knowledge available to people may also be a factor in designating a characteristic good or bad. For example, it is hypothetically possible that we could discover, in three or 30 years, that diabetes produces antibodies that reduce the likelihood of developing heart disease; in that case we might want to encourage the breeding of diabetics and then treat those children for the diabetes, thereby eventually eradicating coronary disease. Something like this is, in fact, the case with sickle-cell anemia. A child with one sickle-cell gene and one normal gene will not develop the disease and will also be genetically immune to malaria.

Today some health centers use genetic counselors to talk with couples who desire to have a baby but who are concerned that their own genetic background might cause the baby to be deformed, mentally retarded, or handicapped. Such counselors can only talk in terms of probabilities; there is little, if anything, that can be promised regarding heredity.

In closing this chapter we would like to point out that, although the eugenics movement is not very lively in the United States, many persons who have never heard the word *eugenics* have developed ideas concerning how they might increase or decrease the proportion of a certain characteristic—physical, psychological, or social—in the population through selective breeding. These people may base their ideas on their understanding of how intelligence, aptitude, and personality are determined—by heredity, by environment, by biochemistry, or by a combination of these three factors. We have discussed some of the ways heredity, environment, and biochemistry may interact; what are your opinions? What would *you* do if you were confident that a good eugenics program would eliminate diabetes or reduce the potential for violence? On what principles would *your* decision be based?

---

# REFERENCES

Ardrey, R. *The territorial imperative.* New York: Atheneum, 1966.

Beach, F. A. The descent of instinct. *Psychological Review,* 1955, *62,* 401–410.

DeFries, J. C., & Plomin, R. Behavioral genetics. *Annual Review of Psychology,* 1978, *29,* 473–515.

Fuller, G. D. *Biofeedback: Methods and procedures in clinical practice.* San Francisco: Copi-Copia Press, 1977.

Hirsch, J. Behavior—genetic analysis and its biosocial consequences. *Seminars in Psychiatry,* 1970, *2,* 89–105.

Huxley, A. Human potentialities. In R. E. Farson (Ed.), *Science and human affairs.* Palo Alto, Calif.: Science and Behavior Books, 1965.

Lashley, K. S. Structural variation in the nervous system in relation to behavior. *Psychological Review,* 1947, *54,* 325–334.

Lazarus, R. S. *Patterns of adjustment and human effectiveness.* New York: McGraw-Hill, 1969.

Lindzey, G., Loehlin, J., Manosevitz, M., & Thiessen, D. Behavioral genetics. *Annual Review of Psychology,* 1971, *22,* 39–94.

Maslow, A. H. A theory of metamotivation: The biological rooting of the value-life. *Journal of Humanistic Psychology,* 1967, *7,* 93–127.

Miller, N. E., & Bannazizi, A. Instrumental learning by curavized rats of a specific visceral response, intestinal or cardiac. *Journal of Comparative and Physiological Psychology,* 1968, *65,* 1–7.

Nagel, E. *The structure of science: Problems in the logic of scientific explanation.* New York: Harcourt Brace, 1961.

Williams, R. J. Biological approach to the study of personality. In E. A. Southwell & H. Feldman (Eds.), *Abnormal psychology: Readings in theory and research.* Belmont, Calif.: Brooks/Cole, 1969. Pp. 306–317.

# CHAPTER 10

## GROUP DIFFERENCES: SEX AND RACE

Few people manage to evade discussing race, ethnicity, and sex. Since most of us identify strongly with both our racial or ethnic group and our sex group, these discussions often have ramifications that extend far beyond the merits of the intellectual positions we maintain. What we bring to these discussions, in terms of implicit assumptions concerning differences among groups and how the differences evolved, affects not only what we say but also how adequately we hear what others are saying to us. We certainly observe differences between groups, but the origins of these differences are frequently obscure. In this chapter, we want to examine such differences and alternative explanations for their occurrences, as well as look into the implications of such explanations.

## MALE AND FEMALE ROLE DIFFERENCES

Different stages are set at birth for males and females. Some of the limitations that arise from these settings are biologically based, while others result from environmental restrictions and from learning patterns that begin almost as soon as the infant begins to breathe. However, it is not certain to what extent biology and inherited characteristics influence the sex-related differences that we observe and to what extent these differences develop through social learning. It is known that sex differences in personality and role behavior are found in every known society throughout history, but we also know that few, if any, of these differences are universal. Even if the same differences between the sexes could be found in all societies, we still could not be certain that the differences are genetically based. And, in turn, in the case of differences known to be genetically based, the differences may not necessarily be universal. For example, although all evidence points to a genetic origin of the average height difference between men and women, many women are taller than the average man.

## PASSIVENESS AND DOMINANCE

One difference that we observe between the sexes in our society concerns passiveness and dominance. Perhaps men assumed the dominant role long ago when communities needed hunters and warriors with great physical strength and speed—a time when women were more restricted than they are today by many pregnancies and by long periods of breast-feeding. Few people or groups give up dominant roles willingly, and men were no different; they kept women in subservient roles long after strength, speed, and the restrictions of pregnancy ceased to be the main factors in determining who will play the dominant role in a society. In fact, the social value system that men developed made a virtue of what perhaps was once a necessity—male dominance.

Another opinion on the development of male dominance notes that throughout history individual women have made great accomplishments and attained positions of power, but that these women were exceptions. These exceptions are used to show that women who have the capabilities can become leaders, but they are also used to imply that most women do not attain leadership because most women lack the capability. A different explanation of the relative powerlessness of women in the past—an explanation that is more in keeping with contemporary thinking—is that learning opportunities for women were so limited that women were unable to compete effectively with men. These limits on education not only prevented women from gaining knowledge and competence, but also reinforced a lesson women learned early in life: in order to be acceptable, women must think and act in ways that preclude many options open to men.

## THE BIBLICAL VIEW OF WOMEN

People often use the same passages from the Bible to support opposing points of view. The following passage is frequently quoted by both proponents and opponents of "women's liberation": "And

God created man in His own image, in the image of God created He him; male and female created He them" (Genesis 1:27). The meaning of the word *man* in this passage appears to be *humankind*, since "man" was created "male and female"; and nowhere in this passage is it implied that men were created more like God than women were. Nonetheless, certain passages in the epistles of Paul can be interpreted as claiming that men are more God-like than women.

It is well known that, according to the Bible, Eve disobeyed God's command and then tempted Adam to disobey. Because of this, Eve is sometimes called a temptress, and, historically, discussions of these passages focus on women as being the downfall of men. Adam, representing men, is seen as sensible and proper; Eve, representing women, is seen as impulsive and seductive. Yet it might be possible to interpret the same passages to mean that woman is curious and seeks new knowledge, whereas man is placid and passive. It is interesting in this light to remember that the result of eating the forbidden apple was the gaining of knowledge of good and evil—the loss of innocence—which suggests that faith was replaced by worldly awareness and curiosity. Tertullian, an early Christian thinker and apologist, berates woman for this:

> *You* are the Devil's gateway. *You* are the unsealer of that forbidden tree. *You* are the first deserter of the divine law. *You* are she who persuaded him whom the Devil was not valiant enough to attack. *You* destroyed so easily God's image—man. On account of *your* desert, that is death, even the son of God had to die [Ruether, n.d.].

To illustrate this point, Augustine draws on a later chapter from Genesis, in which God berates Eve for having taken the apple: "I will greatly multiply thy pain and thy travail; in pain thou shalt bring forth children; and thy desire shall be to thy husband, and he shall rule over thee" (Genesis 3:16).

St. Augustine continued the attack on woman by asserting that women do not reflect the image of God unless they are married or remain virgins. For Augustine, all men reflect the image of God, but women do not if they are single. This emphasis on marriage refers to interpretations of the Old and New Testaments that describe the most important function of woman to be childbearing, but that at the same time condemn female enjoyment of sexual encounters. Women who were not virgins or virtuous, submissive wives and mothers were seen as licentious females who attempted to entice men into unholy carnal relationships. Augustine felt that the nature of woman is to tempt and seduce, but he felt that it is both possible and important for woman to overcome her nature by remaining a virgin or at the very least becoming an obedient wife. Although women were inferior in the eyes of

God and although they tended to behave licentiously, they could be redeemed if they behaved appropriately.

☐ In an earlier chapter, we discussed the historical view that "mind" is superior to "body." In this case, woman is "body" and man is "mind," and the body, which is evil, is seen as trying to seduce the mind, which is virtuous, away from its proper path. Before you assume that these notions are no longer popular, try to respond to the following questions.

1. Is it woman or man who, according to contemporary custom, wants to get married? (Have you heard the expression "A man chases a woman until she catches him"?)

2. How often is it implied that female rape victims actually encourage the attacks?

3. Is man or woman more often associated with strong intellect (that is, mind)? Who is more often associated with strong feelings (that is, body)?

4. On television and in films, what methods do women use to get their way? What methods do men use?

5. Do men or women make greater use of clothing and ornamentation to manipulate the other sex into doing their bidding?

6. Is it man or woman who attempts to manipulate the other into ignoring "important" matters such as work or serious thought, in order to participate in "unimportant" matters such as recreation, love play, relaxation, or the arts? ☐

## BIOLOGICAL BASES OF MALE AND FEMALE ROLE DIFFERENCES

Little doubt exists that fairly consistent concepts of the nature of men and women have evolved in Western culture. The word *nature*, however, suggests heredity, biology, and determinism. To what extent do you think male and female roles and behavior are biologically determined?

There are obvious biological differences between men and women. For example, there are significant differences in anatomical structure, susceptibility to specific diseases, size, and biochemical or hormonal make-up. The question we wish to deal with here is: Did behavioral and role differences between man and woman develop for specifically biological reasons that are still valid today, or do these differences have a psychological, social, or environmental basis? Some studies indicate that women are less aggressive, less dominant, more nurturant, more dependent, less achievement-oriented, and less noisy than men; are these differences, if they exist, functions of heredity or environment?

One line of evidence used to support the claim that women's biology does affect their behavior in ways that are not evident in men concerns the behavioral changes many women experience immediately preceding and during the menstrual period. (If men are affected in this cyclical fashion, either the effects are minimal or they are obscured by other factors.) "Regular, predictable changes occur in the personality of the sexually mature woman, and these changes correlate with changes in the menstrual cycle. The personality changes occur in spite of individual personality difference and may even be extreme; they are a consequence of endocrine and related physical changes" (Bardwick, 1971, pp. 26–27).

However, although some of the observed changes in behavior can be traced to variations in hormone levels, it is possible that the *nature* of the changes is culture-dependent. For example, a young woman who is taught that menstruation is "the curse" may learn to react negatively to its monthly onset, but a woman who is taught that menstruation is an affirmation of a woman's feminine identity may learn to react more positively to its monthly onset.

Perhaps, then, the behavior of women between menarche and menopause is more variable than the behavior of men of the same age, but this hardly speaks to the kind of sex-related behavior differences we noted earlier. Hormone-based behavior variability might help to explain the observations made by some men that women appear inconsistent, moody, or changeable, but we don't know of any good studies to carry these observations beyond the status of folklore.

Among other primates, we find that males are more actively aggressive, dominant, and protective than females, whose main role is to nurture the infants. Young males play more actively than young females; adult males fight more aggressively than adult females. It is difficult (but not impossible) to assume that this behavior arises from social structure and learning patterns; it is easier to assume that male dominance and aggression in other primates are closely connected to size and heredity.

To what extent can we generalize from chimpanzees and apes to people? Although we may observe the same behavior in people and other primates, we cannot exclude the possibility that social structure, rather than biology, has made the human male more aggressive than the human female. Unfortunately, we just don't know much about the origins of differences in male and female role behavior. Although we do know that there are hormonal differences between men and women, we don't know whether they affect behavior in any meaningful and direct fashion; and although we know that sex-role behavior among nonhuman primates displays significant and reasonably consistent patterns, we don't know whether the reasons for the patterns can be used to explain human sex-role behavior.

## FREUD'S THEORY OF
## FEMALE ROLE BEHAVIOR

One especially controversial explanation for some female role characteristics is Freud's penis-envy theory. According to Freud, as young girls become aware that they lack a penis, they develop an envy of boys. Their realization makes them feel inferior, perhaps even mutilated. Girls must therefore sublimate their feelings of aggression, envy, and competition if they are to become what Freud viewed as mature women.

We don't wish to discuss the validity of this Freudian concept here, except to say that we don't accept it. We bring it up because it has had an important influence on the thinking of many people and because it is a good example of a way in which biology can be seen to indirectly affect sex-role behavior. Another example would be the assumption that, although women are not genetically programmed to be protected, they are genetically programmed to bear children, which requires that women be protected.

## INTELLIGENCE
## DIFFERENCES BETWEEN THE SEXES

Analysis of group differences in cognitive capacities between males and females runs into major difficulties. Although it is known that there are differences, we simply cannot determine whether these differences are based on environmental or physiological factors. For example, we have good evidence that women get higher grades during their pre-college years, while men do better in college, but this finding is as readily explained on environmental grounds as on genetic grounds. The same can be said of the tendency of men to do better on tests of numerical ability, spatial relationships, and mechanical aptitude, and the tendency of women to excel in the verbal areas (Maccoby & Jacklin, 1974), although overall differences in intelligence-test scores between men and women are negligible.

Feminists would maintain that the pattern of test results we just mentioned is the result of environmental influences, whereas male chauvinists would maintain that it is the result of heredity. The point to debate in this matter, then, is not *how much* is contributed by heredity and environment, but *whether* heredity contributes meaningfully to differences between men and women (no one questions that environment makes at least some contribution). To attribute to heredity any significant influence on sex-group scores on intelligence and aptitude tests is to accept at least to some extent the principle of genetic determinism.

If the traditional male and female roles are in fact biologically based, then we can defend the ideas that women's place is really in the home, that "anatomy is destiny," that "when women grow up without dread of their biological functions and without subversion by feminist doctrine, and therefore enter upon motherhood with a sense of fulfillment and altruistic sentiment, we shall attain the goal of a good life and a secure world in which to live it" (Rheingold, 1964). We can idealize motherhood and keep women out of the male world of decision making. It would be sufficient that, in the words of a poem by William Ross Wallace, "The hand that rocks the cradle is the hand that rules the world."

If we believe in this school of thought, we would also agree that women should be willing to bask in reflected glory, knowing that the male infants that once lived in their bodies—the infants they loved, nurtured, and reared—will bring them honor. In this case, women would justifiably be limited to the role of helpmate. Being a helpmate, wife, and mother could then be seen as the ultimate freedom, since wives and mothers would not need to become embroiled in the ugly and competitive world of employment, politics, and material achievement. Women by nature would prefer the beautiful, the noncompetitive, and the nurturing qualities of life. Women in this traditional world would also maintain the sanctity of the home by remaining there (at least as long as necessary) to attend to children and household chores and by being satisfied with the knowledge that they are helping to produce a stable society.

## NATURE VERSUS ENVIRONMENT: SOME IMPLICATIONS

We have just discussed the traditional view of male and female roles. Now we would like to discuss some options open to people who believe that male and female role behavior is indeed based on "nature." First, they might agree with the theories of humanistic psychology and work toward enabling women to be themselves and to develop their "natural" interests and abilities. A second option is to attempt to alter the social value system to permit those qualities and tasks that are "naturally" women's to become equal in importance to the qualities and tasks associated with men. The third option is to oppose the oppression and the restrictions suffered by women, even though the results may contradict the "nature" of woman.

If, however, traditional male and female roles are *not* biologically based but are learned as a result of male manipulation of the social environment, then either no exploitation of one sex by the other is justifiable, or each sex has equal right to exploit the other. If you believe in this school of thought you would believe that, given equal opportunity, women can supervise men as well as the reverse. Role differences could disappear; men might not trust the fidelity of their wives any more than some wives believe in the fidelity of their husbands; it would not be assumed that nurses and elementary school teachers are women and that physicians and college professors are men. If role changes did not come about, it would be because of men's entrenched power, not female nature.

People who feel that observed behavioral differences between men and women are primarily a function of social learning have two basic decisions to make: first, what changes, if any, are needed in the present system, and second, how the changes should be enacted. People in this group would find it difficult to believe that women are "naturally" less aggressive and more nurturant than men. If they did believe this, they would be putting women in a Catch-22 position, in which women would be offered the options of their present roles, which are seen as oppressive and restrictive, and egalitarian roles which are "contrary to their natures."

## MEN'S AND WOMEN'S LIBERATION

When the Women's Liberation Movement first began, it concentrated on raising the consciousness of women. Men were seen as the enemy—and often still are. As time went on, however, some recognition was given to the price men pay for their adherence to their own sex-role concepts: men had to be autonomous and nondependent, even when they needed to be dependent; men had to be sexually aggressive or exploitative even when they wanted to be passive or giving; men had to be strong enough to avoid tears, even when they wanted or needed to cry; men could not show or receive physical affection unless it was overtly sexual. In addition, the traditional men's role did not allow men to show interest in poetry, sunsets, concerts, and ballet; expressions of pain, physical or emotional, were inappropriate for them, and achievement on the job was necessary, no matter what the price in time, energy, peace of mind, or simple humanity.

In other words, it was realized that, although women need to be freed from the belief that they are naturally dependent, nurturant, and emotional, men also need to be freed from the belief that being dependent, nurturant, and emotional is contrary to their nature. In this case, the slogan "We shall overcome" applies to the oppressors as well as to the oppressed.

□ Several questions can be raised at this point in our discussion. For example, do "male chauvinists" base their political views of the rights and prerogatives of women on the biological differences that exist between males and females? Do members of the women's movements use as political philosophy theories supporting the idea of the overwhelming significance of environment and social learning in shaping individuals? Are contemporary psychological theories products of a male-supremacy philosophy? Have men been able to control society for many centuries because women are indeed, by nature, dependent, nurturant, and passive? □

There is hardly enough evidence on which to base a final judgment regarding the nature of men and women, but the fight to resolve the social conflicts and the moral questions involved in the Women's Liberation Movement will still be waged, based in small part on facts and in large part on the psychological and economic needs and the philosophical beliefs of the participants. Do you think these questions and conflicts can be settled sensibly? Do you think they can be resolved until the psychological and economic needs of men and women are met (or changed)?

# ETHNIC GROUP DIFFERENCES

Many of the questions we asked about male and female role behavior can be asked about ethnic or racial group differences. Indeed, few issues will produce greater show of feeling in a discussion than the issue of whether differences between racial or ethnic groups are innate and inevitable, or whether they arise from learning situations (which may include living under oppressive conditions). When sex-group differences are discussed, the major emphasis is usually on personality and temperament, although intellectual abilities are also brought up on occasion. When ethnic-group differences are discussed, however, affective or personality considerations are much less important today than intellectual abilities or cognitive styles.

## THE BASIS OF THE CONTROVERSY

What do intelligence-test scores mean? Almost all studies that compare "intelligence" test scores of Whites with test results of Blacks show that the former score higher. That may lead us to believe that Blacks are not as intelligent as Whites, but it is by no means clear just what these tests measure; it could actually be intelligence, but it could also be the ability to function in the White middle and upper classes. In fact, court cases have successfully challenged the use of intelligence tests to place children in various State school systems. The basis of these suits is that, since a disproportionate number of Black children are judged according to these tests to be mentally retarded, the tests are racist. We do know that the tests are fairly good predictors of academic success, however, so that we deduce that

Black children are not as likely to achieve academic success as White children.

What exactly is there about intelligence tests that would discriminate to the detriment of Blacks and to the advantage of Whites? Many studies have tried to find the answer. One study showed that Black children received higher scores when they were tested by Black psychometrists than when they were tested by Whites (Pettigrew, 1964). Another study, done some years ago in Philadelphia, showed that Black children who came to that city from the South had lower test scores when they entered school in first grade than did local Blacks; however, by ninth grade the two groups scored at comparable levels (Lee, 1951). A well-known investigation during World War II showed that, for any one region of the country, White draftees scored higher than Blacks; however, Black draftees from the Northeast achieved better scores than White draftees from the southeast (Benedict & Weltfish, 1943). A later study has shown that the intelligence-test scores of children improve when teachers expect improvement (Rosenthal & Jacobson, 1968)—an expectation that indirectly discriminates against Blacks, since teachers often do not expect them to improve.

One intriguing study of Jewish, Chinese, Black, and Puerto Rican children in New York City showed different patterns of verbal ability, reasoning, numerical ability, and spatial relations. Middle-class Jewish children showed higher verbal ability but lower spatial-relations ability than middle-class Chinese children; lower-class Black children had higher verbal, but lower numerical, ability than lower-class Puerto Rican children (Lesser, Fifer, & Clark, 1965). There have been literally hundreds of studies supporting the idea that ethnic group differences in intelligence are based on differences in learning opportunities.

In any case, we are concerned about whether the bases for any ethnic-group differences on intelligence test scores are environmental—that is, related to health and nutrition, parental and community education, extra-curricular stimulation, material wealth, and the like—or whether the differences are inherited. In this matter, most psychologists would agree with Klineberg (1963): "I can only conclude that there is no scientifically acceptable evidence for the view that ethnic groups differ in innate abilities. *This is not the same as saying that there are no ethnic differences in such abilities.*"

□ What do you think about the matter of intelligence differences among race groups? If psychological differences between ethnic groups have never been satisfactorily demonstrated, do we have the right to act as if they have? □

# JENSEN'S THEORY

Over the years, a small number of respected behavioral and natural scientists have taken a strong pro-heredity view of both race and sex differences in cognitive capacities. This position was advocated by psychologist Arthur R. Jensen (1969) in an article based on his interpretation of his research data. However, according to Hartup and Yonas (1971) and others, the Jensen article and its innumerable rejoinders and counterrejoinders have not led to anything new or of value in terms of either conceptualization, research, or conclusions. In any case, the movement of the debate from academia to the popular media does have major implications: "Hasty and unwise decisions could be made on the basis of these arguments, and we doubt that the population at large is any better informed about the complexities of nature and nurture than previously" (Hartup & Yonas, 1971, p. 354).

What is Jensen's argument? Jensen states that "Since intelligence is basically dependent on the structural and biochemical properties of the brain, it should not be surprising that differences in intellectual capacity are partly the result of genetic factors which conform to the same principles involved in the inheritance of physical characteristics" (Jensen, 1969, p. 32). He agrees that inadequate environment, including substandard nutrition and limited stimulation, is indeed a major factor in lowering intelligence level. However, although Jensen feels that "below a certain threshold (level) of environmental adequacy, deprivation can have a markedly depressing effect on intelligence," he also feels that "above this threshold, environmental variations cause relatively small differences in intelligence" (p. 60).

The key in Jensen's argument is not that environment does not affect intelligence, but that environmental deprivation can only account for lowered intelligence in extreme cases; the population groups in the United States who have suffered only moderate deprivation have not been affected severely enough to account for the differences between their IQ scores and those of other groups. Jensen's most notorious statement was that "there is increasing realization among students of the psychology of the disadvantaged that the discrepancy in their [Blacks' and Whites'] average performance cannot be completely or directly attributed to discrimination or inequalities in education. It seems not unreasonable, in view of the fact that intelligence variation has a large genetic component, to hypothesize that genetic factors may play a part in this picture" (p. 82).

The same issue of the *Harvard Educational Review* that carried the Jensen article carried several commentaries. Hunt (1969) agreed that "the widespread belief in the almost indefinite plasticity of intellect" (p. 278) needs correcting—that is, that there has been too much acceptance of the idea that intelligence can be expanded almost indefinitely by enrichment programs. He disagreed with Jensen, however, that intelligence was "essentially a static function of growth, largely predetermined in rate" (p. 284). Kagan (1969) attacked Jensen's thesis as lacking recognition of the significance of the Black experience in influencing intelligence levels of Blacks. Jensen, he felt, placed far too much stress on genetic limitations on intelligence and far too little stress on the many ways in which environment can function to lower the level of intellectual competence.

Although most behavioral and natural scientists disagreed— often violently—with Jensen, the focus of their anger has been his discussion of group, not individual, differences in cognitive abilities. They feel, like Kagan, that he has grossly underestimated the impact of the environment, including social deprivation and nutritional inadequacies. However, much of the abuse heaped upon Jensen, both by professionals and laypersons, has nothing to do with the logic of his thinking, the adequacy of his research, or even the basis for his data interpretation.

Our concern is not with Dr. Jensen's personal and social values; our concern is with the political and social implications of his work and the furor it has created. Jensen's statements struck directly at the core of many people's beliefs and prejudices, and Jensen set off a political battle lasting several years. His statements, for example, have been used to support the demands of those who oppose school integration and special enrichment programs—although he did not support either integration or segregation in his article—and his name has become a rallying cry for those who oppose his ideas. (In the spring of 1973, several years after publication of Jensen's controversial article, the students at the university where he was teaching voted to condemn him for his views.) In any case, Jensen's paper has forced many people to consider a position that has substantial theoretical and practical importance in psychology and in society, and the unexpected political outcry over this paper has illustrated how impossible it is for theory to remain politically and socially neutral.

## SOCIAL AND POLITICAL
## IMPLICATIONS OF INTELLIGENCE THEORIES

If the intellectual capacity of a person or of a group is genetically determined, programs developed to raise low intelligence levels will have little effect; the ability of a given person or group to absorb, understand, and use information will simply be less than the ability of another person or group. Thus, some people will not do well on intelligence tests, regardless of the kinds of programs, interventions, and so forth that are instituted. In this instance, if a particular group is thought to have more innate competence than another group, an educator or community organizer might treat the groups differently.

If you believe that intelligence level is fixed by heredity, you might not want to marry someone whose genetic structure might produce children of inferior intelligence. As a teacher, you would be satisfied with the modest performance of low-functioning students instead of encouraging high performance; as a parent, you might blame your spouse for having transmitted "weak" characteristics to your children, and you would encourage your low-functioning children to aspire only to low-status jobs with few educational requirements.

Some of the things we just mentioned have happened to many Black, Hispanic, Native American, Puerto Rican, and other minority groups in the United States. However, they happened not because evidence proved that heredity determines group differences in intelligence level but because the biases of decision makers, teachers, community members, and others were so strong that these people functioned as though they had evidence. Indeed, Hartup and Yonas' prediction that people could make rash decisions based on incomplete evidence in this matter has been confirmed, since many of these biased people have ignored evidence that contradicts their beliefs. (Selecting evidence only to confirm a bias has been done by people throughout history and throughout the world; it is not confined to the question of race and sex group intelligence differences in the United States. Prejudice and discrimination are classic grounds for "proving" differences among individuals and groups.)

If intellectual competence were not such an overwhelmingly important attribute in Western society, then the issue of the root of intelligence might be less contentious. As it is, the groups that have suffered from prejudice and discrimination in America contend that their constituents are genetically equal to Whites. They insist that it is the obvious lack of equal opportunity for education, stimulation, encouragement, and so forth, that has led to the group differences found in performance, and they insist on programs to equalize the opportunities and eliminate performance differences among race groups.

Earlier in this book, we discussed political views and assumptions about human nature. Here again it is appropriate to point out how political values interact with views of humanity. Environmental determinists are more likely to support demands for remedial programs for victims of race and sex discrimination, since they believe that environmental factors have caused the intelligence and performance differences and that altering the environment will eliminate the differences. Religious determinists (who, obviously, do not include all religious people) may be fatalistic and assume that the status of all people reflects God's will. Exponents of free will may take the position that Blacks, Hispanics, women, and other groups will gain equality only when individuals act independently in their own interests. Humanistic psychologists would probably combine the idea of free will with environmental determinism and take the stance that the environment must be altered to allow each person to fulfill his or her capacity to act independently to improve conditions.

We can see, then, that political and social liberals would be comprised primarily of believers in environmental determinism and humanistic psychology; they would tend to support the movement for remedial programs to counteract the adverse effects of discrimination and poor environment, and they would support the idea that individual or group intelligence and performance can change. Social and political conservatives, on the other hand, would be comprised mostly of believers in free will and genetic or religious determinism; they would display sympathy for those members of minority groups who "made it on their own" and would doubt the effectiveness of remedial programs in changing any differences in performance or intelligence among groups and individuals.

As you consider the points and questions we have raised in this chapter, keep in mind that, although many people with strong prejudices against various racial, sex, or religious groups draw support from theories that genetic differences among groups do exist, this does not mean that all those who advocate such theories are racists. And that means that for these issues and conflicts to be resolved, the psychological and economic needs of women and men must be met (or changed), and the real philosophical differences must be addressed. How do you think this can be done?

## REFERENCES

Bardwick, J. M. *Psychology of women.* New York: Harper & Row, 1971.
Benedict, R., & Weltfish, G. *The races of mankind.* Public Affairs Pamphlet No. 85. New York: Public Affairs Committee, 1943.
Canady, H. G. The effects of "rapport" on the I.Q.: A new approach to the problem of racial psychology. *Journal of Negro Education,* 1936, *5,* 209–219.
Hartup, W. W., & Yonas, A. Developmental psychology. *Annual Review of Psychology,* 1971, *22,* 337–392.
Hunt, J. McV. Has contemporary education failed? Has it been attempted? *Harvard Educational Review,* 1969, *39,* 278–300.
Jensen, A. R. How much can we boost IQ and scholastic achievement? *Harvard Educational Review,* 1969, *39,* 1–123.
Kagan, J. Inadequate evidence and illogical conclusions. *Harvard Educational Review,* 1969, *39,* 274–277.
Klineberg, O. Negro-white differences in intelligence test performance: A new look at an old problem. *American Psychologist,* 1963, *18,* 198–203.
Lee, E. S. Negro intelligence and selective migration: A Philadelphia test of

the Klineberg hypothesis. *American Sociological Review,* 1951, *16,* 227–233.

Lesser, G. S., Fifer, G., & Clark, D. H. Mental abilities of children from different social-class and cultural groups. *Monographs of the Society for Research in Child Development,* 1965, *30* (4), 1–115.

Maccoby, E. E., & Jacklin, C. N. *The psychology of sex differences.* Palo Alto, Calif.: Stanford University Press, 1974.

Pastore, N. *The nature-nurture controversy.* New York: King's Crown, 1949.

Pettigrew, T. F. *A profile of the Negro American.* Princeton, N.J.: Van Nostrand Reinhold, 1964.

Rheingold, J. *The fear of being a woman.* New York: Grune & Stratton, 1964.

Rosenthal, R., & Jacobson, L. *Pygmalion in the classroom: Teacher expectation and pupils' intellectual development.* New York: Holt, Rinehart & Winston, 1968.

Ruether, R. R. *Misogynism and virginal feminism in the fathers of the church.* Mimeograph, undated, circa 1973.

van den Berghe, P. L. *Age and sex in human societies: A biosocial perspective.* Belmont, Calif.: Wadsworth, 1973.

# CHAPTER 11

## DEVELOPMENT AND SOCIALIZATION

If you don't know where you're going, any road will take you there. What road brought you to where you are today? How did you come to be the person you are at this moment? To what degree are you the product of your genetic inheritance? How influential was your early social environment? To what extent was motivation a factor? How about your mood and temperament? Intellectual abilities? Physical appearance? Social roles? Possible sources of deprivation? And in what ways did all these interact dynamically with one another?

Our discussion in the remainder of this book will become less explicitly philosophical and more psychological, but we will continue to focus upon the notions of values and success. The questions we have raised in the first ten chapters will be found to underlie many issues in psychology.

## SOCIALIZATION AND SOCIAL CHANGE

Conflict between generations is an ancient phenomenon. The young ape who challenged an aging leader for dominance in the troop may well have been the progenitor of the contemporary young militant (or the passive drop-out) who challenges parents and community leaders for control of society and its institutions. (You may not think

**145**

of a drop-out as challenging for social control, but give it some consideration.) Eventually, of course, the young will triumph, because the old must inevitably give way at their deaths, if not before.

However, the leaders, the parents, the socializers have at their disposal one powerful weapon to use in maintaining control even after they have lost their personal power. These are the people who establish the institutions through which the young must travel in order to gain entrance and acceptance in the community. It is the parental generation that dominates schools, neighborhoods, churches, health and mental-health facilities, jobs, and—probably most important of all—families. It is through the family, probably more than through any other source, that new generations develop their values, evolve their motives, work out their future relationships. It is through families, probably as much as through formal schooling, that traditions, customs, and loyalties are handed down. And the young, for the most part, abide by the customs, take on the values, and support the institutions handed down to them.

With such complete control over the sources of socialization and communication, the generation in charge should have no difficulty in making its successors carbon copies of itself. Yet somehow, in ways that are not really understood, the social dynamics of institutions, technology, family relationships, political circumstances, and so on, do produce some degree of social change. This gradual change may be insufficient for the more aggressive of the young and overwhelming for the more frightened of the old, but it does occur. Despite the strong influence of the parental generation, children are never carbon copies of their parents; they are always themselves.

Some of the reasons for this inevitable change are these. First, no family, community, or society exists in total isolation today, so that competing values are always in evidence. Second, since the socializing process is only imperfectly understood, no one knows how to use even total control of all the socializing inputs to gain total control of the individual. Third, within any family, community, or society there are conflicting currents that communicate alternative ideas to the persons being socialized. Fourth, if there is—as the humanistic psychologists contend—any such thing as an individual's nature, certain kinds of socializing pressures just will not work effectively because they run counter to an individual's nature. Fifth, if a great deal of personality development occurs during the early months of life, so that certain potentialities for later behavior are built in at this time, subsequent unlearning of these patterns will be extremely difficult. Consequently, socializing pressures that work against what has been learned in infancy may not be effective. Sixth, many socializing agents obviously use inappropriate techniques—perhaps because the techniques had worked previously, perhaps to express their own anxieties, perhaps because they are confused or simply not knowledgeable, or for any of a variety of reasons that you might care to add.

Changes that occur in the relative power of the family undoubtedly will bring changes in other roles and relationships. Recent history has seen an expansion of the proportion of children attending school (an institution under community rather than family control) and an increase in the length of time that children attend. In addition, increased use of child-care facilities brings children under the influence of adults outside of their families at an earlier age than ever before. At the other end of childhood, the lowering of the age of legal adulthood brings people permanently out of familial control at a younger age as well. As parents increasingly turn their children over to institutionalized influences, they may well be weakening their hold over their children and strengthening the hold of governmental policy makers. It is still too soon to evaluate the long-range effects of the development of child-care facilities and the reduction of the age of legal adulthood on other social customs or on parent/child relationships.

The attempt to understand the process of socialization, then, is an attempt to understand a double-barreled question: how people learn to behave, feel, think, perceive, and perform roles according to the expectations of their various social groups, *and* how they learn to behave, feel, think, perceive, and perform roles that *differ* considerably from those expected by their various groups (after Mussen, 1967).

In considering the process of socialization, it is important to remember that the child, even the infant, is not merely a helpless and passive entity that is molded by an overpowering social and psychological environment. The infant impinges on the environment. Children behave in many ways that influence their parents, who, in turn, influence the children. The cry of a baby, no matter what the cause, affects parental response; a baby perceived as cute elicits different parental reactions than one perceived as homely; an infant who cries a great deal or is "cuddly" creates a different home atmosphere than an infant who cries very little or is physically aloof from parents. No discussion of socialization should fail to take into account that infants and children have power and influence of their own.

# THE MEANING OF WHAT
# WE HAVE UPON ARRIVAL

The influence of the environment before birth is minimal but most certainly real. To think of all behavior at birth as being the outcome of purely genetic factors is to ignore nine months of development. At the extreme, serious physical and intellectual deficiencies can be caused by a variety of environmental conditions—for example, oxygen deficit, blood abnormality, x-rays, hormone and dietary inadequacies, and incompatible blood typing between mother and father. There is also some evidence that chronic emotional stress undergone by the mother may have a harmful effect upon the unborn child.

Given the present biomedical assumptions about the effects of maternal behavior on the subsequent physical and intellectual capacities of the infant, what responsibility does an expectant mother have to her future offspring? The same question might be directed to the community: What responsibility does a community have to the future offspring of its citizens? Is it enough, for example, to make maternal and child-care clinics available to the public? In the United States, most communities have one or more clinics providing service without charge or with only a minimal fee, yet the infant-mortality rate ranks above those of many other nations, the rate being much higher for non-White ethnic groups than for Whites. Do these figures suggest that the community is not trying hard enough to reach expectant mothers? Do they indicate that parents are not sufficiently concerned for their infants? Where does the responsibility lie for the well-being of newborn infants?

Of course, you might contend that these questions imply the unwarranted assumption that a low infant-mortality rate is desirable. You might argue that infant deaths weed out those infants who would not have been strong anyway, or that prenatal maternal care is quite adequate in our society, or even that overpopulation requires a reduction in maternal and child-health services.

Or perhaps you would argue that the only real responsibilities belong to the parents-to-be, not society. Yet even here the questions are difficult. Is the pregnant woman morally obliged to avoid smoking because nicotine affects the birth weight of infants, even though there is no evidence that permanent harm is done? Since some drugs—heroin, certain diet pills, tranquilizers, etc.—taken during pregnancy do affect the fetal bloodstream, at least temporarily, what responsibility does the mother have? Does her responsibility differ if she is not married to the father? If she despises the father? Or are her feelings about the father totally irrelevant? How about her feelings about the fetus and her impending motherhood? (We bring up the issue of responsibility to others at this point in a rather unusual context. However, we will return frequently to this issue of responsibility throughout the book.)

At the time of conception, many characteristics of the future person are established. Some of these, such as eye color, are impossible to alter in the years ahead. Some, such as head shape, can be affected only by illness or accident. Some, such as facial appearance, height, and bone size, can be influenced by subsequent environment, although for most persons the genetic transmission is of overwhelming importance. Thus, by the time infants are born, they are already set upon their future course in terms of their physical characteristics. In addition, they have also inherited susceptibility to certain illnesses, perhaps significant or insignificant physical disabilities, and numerous characteristics that mark them as being members of particular racial, national, ethnic, and sex groups.

These characteristics are valued differently in any given society, in any community within a society, in any family within a community. Eye color, head shape, skin color, hair texture, or height have almost nothing to do with people's behavior *except* as these characteristics are valued by their culture, community, peers, and family.

Consider the seemingly neutral characteristic of height. For the past several decades, Americans have gleefully watched the average height of men and women go up. Americans were getting bigger and bigger, which, it was assumed, implied that they were getting better and better. After all, their bigness was undoubtedly caused by better medical care and better nutrition; it coincided with a longer life expectancy; it was "obviously" good. Then people began to ask: Why is it good to be big? Of course, size helps a little in winning some international sporting events, but it also means that Americans must consume more food, use up more hides to make the leather to cover larger feet, produce larger automobiles and larger beds and larger airplane seats and larger bus seats and . . . . This line of questioning is rarely pushed very far, because people who are tall (but not too tall) are considered to have an advantage. Because of the values of society, an otherwise useless physical characteristic becomes an important part of a person's body image and thus of the person's self-concept.

Your physical appearance is not something you have earned. You never worked for it, nor were you gracious or brave or clever or cruel enough to have been given it. It was programmed in at conception and developed in subsequent years. Of course, within limits you are able to have some influence on your appearance. You can partially determine your weight; you can style your hair and alter its color; you can use cosmetics; you can dress to emphasize or deemphasize certain physical aspects. Essentially, however, your physical appearance was given to you well before you were capable of doing anything good or bad, right or wrong. Yet, if your culture and community define your physical appearance as attractive, you will be accorded a much different treatment than if you are perceived as plain or unappealing.

□ It has been suggested that, by the age of 40, a person has the face he or she deserves. Do you believe that the stresses we encounter, the kindness or cruelty we exhibit, are reflected in our faces? Would you disagree with the first sentence in the previous paragraph in that regard? How do you think others around you have evaluated your physical appearance? What effect has your perception of that evaluation had on you? Does your life experience reflect itself in your face? Your body? □

# EARLY DEVELOPMENT

Although biological factors and genetic transmission influence the direction that socialization will take, the process itself is strictly a function of learning. Early development, however, is not strictly a function of learning. Some kinds of behavior appear to emerge when the organism has matured to a particular point, without regard for learning. Walking, for example, would probably occur at roughly the same age regardless of whether there was any attempt to teach the child. Eager parents may speed the process up a bit—if their very eagerness does not introduce anxiety and thus slow the process down—but by the age of 2 children can usually walk regardless of whether their parents have encouraged, discouraged, or ignored walking. Walking is therefore said to be the outcome of maturation, a process that might be likened to the unfolding of a flower. Unless something intervenes to limit a child's ability to learn to walk, the child will learn when he or she is ready and not much before.

## *LEARNING*

The amount of learning accomplished by normal children during the first year of life is truly remarkable. They learn to relate visual stimuli to tactual stimuli; they learn to associate certain sounds and sights with subsequent sensations, such as being fed, being handled, being bathed; they learn to swallow, to creep and crawl, to feel pleased when a particular configuration of stimuli occurs and perhaps to feel fearful in response to another configuration; they learn to understand the meaning of some words and voice tones; they learn to grasp objects; and so on through a very long list.

In order for learning to occur, several basic conditions must be present. First, biological development must have reached the stage at which the child is capable of performing the task. At 6 months of age, infants' legs have not developed physically to the point where they can walk; 2-year-olds lack the physical maturation and coordination to ride a tricycle; 3-year-olds are normally far-sighted and therefore unable to make out letters unless they are quite large, which makes reading impossible without special materials (Strang, McCullough, & Traxler, 1967).

Second, cognitive capacities must also have developed to the stage where learning is possible. The brain, which is obviously part of the body, develops over time. Some parents' claims to the contrary, 3-week-old infants do not have the cognitive capacity to recognize their parents or to differentiate their mothers from their fathers; 3-year-old children lack the cognitive maturity to write a novel.

Swiss psychologist Jean Piaget has observed that there are very definite cognitive stages children go through. Until a child reaches a certain stage, there are things he or she simply cannot learn. For example, 2-year-olds cannot understand that matter is not created out of nothing and does not disappear. If you doubt this, the next time you are faced with a 2-year-old who has one cookie but wants two, try taking the one cookie the child has and breaking it in half. We predict that the child will happily assume that he or she now has been given two (Piaget, 1954).

Third, learning also depends upon attention. A child who is not attending to a potential learning situation is unlikely to learn. Since children often have short attention spans, they are more difficult to teach in the formal sense.

Fourth, there is the role of motivation. Whether any learning takes place without motivation to learn is a matter of some debate. Considerable evidence suggests that learning can occur without motivation—for example, two events follow each other in time or two objects are adjacent in space on occasion after occasion. Even though the observer may not be motivated to learn to associate the two occurrences, learning is likely to take place. Thus, whether motivation is absolutely necessary for learning is still uncertain. That motivation is one of the major factors in *how much* learning takes place is, however, undebatable.

Fifth, reward or reinforcement must be considered among the primary factors in learning. Some theorists insist that no learning can occur without reinforcement; others refuse to accept this extreme position. No one, however, appears to doubt that reinforcement is intrinsic to much human and animal learning. Young children, in learning to talk, make many random sounds, some of which elicit favorable responses from people in their environment and some of which probably strike them as sounding a great deal like sounds they have heard these people make. If the response of the people in their environment or the hearing of a familiar sound is felt to be positive, it is a reinforcement that rewards the use of that sound in that circumstance. In the future, the sound is more likely to be repeated in that circumstance, and, since the same reinforcements are likely to occur again, continuous learning occurs. On the other hand, many other sounds that do not receive reinforcement eventually drop out of children's repertoire; the ability to make some of these sounds later is actually lost.

Reward or reinforcement (these are not identical concepts, but they are closely related in this context) can consist of a smile, food, absence of punishment, the satisfaction of feeling a job is well done, the promise of security, a gesture of love, or even—for some persons—being disciplined.

Those who argue that reinforcement is necessary for learning tend to support a fairly extreme determinist approach to human behavior. They use such concepts as behavior modification and shaping, and they tend to approach human behavior as something that can be altered through outside interventions. The term *shaping* recalls the process undertaken by a beautician in styling hair. The application of the metaphor to reinforcement theorists is not entirely facetious, since they appear to think of people's behavior as being shaped by environmental forces in somewhat the same fashion as a head of hair is shaped by a beautician.

Their opponents agree that reinforcement influences behavior, but they argue that the relationship between reinforcement and behavior is so far from one-to-one that other concepts would be more fruitful in explaining people's actions.

Another way of phrasing this basic condition for learning, one that would probably find general acceptance, is that environmental conditions must be appropriate for the learning to occur. If maturation were sufficient, little structuring of the environment would be necessary. And if a rich environment were sufficient, the level of maturity would be irrelevant. In essence, then, for learning to take place, an individual must be ready to learn and the environment must provide the wherewithal to permit the learning to occur.

## HUMAN DEVELOPMENT
## AND MORAL BEHAVIOR

Preschoolers, at least in our society, tend to be highly possessive. One 3-year-old, who had two 5-year-old friends playing in her room with her toys, spent most of her playtime racing from one friend to the other, shouting "Mine! Mine!" and grabbing the toys out of their hands. Children at this age have only the most rudimentary idea of morality and often simply cannot grasp the idea of sharing, however much parents may attempt to get it across. They have just recently mastered the notion of possession, and it is quite a feat of abstraction to realize that the toy is still theirs even though the child over there is playing with it.

According to Piaget, around the age of 5, children become moralistic to the point of rigidity. Their perception seems to be that all rules—from the rules of a game to moral rules—exist all on their own. Just as transgressing the rules of a game is a black-or-white, absolute thing ("You cheated!" "I did not!"), so the transgression of a moral rule is absolute ("It's not fair!"). And, just as children tend to overgeneralize grammatical rules (if the singular of books is *book*, isn't the singular of cheese *chee*?), they overgeneralize moral rules ("It's not fair that he got seven grapes and I only got five!").

This kind of thinking typically continues until adolescence, when young people begin to realize that interpersonal relationships require reciprocity based on mutual accommodation. In the face of this, the teenager will realize that parents cannot have absolute moral control. This really hits home when the moral fallibility of parents becomes evident. At this time, moral accountability is normally shifted from family to society. (At least it is in our culture. Things get a bit more complicated in cultures with extremely strong family or clan ties.)

Children's *observance* of rules also develops with age but does not completely parallel their *awareness* of the rules. That is, in some ways children practice rules of morality before they are consciously aware that the rules exist and certainly before they can express the rules in words. At the same time, rules are often understood and readily verbalized but not followed in practice. Both of these sets of circumstances are undoubtedly familiar to you.

Beginning with the studies by Hartshorne and May (1926), results of research have consistently shown that people whose behavior is considered moral in one situation are not necessarily those who behave in a morally approved way in another situation. The more similar the situations, the more likely people are to behave in similar fashion. And this is true of all ages, not just children. The person who assiduously follows all the rules of the road in driving may never think of returning overpayments at the supermarket; the student who never cheats on examinations may lie to his lover without batting an eye; the professor who reimburses her secretary's petty-cash fund for every stamp she takes for personal use may withdraw expensive books from the university library and never return them. It is not that relationships between different kinds of moral behavior do not exist, but that their relationship is not at all obvious. Nonetheless, children and early adolescents believe that rules are extremely necessary, and they feel that the evil nature of humanity would hold sway were rules done away with (Tapp & Kohlberg, 1971).

# LATER DEVELOPMENT

Development is commonly seen as occurring primarily or completely during the early years, but this is far from true. Development continues throughout the life span. The notion that behavior and personality are set in concrete after the first few years is dangerously misleading.

In each phase of the life cycle, different behavior patterns are seen as age-appropriate. Socialization into these patterns occurs in much the same fashion as during the early years. Learning the expected behavior for a work role probably begins early in life, but 12-year-olds have hardly been effectively socialized to their future roles as full-time workers. Such socialization does not occur for many years. When it does take place, it takes place slowly and only after actual experience with work. Teenagers on their first jobs build upon what they have learned from family members, friends, teachers, counselors, and the media, incorporating these teachings with the experiences and social relations associated with a part-time after-school job. Later, on their first full-time jobs, they broaden their awareness. Even ten years and, perhaps, several jobs later, their development is still occurring. Their socialization now may involve a supervisory role and greater job responsibility.

As the years go by, concern for the work role is slowly replaced by anticipation of the retirement role. Retirement may or may not be a happy event, but it is inevitable for most workers, whether as the result of ill health, personal preference, outmoded skills, or simply age. A new role confronts persons approaching retirement, who may begin to perceive themselves as "pre-retired" well before their actual retirement (even though some people avoid even thinking about retirement planning until they wake up one morning to find that the alarm clock no longer needs to be set).

Neugarten and associates (1965) have pointed out that some people look upon themselves as ahead of schedule, while others perceive themselves as being on time or running late. A 6-year-old child in third grade is ahead of schedule, as are a 22-year-old physician, a 19-year-old mother of two children, a 36-year-old president of a multi-million-dollar company, and a 44-year-old navy admiral. There is pressure on people who run ahead of schedule, since their tasks are seen by others as being more appropriately accomplished by older people. They must enter into role behavior that their age peers have not yet encountered, so those people to whose behavior they must gear themselves are considerably older than they. And they may well be resented as well as respected for their accomplishments, since they are out of step with their schedule.

Persons behind schedule are often subjected to even greater stresses. The mere fact that they are behind time is often taken to indicate some kind of inadequacy. In addition, they have less time to make use of whatever position they are heading toward. The 40-year-old college freshman, the 9-year-old physically handicapped child entering first grade, the 46-year-old housewife now embarking on her first full-time job, the 37-year-old man marrying for the first time; all these people will have to cope with being one of the oldest in their groups. They also will meet prejudice and discrimination as they become socialized to their changing roles. Moreover, the guidelines for these roles are geared to younger people; how do a 30-year-old professor and a 40-year-old sophomore address each other?

The behavior socialized is no longer toilet training but work habits or marital relations or parental functioning; the socializing agents are no longer parents and teachers but employers, co-workers, peers, and (perhaps) television; the socializing practices do not include physical punishment but involve promotions, salary increases, community acceptance, reactions of neighbors, respect from spouse and children. But the process is still that of socialization.

☐ What roles or kinds of behavior have you been socialized to during the past year or so? How well has the process worked? Do you think it's possible to avoid socializing others to age-related roles? Would that be a good idea? ☐

## SOCIAL IMPLICATIONS

Like physical attractiveness, intelligence and ability to learn verbal and abstract concepts are highly valued in our society. Moreover, children who appear to be ahead of their age peers in their development are also valued. Walking at 10 months, speaking entire sentences at 16 months, reading at 3 years, all are looked upon with great favor, while children whose development is slow may aggravate their parents and embarrass them in front of their more competitive friends. To some extent, the value attached to precocious development results from the assumption that it is predictive of high competence in the capacity that seems ahead of schedule; to some extent, in our relatively competitive society, it results from the desire to be better at whatever is at issue at any age.

Whatever the bases for these values, the outcomes are worth contemplating. Children mature biologically and cognitively at a certain rate; to a large degree, this rate of maturation cannot be speeded up. This does not mean that 3-year-olds cannot be taught to read. It does mean that the job of teaching them to read a book will probably take much longer and be much more difficult than it would be at the age of 5 or 6. By the time a child is 8, it may be a matter of indifference whether reading began at 3 or at 6, assuming that, as a 3-year-old, the child was read to and was otherwise involved in tasks that would lead to reading.

Similarly, individual children mature biologically and cognitively at different rates. The averages and the charts are useful only as general indicators; thus, children whose development is far behind the average for their age group might be watched more carefully and, if maturity seems definitely retarded, taken to a specialist in child growth. It is common for parents and others to pressure infants and young children to live up to published averages or to permit children to use the rate of their maturation as a basis for self-evaluation, but we suspect that these practices are not very healthy for either the parents or the children. If a child is ahead of schedule, the parents may praise themselves; if the child is behind, the parents often blame the child, although they still feel an undercurrent of personal responsibility.

In our society biological maturity, cognitive maturity, long attention span, and motivation to learn are all valued. One reason for this is the belief that early development of competence in these areas will lead to qualities that, in turn, will lead to success as defined by our society. And here we return to the theme with which we began—that the way you define "success" is a pervasive influence in your life.

□ Can you picture a society in which one or all of the four qualities just mentioned are not valued? How about a society in which children are expected to *avoid* excelling in any way, in which a person who wins too many races or shows too much desire to be a leader is ostracized? How about a society in which attentiveness is perceived as indicating overinvolvement, in which the norm is: stay cool, don't show that you care, remain uninvolved, be casual, indicate that you would just as soon be somewhere else? How about a society in which "good" children are those who do not care to move physically away from the immediate area of their parents' care? If biological maturity were a little longer in coming, the child would be helpless a little longer and, therefore, "good" a little longer. Perhaps some of the examples sound familiar. Often the very things we take most for granted are contrary to the "givens" of another society. □

## SOCIAL IMPLICATIONS OF REINFORCEMENT

The social implications of reinforcement or reward deserve special attention. Parents and other caretakers reward behavior in children, and these rewards help determine how the children will behave the next time the situation arises. They also influence how the children feel about the persons providing the rewards, how they feel about themselves, and how they feel about the world in general. Experts in behavior modification make a point of their ability to elicit wanted behavior by reinforcing those responses that they wish to have repeated, while leaving unreinforced those acts they wish to see stopped.

In terms of reinforcement, then, *success* is defined by the persons who are modifying the behavior. Essentially, these persons decide the goals of the learning process, although sometimes the people with whom they are interacting can leave the scene if they dislike what is happening to them. But much more important than the role of professionals in behavior modification is the way we all use reward and reinforcement to influence the behavior of others. When someone tells a poor joke, you don't laugh; when a speaker bores you, you begin to count the holes in the soundproofed ceiling; when children interrupt, you ignore them and continue to talk; when a stranger offers your 3-year-old a piece of candy, you grab your child by the hand and march away. Each of these acts is meant in part to affect the subsequent behavior of the person you are responding to. *You* have defined success as not telling dumb jokes, not giving dull talks, not interrupting, not making friends with strangers. Do you have the right to attempt to influence behavior in these fashions?

Consider the situation in which your control of rewards is much more profound—for example, when you are acting in the role of a parent, a supervisor, a clergyman, a social worker, a teacher, a shop steward, a personnel interviewer, a psychotherapist, a caretaker of children, an aide in a convalescent-care facility. In these situations, you can provide rewards and non-rewards on an ongoing basis. You have enough control to force others to bow to your demands, at least at a superficial level; by offering your reinforcements at frequent intervals, you may even have a major impact upon behavior. Now you are faced with a different kind of ethical and moral consideration. Now you have the chance, at least potentially, to alter behavior in a given direction. Now your definitions of success may indeed be imposed upon others.

So now we ask again, do you have the right to attempt to influence behavior in this way? We suspect that you readily agreed when we said at the start of this book that "success" must be defined by each person as an individual, that you need to be successful according to your own standards, that your behavior should be effective in your own eyes, that you need to have integrity, to feel like a whole person, to be true to *your* self. Now we see that it is almost impossible for one person not to impose standards of success and effectiveness on another! How can we have it both ways?

As a parent, you reinforce smiling and you punish, or leave unreinforced, whining; as a teacher or a nurse's aide, you might reinforce docility and quiet while punishing restlessness and noise; as a clergyman you reward church attendance and prayer; as a shop steward, you reward exploitation of grievances and punish passivity in the face of management pressures. You have defined success and are acting upon it, but your actions also affect others. You have some control over one of the basic conditions of learning, and you are using it to lead others to your goals.

Of course, you never have complete control over the behavior of others. You've probably been frustrated to find how little influence you often have. Parents and teachers frequently comment upon their lack of success in directing the lives of their charges. Nonetheless, you do have the potential for influence. This potential brings with it the obligation to recognize who you are, where you are going, what defines success for you, and what you are doing to others as a result. Perhaps most important, it brings the obligation to continually ask yourself what you have the right to do to whom.

## REFERENCES

Hartshorne, H., & May, M. A. Testing knowledge of right and wrong. *Religious Education*, 1926, *26*, 539–554. Also *Studies in deceit*. New York: Macmillan, 1928.

Mussen, P. Early socialization: Learning and identification. In G. Mandler, P. Mussen, N. Kogan, & M. A. Wallach (Eds.), *New directions in psychology: III*. New York: Holt, Rinehart & Winston, 1967.

Neugarten, B. L., Moore, J. W., & Lowe, J. C. Age norms, age constraints, and age socialization. *American Journal of Sociology*, 1965, *70*, 710–717.

Piaget, J. *The construction of reality in the child*. New York: Basic Books, 1954.

Strang, R., McCullough, C. M., & Traxler, A. E. *Improvement of reading* (4th ed.). New York: McGraw-Hill, 1967.

Tapp, J. L., & Kohlberg, L. Developing senses of law and legal justice. *Journal of Social Issues*, 1971, *27*(2), 65–91.

# CHAPTER 12

## SOCIALIZATION
## AND MORAL VALUES

How does socialization occur? We begin with an infant who lacks any social values or awareness of human relationships, and, in a relatively brief period of time, we have a child who boasts a complex network of values and an extremely sensitive awareness of relationships. What is the process that enables the socializing agents—most probably the parents at this juncture—to get their messages translated into behavior on the part of the child? Equally important, how is it possible that, to a considerable extent, these values and relationships are internalized by children as their own? Children do more than imitate their parents or even identify with them; they assimilate many of their parents' thoughts, feelings, and behaviors to the point that these become their own thoughts, feelings, and behaviors.

When behavior is elicited through outside demands—for example, through threats, bribes, or coercion—it usually ceases or drastically alters when the outside demands cease. On the other hand, when behavior results from internalized values, the task of changing it is much more complicated and often impossible. Knowing this, persons who wish to influence social or personal change frequently try to reach the socializing agents.

Most writers have emphasized socialization in children, thus ignoring one of its vital characteristics—the fact that it is a constantly changing and developing process. It is true that certain values and relationships are developed very early in life and are likely to resist change, but others are in a constant state of flux and can be affected by changes in others as well as by personal maturation. For example, are your religious values the same today as they were ten years ago? Consider the sexual behavior you now believe is appropriate for someone of your age, sex, and marital status: how closely do your views resemble the ones you would have predicted for yourself a decade ago?

# PATTERNS, AGENTS, AND PRACTICES

In studying the socialization process, three matters must be considered, regardless of the age of the person being socialized: (1) the behavior patterns to be socialized, (2) the agents participating in the socialization process (for instance, parents, peers, teachers, television programs), and (3) the techniques and practices through which the socializing occurs.

In each of these matters, the values of the culture, the community, and the family are displayed. Choice is involved. (Whether or not you are a determinist, and, if so, how strong a determinist you are, will probably influence your reactions to the following statements.) In the United States and Canada, neither the behaviors to be socialized, nor the socializing agents, nor the socializing techniques are fully predetermined; exposure to a variety of partially conflicting views is virtually inevitable. Even in more isolated cultures, not all infants receive exactly the same kind of socialization.

You express your values in your selection of those patterns of behavior you wish to socialize into others. For example, are you highly concerned with toilet training? Do you see your child's training as reflecting upon your competence as a parent? As getting rid of an unclean and messy task? As eliminating a health problem? Lest you suppose that everyone sees toilet training in the same way, consider that in a great many cultures parents do not give toilet training nearly the importance that parents in our culture do. Even within the North American countries, there is evidence of social-class differences in the application of early toilet training procedures.

Our point, however, is not that early toilet training is good or bad, but that the tendency of so many people in Western culture to focus upon toilet behavior as one of the most necessary behavior patterns to socialize is the result of our cultural values. We might have picked swimming, learning to feed oneself with utensils, differentiating colors, or moving the body in time to music, but in our culture these concerns are normally seen as minor in comparison to controlling the elimination process.

Just as our value system determines which behaviors receive most emphasis in the socialization process, so too our value system also selects the socializing agent. In most instances, the first socializing agents are the parents. Input, normally of a less influential nature, also comes from brothers and sisters, grandparents, and other relatives; sometimes close family friends, servants, child-care personnel, and others are also important socializing agents.

Several pressures appear to be operating against the existing family structure, however. These pressures include higher divorce rates, greater opportunity for egalitarian sex roles, greater use of child-care facilities, greater freedom to obtain abortions, development of communes and other extended family arrangements, lowering of the age for the beginning of formal education, lowering of the age of legal adulthood, pressure on welfare mothers to find jobs, and increase in the number of families in which both parents work. In addition, the requirement that all children must attend school places much more power in the hands of teachers as socializing agents. Since the movement toward compulsory education coincided with reduced social pressure to attend church, the socializing influence of the clergy has possibly diminished as that of the educators has increased. And we shouldn't overlook the role of physicians and psychologists; after all, who writes most of the books telling parents how to rear their children?

Finally, the specific practices and techniques used to produce the desired socialization also depend upon the values of the socializers. These values determine whether the socializing agents follow a humanistic psychological approach, a psychoanalytic model, or a behaviorist model; whether the techniques of socialization include strong and even painful punishment; whether shame and guilt play important roles in the process; whether internalization or external control is emphasized. The experiences, belief systems, goals, and personalities of the socializing agents all interact to produce the socializing techniques. Few socializing agents sit down and logically set up their techniques to accord with their goals and personalities; usually their choice reflects implicit assumptions rather than a detailed, explicit philosophy.

One socializing agent will be nurturant, careful, warm, and overprotective, while another will be casual, aloof, and demanding. Both may say that one of their major goals is to teach those they socialize to act independently, but each obviously has different implicit assumptions about human behavior, and each is undoubtedly expressing an individual personality and value system in his or her choice of techniques.

☐ Can you recall the socializing styles your parents used? How well did they work in achieving your parents' goals? How do your own approaches differ? □

## DEVELOPMENT OF CONSCIENCE

Control over behavior can be based upon fear of punishment, but that requires that a reasonably good chance of being caught exists. Control can be based on worry about bringing shame to the family, but this assumes that people will find out about the shameful behavior. Control can be based upon internalized values that prevent a person from performing the "wrong" behavior to begin with, but this demands that the person's conscience be sufficiently developed to serve as an internal control. When all three controls are in operation, it is probable that control is quite effective. However, we cannot evaluate the success of a control system unless we have a good understanding of the nature of the proscribed behavior. For example, when the motivation to behave in some way that is socially condemned is strong, the controls must also be strong to keep the behavior from occurring. In spite of the many controls that punish certain kinds of sexual behavior or various forms of cheating and stealing for financial gain, people still cheat, steal, and behave promiscuously. The potential rewards obviously outweigh the fear of punishment, the shame, and the guilt. On the other hand, most people dress appropriately for church. Even though the punishment, shame, and guilt incurred by improper dress in church are much less than those incurred by, say, sexual transgressions, the reward for the "good" behavior is also much less. That this matter is highly complex, however, is shown by such widespread phenomena as cheating on college exams or shoplifting. These transgressions continue to occur even though the potential punishment usually outweighs the potential gain. Even the shame and guilt that should serve as controls in these circumstances often do not. Yet the same person who readily cheats on exams or steals from supermarkets might feel physically unable to spit on a crowded sidewalk, despite having a mouth filled with phlegm. This rather unpleasant image is used as a particularly graphic example of the power of shame and guilt, even when consequences are relatively minor.

Since a society maintains itself through socialization of its newcomers, it is vitally important to most adults that the young remain controlled by the socializing agents. Control is maintained by teaching the young to fear punishment and to believe that punishment for evil acts is imminent, by teaching them to avoid shame and to believe that the reputation of wrongdoers is quickly destroyed, and by trying to instill a strong sense of internal controls. Then the socializing agents leave the young to their own devices, secure in the belief that these internalized teachings can take the place of constant external supervision. Thus parents transmit their values to their children; jobholders transmit their values to new employees; older students socialize new ones; members of the American Medical Association, Boy Scouts, Marine Corps, American Civil Liberties Union, Actors Equity, Oakland Raiders, John Birch Society, and Great Neck Home Owners Association try their hand at socializing the prospects and neophytes. Yet, as we all know, people constantly behave in ways that risk punishment, promise shame, and produce guilt.

# IDENTIFICATION AND IMITATION

Fortunately for the socializing agents, they are not working unaided. In many, perhaps most, situations, the people being socialized are very cooperative in expediting their socialization through the related but very different processes of identification and imitation.

## *IDENTIFICATION*

Identification is closely related to internalization and undoubtedly underlies it in many ways. Based upon the psychoanalytic writing of Freud, the term *identification* refers to "the process that leads the child to think, feel, and behave as though the characteristics of another person . . . belong to him" (Mussen, Conger, & Kagan, 1974, p. 395). We would substitute the word *individual* for *child*, since identification is not limited to childhood.

For children, identification most frequently occurs in relationship to parents. A young boy, for example, observes the ways his father behaves, how this behavior seems to differ from the ways his mother behaves, how his father responds to his mother, and how his mother responds to his father. These sets of integrated observations provide the framework for his own subsequent behavior, especially his sex-role behavior, and may determine how he will respond to women and how he will expect women to respond to him. A similar identification occurs between a young girl and her mother.

In the classical situation postulated by Freud, young children develop a strong desire to possess the opposite-sex parent (Freud assumed a sexual component in the desire, but there is no reason why the paradigm won't work with the concept of social possession). Children compete with the same-sex parent for the attention and affection of the opposite-sex parent (if you don't believe this, watch how young children respond differentially to adults of different sexes and how much tease and play is involved). Eventually, however, children recognize that competition cannot work. They may become very angry with their parental rival, but they fear that any expression of this anger will be dangerous. (Freud called this fear the fear of castration, a term that is somewhat awkward for little girls.) Still wanting to possess the opposite-sex parent, children take the one road remaining: they develop characteristics that permit them to be like the victorious parent, so that, symbolically and perhaps actually, they can enjoy the same success as the same-sex parent.

One author describes two general types of identification. The first is *identification with the aggressor*, in which children (almost all sources describe the process of identification as though it ceased to be operative at age 12) are fearful of possible punishment from parents and thus avoid punishment and gain parental approval by becoming like the same-sex parent. The second type is termed *developmental identification*, in which children are anxious over the possible loss of parental love and become like the parent to reduce the anxiety and retain the love (Hoffman, 1971).

Other authors touch on additional aspects of the identification process. One theorist (Mowrer, 1950) postulates that love, affection, and respect underlie identification. Another (McGinnies, 1970) puts the spotlight on imitation and offers a framework of positive control and aversive control, occurring through the reinforcement of preferred behavior and the nonreinforcement, or negative reinforcement, of nonpreferred behavior. A third approach (Whiting, 1960) is that identification occurs because of envy of power or status. That is, children envy the way in which parents appear to have control of so many resources, both material and human, and identify with parents in order to feel that they share this control. In addition, two of the conditions Freud outlined for identification are salient (Hall, 1954). First, a person with a particular characteristic—being female, owning a Ford, having the flu—tends to identify with others who have the same characteristic. Second, a person who *wants* something that others have may identify with those who have it, hoping to achieve the desired object.

Children's identification with parents is far from total, as any frustrated parent will confirm. It is affected by two important factors: (a) the reward system of the people and institutions in the broader society outside the nuclear family and (b) the individual personality and needs of each child. Given a reward system and a personal need system that may work against children's identification with parents and parental values, it is important that these values undergo a continuing pattern of social reinforcement and support.

Children are immersed in a social system that extends far beyond the input of parents. These other people and forces are part of a child's world and leave their imprint on the child. Children also identify with people other than their parents, although usually with less intensity. Later they identify with groups and organizations—peer groups, religious denominations, political parties, social clubs, ethnic groups, neighborhoods, union locals. Although the term *identification* is used slightly differently with respect to these situations, individuals apparently do respond to their image of what is expected of a member of each of these groups. That is, instead of identifying with one person, they identify with a generalized person, made up of a blending of many actual persons plus assumptions about people they have never even met. Then they are led to think, feel, and behave as though the characteristics of this generalized person belonged to them.

In addition to these social influences, individual differences in hereditary and biological characteristics also help to keep identification with parents below 100%. In the final analysis, we should not be surprised that children are not replicas of their parents. Rather, we should wonder at the audacity of those who continue to seek ways of completely understanding and predicting human behavior, in spite of the immense difficulties.

## *IMITATION*

Another important component of socialization is imitation. Some imitation is undoubtedly a kind of social facilitation, in which the mere fact of being in the presence of many others who are doing something will lead the individual to do it also. If you see many people congratulating a friend, walking quickly, talking loudly, or complaining about the weather, you tend to do the same thing. You become caught up in the spirit of things and act as the others do. Watch what happens at a busy corner when one person begins to cross the street against the light.

The more usual notion of imitation is choice-matching imitation. This is the process of learning to do what someone else is doing through external reinforcement for appropriate actions (Aronfreed, 1968). A certain amount of trial-and-error and feedback may be involved prior to correct performance, as in imitating a piano teacher's hand movements or the accent of a new television star. Also, whether the model being imitated is rewarded or punished for the behavior influences the likelihood that the child will repeat the act (Aronfreed, 1968). Since children mimic the behavior of their parents, an astute observer may learn a great deal about what is going on at home by watching the children play.

# CONFORMITY OR INTERNALIZATION

Virtually everyone seems to be opposed to conformity. Only when you begin to probe do you learn how varied are people's perceptions of what constitutes conforming behavior. You may well end up with the feeling that conformity is a derogatory term applied to anyone who, as a member of some group or assortment of persons, behaves in ways the speaker doesn't like. Wearing beards, joining a college fraternity, avoiding picket lines, encouraging school achievement, voting for members of the two major parties, studying business administration, wanting to earn a lot of money, not wanting to earn a lot of money—all have been used as examples of conformity.

Beloff (1958) makes a useful distinction between two types of conformity. *Conventional conformity* refers to behaving as others of a similar background behave. The behavior is seen by the actor as appropriate; it is based upon views and values that have been effectively internalized. *Yielding conformity* refers to giving in to social pressures, regardless of one's personal values. It involves pretense, or incapability to assert one's own views. We all display yielding conformity at times; perhaps we wish to avoid an argument, or perhaps we're embarrassed because we favor a view that many others oppose. We probably display this type of conformity a great deal more than we like to admit. Frequent resort to yielding conformity works against being what Jourard (1968) calls an authentic person. We are not what we try to seem.

Clearly, there is an important difference between behaving according to internalized values (conventional conformity) and behaving without regard to one's own values (yielding conformity). In the first instance, you may criticize people as being "conformists" because you feel that their internalized beliefs sound too much like a party line, too similar to the beliefs of some Establishment, or too little given over to critical evaluation. In the second instance, you may call people "conformists" because you feel that they are keeping up a pretense. The first type of criticism may reflect only a difference in values; you might not apply the label of "conformist" to someone whose values conform to your own! The second type of criticism is directed at the *authenticity* of people's behavior, whether or not you agree with their professed values. We need to be aware of whether we are criticizing someone's "conformity" only because we happen to disagree with the person's values.

# THE NATURE OF GUILT

Guilt has many meanings. Consider the following cases.

In the trial of Leopold and Loeb for the murder of Bobby Frank, little doubt existed that the two students had committed the murder. They were convicted and imprisoned on the grounds that they were guilty of the crime.

In the war-crimes trials of Nazi leaders and their followers after World War II, many Germans convicted of a variety of crimes, including murder, were imprisoned or executed. Although many pleaded that they had been helpless in the face of the Nazi establishment—that they had been forced to commit the crimes—they were still considered to have guilt on the grounds of individual responsibility.

Shortly after the 1965 riots in the Watts ghetto of Los Angeles, many community leaders claimed that all persons in the country, through omission or commission, shared in a collective guilt for the conditions that led to the riots.

In *The Trial*, by Franz Kafka, Joseph K. is accused and convicted of a crime without ever being informed of the nature of the crime. People treat him as though he were guilty, and he assumes that he must be guilty. His guilt is a terrifying, destructive feeling, all the more anxiety-provoking since the objective basis for it is beyond his determination.

A man seduces a young girl with claims of his love, takes her to bed, and then cannot consummate the action. He is rendered impotent by his guilt.

As these examples show, guilt comes in many packages. It is a label attached to a person for an action the person has committed or is believed to have committed. It is also a feeling people have when they believe that they have violated some value that they have internalized. These two meanings are obviously connected, since feelings of personal guilt usually result from doing something that others would label as wrong. For the present, our main concern is conscience-induced feelings of guilt.

The paradoxical nature of guilt is well expressed in these two statements:

> No feeling is so agonizing to a well-socialized person as acute guilt, except perhaps an acute anxiety attack. Since guilt is such a powerful feeling, it incites the person to do something quickly in order to get rid of its pain [Jourard, 1968, p. 256].

> ... the motivation to avoid guilt is insufficient for resisting temptation and ... other personality and situational variables should be considered [Hoffman, 1971, p. 238].

Both statements can be true. Hoffman points out that even people with "well-developed moral commitments" can handle strong feelings of guilt through defense mechanisms, so that, at least consciously, guilt is not felt. Others have inadequate inner controls to refrain from the guilt-producing action; consequently, they both behave immorally *and* feel guilty for it. In spite of the pain, the act is committed, and the person either lives with the pain or defends against it.

Many religions, like other institutions, use guilt and freedom from guilt to control behavior. The Christian religion can be seen as emphasizing demands for moral behavior and the guilt of those who fail to live up to its standards more than other religions do. It does this by focusing not only on overt behavior but on the feelings that underlie the behavior. In other words, it demands not only purity of behavior but purity of motives. For example, it is insufficient merely to avoid promiscuous sexual relationships: "I tell you that anyone who looks at a woman with desire has already committed adultery with her in his heart" (Matt. 5:28). St. Augustine elaborated on this teaching by claiming that virtues pursued for the purposes of self-aggrandizement and self-love become vices (a theme echoed by Kant in a nonreligious context over a thousand years later).

Religious precepts are often perceived as constituting the ideal, against which human beings are expected to fail while constantly attempting to improve. On the one hand, Christianity, with its emphasis on all-forgiving love, turning the other cheek, and so on, probes beyond behavior and into thought and feelings. Even to *think* evil thoughts is sinful. On the other hand, Jesus is seen as forgiving and His forgiveness can provide life eternal.

Conflict has occurred between religious teaching and the practice of psychotherapy because of a difference in values and views of guilt. In some instances, the kinds of behavior that psychotherapists have tried to free from guilt have been the same kinds of behavior that more traditional persons wished to eradicate altogether. Clashes between religious adherents and supporters of psychotherapy were once common but have been steadily diminishing over the past several decades.

## DEVELOPMENT OF GUILT

Children become aware that they are observed, evaluated, and punished for stepping outside the bounds of acceptable behavior. As they internalize the values and standards of parents and others in the community, they also take on the role of observing, evaluating, and punishing (Janis, Mahl, Kagan, & Holt, 1969). In so doing, children observe their own behavior, evaluate it, and institute punishment when it is "bad"—that is, when it violates their conscience. The punishment is guilt.

Reactions to guilt have been described under three basic headings. First, we may accept responsibility and attempt to make compensation. We condemn ourselves, apologize, do something to make it up to the victims, real or imagined, or—in more dramatic instances—find some way of being punished. Whenever a major crime or murder is publicized, a number of confessions appear from people who seem to be seeking punishment for their own self-defined crimes. The Catholic Church, through its confessional and opportunities for penance, recognizes the need to compensate; Alcoholics Anonymous require, as part of their program, that a member seek out each person he or she has wronged and apologize or make some sort of restitution.

Second, we may direct guilt feelings away from ourselves and toward others whom we claim are blameworthy. This is an example of the defense mechanism of *displacement* or *projection*. The actor misses an entrance and blames the set designer for not constructing the set in such a way that he can watch the action; a passive and uninvolved student feels guilty for not participating in campus action and claims that the active students formed an impenetrable clique.

Third, we may justify the guilt-producing actions or rationalize away the serious nature of what we have done (after Janis et al., 1969).

These three responses to guilt parallel Rosenzweig's categorizing of responses to frustration. Rosenzweig applied the terms *intropunitive, extrapunitive,* and *impunitive* to these responses; you should have no trouble fitting these terms to the three reactions to guilt we have described.

## GUILT DIFFERENTIATED FROM SHAME

Guilt and shame both serve the purpose of reducing behavior that is socially disapproved of; both are usually learned from parents and other important figures in early life and throughout the life span; both are influenced by relationships and by roles. But they are not identical.

Guilt is the result of violating our own set of standards, our conscience. It operates regardless of the presence, or even the awareness, of others. It is based upon internalized values and represents our own control over our own behavior. Shame is the feeling of remorse that arises when we believe that we have brought discredit to ourselves or to others with whom we identify. Shame will not occur unless we believe that others are aware of the shameful act. Shame represents the control of others over our behavior.

You might feel guilt for harboring a sexually lustful desire, but you will not feel shame unless your lust becomes visible to someone else. You might feel some shame for being unsuccessful on a job and yet feel no guilt (because you did the best you could in the circumstances). Although guilt is a more common social control than shame in most Western nations, the reverse is true in much of Asia. In Japan, for example, a high school student who fails his exams may have a desolating sense of shame for himself and his family; a mother may feel horribly shamed if her son is arrested for criminal behavior; an employee may feel shame if the boss is fired for incompetence.

Sexual behavior, wishes, and fantasies often produce guilt. Because so many taboos surround all forms of sexual behavior, society works very hard—and usually very effectively—to socialize young children into the sexual mores of the community. Normally this job of socialization is successful: children internalize a strong set of values concerning when and with whom sexual behavior is appropriate and inappropriate. However, since the physiological sex drive and the social rewards for participating in active sexual behavior are also very strong, a conflict situation frequently arises. When the sexual drive overcomes the internalized restraints and forbidden sex takes place, guilt is a very common result. Even sexual wishes and fantasies, because they are believed to be evil, may disturb the conscience.

Sexual behavior outside of marriage brings shame when others find out about it and condemn the participants. In days gone by, many girls avoided premarital sex because they feared for their reputations. Today shame is less likely to result when age peers learn of sexual behavior, but a measure of shame may still be produced by the condemnation of middle-aged and older persons who still disapprove of premarital sexual relationships.

## DANGERS OF GUILT

Guilt has its hazards. Feelings of guilt can be greatly disproportionate to the objective reality of the acts performed. Many persons develop an overly rigid, overly demanding, overly critical conscience, perhaps because some parents set impossibly high standards their children must meet to gain their love, perhaps because some parents set such confusing or conflicting standards that their children cannot cope with them and develop their own highly rigid conscience structures, perhaps because some parents communicate to their children a feeling of low self-worth, a very inadequate self-concept, so that the children feel they must have done something wrong to be so poorly esteemed. Whatever the reason, many people do feel guilty about insignificant acts, and many feel disproportionately guilty about all improper acts.

We all have guilt feelings not only about the things we do but about the things we do not do. In addition, we feel guilty over our thoughts, our fantasies, our wishes, our unexpressed hates and angers, our uncommitted acts of lust and sexuality. When such guilt begins to have a seriously inhibiting effect on personal functioning, it becomes dangerous.

Manifestations of exaggerated guilt appear in many kinds of behavior pathology. To select a classical example, highly compulsive persons who constantly feel that their hands are unclean and need to be washed are very likely symbolically cleansing away guilt. A paranoid person who complains about the laser beams that induce homosexual fantasies is responding to intense feelings of guilt about personal homosexual inclinations. A dark-skinned child born into a family of light-skinned parents and siblings may come to feel that her dark skin is a sign of wrongdoing, a punishment for a sin she cannot comprehend. She may express her sense of guilt by a violent display of prejudice against members of dark-skinned ethnic groups.

These cameos are just brief examples of the potential cost of exaggerated guilt. One of the functions of psychotherapy is to reduce guilt and to bring it in line with reality.

## GUILT AND FORGIVENESS

When people see themselves as having failed according to some internalized standard, they will think less highly of themselves; their self-concept will be that of less adequate people. Guilt therefore works against self-esteem. To improve self-esteem, which appears linked to effective behavior and enjoyment of life, guilt must be reduced. On the other hand, to eliminate all causes of guilt is to socialize people without any sense of right or wrong.

Christian theology places forgiveness in the hands of God, or Jesus, who can then absolve a person of sin and guilt. One fallen-away Catholic psychologist bemoaned the unexpected cost of leaving her church: "When I used to go to confession and be absolved of my sins, I left services with a feeling of well-being that I have never been able to recapture. Now I need my own psychotherapist to absolve me. I don't feel so totally freed, it is much more painful and time-consuming, and it costs me a small fortune."

Once the function of absolution is taken away from the church, it is another person—or, in a sense, oneself—who offers absolution for sin and guilt. This shift alters the world from God-centered to human-centered. It also gives some human the responsibility for deciding what behavior is wrong and requires absolution or what to do in order to be absolved.

By what authority does another human forgive us and wash away our sins and guilt? Can we accept another person as an authority to help us overcome our guilt, even one who is seen as representing the general community or as the gatekeeper to mental health? Can we accept our own judgment in determining the degree of rightness and wrongness of our actions? Jourard suggests that healthy reactions to guilt are either to get rid of the guilt feelings by behaving in conformity with our conscience or else to alter our conscience. But this presupposes that our internalization of values is only relative, not ultimate. In the same vein, Roger Brown (1965) states that one of Freud's most important contributions was the proposition that "morality is not instilled by God but is acquired from society and more directly from two parents" (p. 351)—again implying a relativity of values. We would state the point a little differently, since we do not know whether moral *values* are in any sense relative. We do think, though, that people's moral *beliefs* are relative and, at least in part, socially transmitted. As society and people change, we can expect people's moral beliefs to change, too.

Faith in sacred rituals and persons must now share the altar with faith in the psychotherapeutic process and in the significance of the self. Guilt emanating from sexual and aggressive thoughts and behavior no longer requires Christian faith to resolve; these desires are explained as natural, not because human nature is imperfect, but because we are entitled to such satisfactions, at least within limits.

It is up to you to evaluate for yourself the views implied by contemporary religious and psychotherapeutic practices, and then to choose between them or to reconcile the two in some fashion. We suggest that your reflection include the concept of *appropriate guilt*. By *appropriate guilt*, we mean that the feelings of guilt engendered by immoral acts should not be incapacitating but should be sufficient to restrain us from repeating the same act. Appropriate guilt should, if possible, lead to some form of restitution or compensation to injured parties as well.

☐ You may have noticed that we dodged two controversies in the preceding paragraph. First, we referred to guilt as being engendered by immoral acts but said nothing about immoral feelings, values, or fantasies. Second, we suggested some form of restitution to others, in case the immoral act had a victim; some may hold that one's conscience can be violated irrespective of effects upon others. For instance, can we feel *appropriate guilt* for not having studied enough, for smoking too much, for wasting time watching third-rate television rebroadcasts? How about for not making use of our talents, for wasting our personal capacities, for ignoring opportunities to increase our own life satisfactions? ☐

# REFERENCES

Aronfreed, J. *Conduct and conscience: The socialization of internalized control over behavior.* New York: Academic Press, 1968.

Beloff, H. Two forms of social conformity: Acquiescence and conventionality. *Journal of Abnormal and Social Psychology,* 1958, *56,* 99–103.

Brown, R. *Social psychology.* New York: Free Press, 1965.

Hall, C. S. *A primer of Freudian psychology.* New York: Mentor, 1954.

Hoffman, M. L. Development of internal moral standards in children. In M. P. Strommen (Ed.), *Research on religious development.* New York: Hawthorn, 1971.

Janis, I. L., Mahl, G. F., Kagan, J., & Holt, R. R. *Personality: Dynamics, development and assessment.* New York: Harcourt, Brace, & World, 1969.

Jourard, S. M. *Disclosing man to himself.* New York: Van Nostrand Reinhold, 1968.

McGinnies, E. *Social behavior: A functional analysis.* Boston: Houghton Mifflin, 1970.

Mowrer, O. H. *Learning theory and personality dynamics.* New York: Ronald Press, 1950.

Mussen, P. H., Conger, J. J., & Kagan, J. *Child development and personality* (4th ed.). New York: Harper & Row, 1974.

Whiting, J. W. M. Resource mediation and learning by identification. In I. Iscoe & H. Stevenson (Eds.), *Personality development in children.* Austin, Tex.: University of Texas Press, 1960.

# CHAPTER 13

## SOCIALIZING FOR AGGRESSIVENESS AND DEPENDENCE

The goal of socialization is to channel behavior into acceptable paths. This goal is not fully achieved by any society, since neither the socializing agents nor their techniques are more than moderately successful. This chapter will discuss socialization in regard to two areas of primary concern: aggressiveness and dependence.

## AGGRESSIVENESS

Every society has a norm for the degree and kind of aggressive behavior it prefers, and every parent or other socializing agent has his or her own norm. In most instances, these norms are not far apart. Each society and each parent also tolerates a certain degree of deviation from the norm, and each is willing to practice its most effective techniques to keep those being socialized within the limits set by that tolerance.

Views of aggression are inevitably mixed. If a society encounters more aggression than it can cope with, it may enter a period of violence that is very destructive to its members, both physically and psychologically. On the other hand, if a society consists of highly submissive and docile persons, it may be unable to defend itself against outside intruders.

Rather than talk about aggressiveness as though it were a unitary phenomenon, we might be better off offering a profile of aggressiveness. Aggressive behavior can be purposeful or accidental. Aggressive outcomes can be the entire point of the behavior, as in tire slashing by vandals, or a by-product, as in a boxing match staged between two friends. Aggression may or may not lead to injury, either physical or psychological (Feshbach, 1971). It may represent an act of hostility, or it may be more nearly synonymous with self-assertiveness.

In any society or group, some forms of aggression are treated punitively, some are permitted, and some are encouraged. In our culture, aggressive selling, aggressive athletic competition, aggressive pursuit of high grades, aggressive (but not violent) pursuit of sexual relationships are all permissible and occasionally even rewarded. (Note the heavily masculine orientation of approved aggression, and consider the public response to women who are aggressive in just these ways.)

Of course, neither societies nor individuals are consistent in their views. Aggression and even violence done in the name of a popular social cause may be indulged, while the same action performed in the name of an unpopular cause is punished. The same society that encourages boxing or bullfighting, wars of conquest or defense, or the private possession of firearms may also invest great time, money, and effort in reducing aggressiveness in children's school behavior, in crimes of violence against persons, and in parents' disciplining of their children. In London, for example, with its international reputation for having police who work with a minimum of violence, a law to prohibit caning of children under 12 by teachers was met with great opposition when it finally passed *in 1971.* Yet the English eliminated capital punishment years ago.

Usually the concept of aggressiveness refers to the act of striking out when provoked (as in anger or fear) but does not include the desire to do injury to another. "When anger is elicited in the young child, he has a drive to hit rather than to hurt. Although by maturity anger has become closely associated with the motive to inflict injury, these response modes can still occur independently" (Feshbach, 1971, p. 284).

## DEVELOPMENT OF AGGRESSIVENESS

Whether aggressiveness might stem from instinctive or innate drives has already been discussed briefly. Much aggression is the result of frustration, which arises when we are unable to attain a goal that we consider important. (This is, however, much less true for the kind of aggressiveness that is similar to assertiveness.) The direction of the aggression, as well as its degree and mode of expression, vary as a function of the individual and the situation. Sometimes we direct aggression at ourselves, as if through self-blame for failure; sometimes we direct aggression against other people or even against inanimate objects; and sometimes we simply turn aggressive feelings aside.

Frustration does not always cause aggression, nor is aggression caused only by frustration. Research suggests that children become more aggressive when they are exposed to aggressive models (Hanratty, Liebert, Morris, & Fernandez, 1969). However, much of the seemingly aggressive play of young children, which can include absolutely grotesque imagery, should not be interpreted as actual aggressive behavior but rather as harmless role-playing. It is important to be able to distinguish innocent play from identification with a model. Further, although it appears important to present children with models of behavior of the sort we want them to internalize, we cannot self-consciously set out to act as role models for children; they almost always see right through the charade.

Although the potential for aggressive behavior, and probably for violence also, exists within each individual, aggressiveness is expressed only under certain circumstances. Such circumstances are not uncommon. When children strike out because of anger or frustration, it sometimes happens that subsequent attacks upon them diminish. Children are also likely to be reinforced for counter-aggression by social values that encourage retaliation in the eye-for-an-eye and tooth-for-a-tooth sense (after Feshbach, 1971). Producing a toll on the other person that is roughly equivalent to the pain and anguish received is more acceptable (in our society) than exacting greater revenge, although the latter is not uncommon. Unequal revenge seems especially to be tolerated when we can inflict it without further counter-retaliation.

□ An intriguing question may be asked in this regard. Assume that another nation has just sent nuclear bombs that have destroyed most major cities in the United States, killing as many as half the people in the country. It is within your power to press the button that would retaliate. Would you destroy the same proportion of the enemy? More? Less? All? None? Obviously, you would be moved to aggressive feelings. Considering your *values*, how ought you to deal with those feelings? Again, we see how your philosophy interacts with your psychology to produce your behavior. □

Among the most important causes of the anger and frustration that lead to aggression are violations of self-esteem through insult, humiliation, or coercion (Feshbach, 1971); other sources of frustration are embarrassment, loss of face, shame, and guilt. However, aggression need not arise from anger and frustration. Aggressive acts can result from greed, lust, or desire; from obedience to higher authorities that order aggression; from attempts to gain in a competition; and from being aroused by observing violence (in this connection you may recall our earlier discussion of censorship).

Should aggression be reduced? If so, how? There is good evidence that attempting to reduce aggressive behavior by force often increases frustration and anger, thus leading to more aggressive behavior. Of course, if the force is powerful enough, the aggressive behavior might be channelled in another direction. Permitting aggressive behavior to be expressed may allow an adequate release of tensions and thus reduce the frustrations and anger; on the other hand, if it is perceived as reinforcing the aggressive action, an increase in aggressive behavior could readily occur (Berkowitz, 1970).

The roots of later aggressive behavior are sometimes believed to reside in the very early experiences of infants. Infants may experience frustration because their wants are not attended to quickly enough. Since much of this frustration may be associated with either the presence or the absence of parents, it is easy to see how aggressive and angry feelings are mixed in with love feelings for these same people. A large number of books and articles have been written about specific socializing techniques, such as early or punitive toilet training or inadequate physical mothering, as leading to lowered tolerance for frustration at later ages. The results, as you might suspect, are more complex than they initially appear. Extremely rigid and punitive approaches, for example, may inhibit aggression expressed toward the parent but lead to its indirect expression or displacement. The same may occur in adults. Consider, for example, what occurs in prisons when the inmates are too fearful of directing their anger toward the guards and turn on one another instead. Undoubtedly, methods of parental discipline interact with the emotional climate in the home, as well as with the sex of the child and other factors, in their effect upon the behavior of children.

As children develop relationships with people other than their parents, these relationships begin to account for more of their frustration-induced aggression, as well as aggression that is based on imitation or observation. Aggressive behavior often ends in satisfaction, even though punishment for the aggressive behavior is part of the package. Aggressive children may get the attention desired and also get the toy; or they may turn their parents into shouting, screaming, hysterical persons or whining, tearful, self-pitying ones—which, for reasons parents can never understand, may be just what the children desire.

Play with other children, including brothers and sisters, produces many frustrating situations. Children cope with these situations in a trial-and-error fashion, based in part on frustration tolerance and prior learning, and slowly develop methods of reacting to these frustrations. Although people probably do develop some response patterns for dealing with frustration, these patterns are sufficiently influenced by the immediate circumstances that it becomes difficult to predict what a given person will do in the face of a given frustration. For example, the response pattern for a 3-year-old boy may be to grab any toy he wishes, but he may modify this response when playing with his cousin, to whom he defers from affection, or with his older sister, to whom he defers from the valid fear that he will get slugged.

Socialization for coping with aggressive feelings begins in childhood but does not cease when childhood is over. A new salesman, a young teacher determined to become principal, a government worker who wants to become supervisor, a shop steward who wants to get a grievance settled on union terms, a newspaper reporter trying to investigate a scandal, a traffic policeman: all these people must learn new kinds of aggressive behavior in response to new kinds of frustrations, models, and desires.

## VIOLENT BEHAVIOR AND SOCIALIZATION

Feshbach (1971) writes: "The widespread concerns and outcry regarding Violence, writ large, are really concerns about particular forms and uses of violence" (p. 289). Results of violence become part of the definition of the act itself. An attempted murder is held to be less serious than an actual murder. The motives for the violence are also important. Violence used in supporting the social order is normally looked upon as much more appropriate or necessary than violence for personal gain (Feshbach, 1971). Conversely, revolutionaries may also oppose violence for personal gain while viewing it as a necessary means of creating change.

Certain forms of violence are often encouraged: "Whether physical force is good or bad is always decided in a culture value setting" (Wolfgang, 1970, p. 170). Thus, parents are permitted to use violence—painful physical punishment—to discipline children. Limits, of course, are placed by the society on how far this parental violence can be carried, but the number of battered children shows that many parents are unable to abide by these limits.

When parents apply physical force, however, they are also serving as models to their children. They are teaching that strength and power are sufficient bases for getting one's way. It is ironic that parents often hit their children as punishment for hitting or yell at children to stop yelling. It is questionable whether children are actually socialized by these behaviors to avoid hitting and yelling, or whether they are merely made aware that certain actions are appropriate only when one has status and power. (We doubt that any parent is totally free from occasionally falling into this kind of behavior. You might ask yourself how—and whether—children can be helped to deal with it.)

☐ Have you ever responded with murderous fantasies to being cut off while driving? Or been infuriated by slanderous and untrue comments made about your sex or ethnic group? Or found yourself ready to begin shooting when you observed a young child being viciously teased by several other children? If you were tired or hungry or tense, were you all the more ready to break out the machine guns and fire away? Sometimes frustration is so great that any one of us might respond with extreme violence, were it not for the contact with reality that enables us to realize the fruitlessness of such behavior. And what happens to those whose contact is so tenuous that it breaks under the pressure of frustration and anger? Perhaps your own feelings can provide you with better insights into the fury that leads combat soldiers to kill and torture their prisoners, or the hatreds that develop between groups such as prisoners and guards, or even the aimless viciousness of people who select random victims to kill. For all of us some of the time and for some of us all of the time, the philosophy of an eye-for-an-eye seems stronger than that of forgiveness. ☐

Middle-class families tend to socialize their children to refrain from physical violence, but they rarely discourage verbal violence. Lower-income children, although more capable of both handing out punishment and accepting it in physical combat, are often unable to cope with the aggressive verbal witticisms that middle-class children use. Consider the following experience of one of the authors (R.K.):

> At the ripe old age of 19, I was working in a state mental hospital as a recreation aide. A co-worker of mine was a well-meaning but not overly intelligent ex-prize fighter. He outweighed me by a good 50 pounds and could probably have pounded the daylights out of most men 50 pounds heavier than himself. Although good-natured, he could not understand the problems of the mentally ill. Whereas I was basically popular with the patients, he managed to irritate virtually everyone, in spite of his good intentions.
> One day, after his insensitivity broke up a patient softball game, I muttered some very uncomplimentary comment. This pushed him past his breaking point, and he immediately strode over to me and threatened, in front of the patients, to beat me to a pulp. I realized immediately that each of us had face at stake. He was trying to salvage psychological face, while I was hoping to salvage physical face. The conversation, much abbreviated, went something like this.
> *Him:* I'm going to beat the shit out of you.
> *Me* (smiling wanly): What will that prove?
> *Him:* That I'm the better man.

*Me:* Okay, I tell you what. I will admit right now that you can beat the shit out of me. I admit it. You are a better fighter than I am.

*Him:* I'm going to beat the shit out of you.

*Me:* All you will prove is that you can hurt me, which we already know, and that you are a better fighter, which we already know. It won't have anything to do with who the better man is.

*Him:* Ahhhhhhh!

And he walked away. While he was threatening to do physical violence to me, I attacked him verbally. I began by insulting him, then I embarrassed him before the patients (which bothered him much more than it would have bothered me), and finally I deprived him of his major claim to masculinity and personhood—the meaning of his physical strength. I was clever, and I had to be in order to save myself a possibly serious beating, but in the process I was very cruel indeed.

## SOCIAL IMPLICATIONS
## OF AGGRESSIVE BEHAVIOR

What kinds of aggressive and violent behavior, under what kinds of circumstances, do you consider justified? What do you consider to be unjustified? What are the gray areas?

The social implications of aggressive behavior have concerned humanity for centuries. For example, many of the Ten Commandments are concerned with aggression. Our entire legal system and our entire military program are both primarily concerned with protecting people from the aggressive behavior of others, although indirectly both the courts and the military may also produce aggression and violence.

Are there times when aggressive behavior is appropriate? Most people would say yes. Are there times when violence is appropriate? Is violence turned against self ever permissible? How about the killing of others? For money? For love? For freedom? "When, in the time of your life, you must kill, then kill," says a character in a play by Saroyan, and he subsequently kills a man whose brutality has caused the destruction of others. Is such violence justifiable? Should a Hitler or a Stalin be killed? Would you be willing to do the killing?

You might also need to ask yourself how your views on violence are influenced by other values. Berkowitz (1968) points out that the reports of two presidential commissions made somewhat conflicting recommendations, yet both sets of recommendations were lauded by liberals and condemned by conservatives. In the former report, the claim was made that the evidence for *sexual* arousal through the viewing of pornography in the media was negligible and that extensive freedom from censorship should be granted; in the latter, the claim was made that the evidence for *aggressive* arousal through the viewing of *aggressive* behavior in the media was sufficiently impressive to warrant curtailing the freedom of the media. Yet, by and large, the evidence was quite similar in both situations. The outcomes of sexual and aggressive acts differ, of course, and some people feel that aggression is more destructive than sexual behavior, while others take exactly the opposite position, but those stands are based on personal values, not behavioral studies. Enter philosophy—again!

# DEPENDENCE

Like many hypothetical constructs, dependence is a much more complex concept than it might initially seem. It involves the wish to be cared for, helped, comforted, protected, supported, or emotionally close to others (Mussen, Conger, & Kagan, 1974). It can refer to a relationship, a condition, a personality characteristic, or a particular example of behavior. Dependence can be mental, physical, economic, or social; cognitive or emotional; real or pseudo; healthy or unhealthy; manipulative and exploitative or manipulated and exploited. We are all dependent on others and have others dependent on us.

Dependence must be differentiated from submissiveness. The former involves the need for support; the latter implies docility. A dependent relationship is a highly demanding relationship, because the dependent person needs to draw strength from the person depended upon. A submissive relationship is not especially demanding, because the submissive person is neither demanding nor manipulative. Children are dependent on their parents, and the elderly upon their adult children, for many kinds of support; in many instances, adults are dependent on their children for love and the feeling of being meaningful and on their parents for a sense of responsibility. In these ways, people are interdependent.

## DEVELOPMENT OF DEPENDENCE

There is little difficulty in tracing the origins of dependence to the beginning of life. As Goldfarb (1969) has said, "dependence is biologically determined but culturally reinforced and perpetuated. The infant is naturally dependent upon his parents for food, warmth, comfort, and protection, [and] has instinctive ways of signaling discomfort and tension in order to obtain help" (p. 3). It is this high degree of dependence that provides parents with so much power over their children, at least in the initial years. Parents not only control the rewards and punishments but provide the most available models for identification and imitation. In addition, children are highly dependent on their parents for information concerning the environment and for interpretations of this information.

Over time, the dependence of infants on their parents is less tied to immediate physical needs and more related to developing feelings of affection. Initially the infants respond to the satisfaction produced by being fed, kept warm, and being touched and cuddled. Slowly they learn to associate these positive feelings with the presence of their parents. Eventually the stimulus previously associated with need satisfactions becomes satisfying in itself; that is, the mere presence of the loving parent is reassuring. Thus children become strongly attached to their parents and come to need not only food and warmth and physical affection but also their parents' presence. This need produces a high degree of dependence on parents.

Since the parents become the dominant persons in a child's life, the child is immensely interested in pleasing them. As children we imitate our parents and express ideas that are consistent with theirs, partly because we wish to gain their approval and partly because these are the ideas that we have primary access to. As we continue to express these ideas and to identify with our parents, their ideas and values become our own; they are internalized.

Children who have no dependence on their parents are not very likely to internalize their parents' values. It's possible that, if child-care centers multiply and parent-child contact is reduced, children may become less dependent on their parents and more dependent on the center staff and the other children.

We have already noted the mixed messages children receive about aggressiveness. On the one hand, parents usually make a concentrated effort to eliminate behavior in their children that they deem overly aggressive; on the other hand, the parents' behavior is often filled with aggression, and the media and other readily observed settings frequently reward aggressiveness. Much the same is true of dependence. Certain types of dependent behavior are negatively reinforced, with the hope that they will disappear. Children in our culture are weaned from the breast to the bottle and then from the bottle to the cup at an early age, much earlier than in most of the world. Many mothers are very explicit in insisting on early weaning to diminish their children's dependence on them and to increase their own freedom from their children's demands. Many new mothers do not breastfeed their children at all, in spite of the encouragement of mental-health experts, often with the explanation that breastfeeding ties them down too much.

A classical study of child rearing, written about 30 years ago, compared socialization practices in the United States with those of other societies. The evidence indicates relatively little change since that book was written. The authors (Whiting & Childs, 1953) point out that parents in the United States push their children from them at a much earlier age than in most other societies. In the U.S., to be tied to a mother's apron strings is considered terrible even by young children, but Japanese children at the same age are often literally tied to their mother's "apron strings" (actually the mother's sash).

□ What do you suppose are the effects of these different practices on children? Which do you think is more desirable—to wean children from dependence on their mothers and fathers as early as possible, or to allow dependence to continue to a later age? What values are presupposed by your answer? □

## DEPENDENCE AFTER CHILDHOOD

Although dependence in certain kinds of behavior is discouraged in our society, other kinds of dependence are actually encouraged. Teenagers, for example, are not encouraged to leave home, nor are young adolescents given the opportunity to be financially self-supporting. Legal and social restrictions purport to tell young people what movies they cannot see, what beverages they cannot drink, what sexual relationships they cannot have, what they cannot smoke, what jobs they cannot take, and what family relationships they cannot establish. Even parents who delight in telling their friends that they want *their* children to learn *how* to think, not *what* to think, often pull back abruptly when their children begin to challenge parental values.

Dependency relationships exist throughout life, although they change in nature. Feelings of being dependent on parents undoubtedly persist in adulthood, even when the needs for nurturance and support are supplied by spouse, children, and others. When the parent-child dependence relationship reverses during the late aging process of the parent, both parties often find the adjustment process extremely difficult. (See Chapter 15 for a further discussion of the relationship between adults and their parents.)

## SOCIAL VALUES AND DEPENDENCE

Although dependent persons are provided with much of the strength and succor of the persons they depend upon, being dependent is a one-down position. The dependent person is vulnerable with respect to the stronger party in a relationship, a situation that can readily produce anxiety. Many people attempt to avoid dependence for this reason, among others, even though totally independent people are virtually unable to exist in a society. People who have strong dependency needs that they are reluctant to express often repress them. But the needs won't stay repressed for long and often find expression in such things as psychosomatic complaints or other symptoms of stress.

This line of thought has contemporary relevance. Many people today contend that children should have less contact with their parents and more contact with a variety of other persons, either through a communal living arrangement or through increased use of child-care facilities. If the ideas we have been discussing are valid, then these children can be expected to be less likely to adhere to their parents' values and more likely to internalize values from the other important people in their lives. One might respond by stating that this is, in part, why it is advantageous to distribute young children's affectional relationships among more people; children will thus be exposed to a greater variety of values and be in a better position to adopt values that are comfortable and appropriate. The alternative response is to be concerned that children will respond not to the values themselves but to the warmth and personalities of the socializing agents. Therefore, they will not be selecting compatible values, but rather internalizing the values of compatible persons. Often, of course, parents place their children in settings in which the values of the socializing agents are very similar to those of the parents. In that case, children will have numerous people with whom to identify, even though the range of values is not great. Nevertheless, dependence upon the parents will be weakened, and other agents will have greater influence.

## WHEN PEOPLE HAVE POWER

Power is inevitably involved in a dependency relationship. Being dependent on someone gives that person power over you, which is a justifiable cause of tension in you and of concern in the person you depend upon. Abuse of power in such relationships is common. A young woman, knowing that a particular man is very much in love with her, teases him about his intentions, until he is faced with the dilemma of giving up his pride or sacrificing any chance for an ongoing relationship. Or the charge attendant in an institution for the mentally ill refuses movie privileges for patients who do not abide strictly by his rules. Or a father manipulates his children into competing with one another for his time and affection. There is an obvious extension of these examples to military commanders, jail guards, social workers, teachers and professors, and so on.

Numerous kinds of power have been described (Raven, 1965). People who control the flow of information have power over those who depend upon the information. Censors, writers, and publishers all have this kind of power; under some circumstances, so do parents, teachers, government workers, and many others. Coercive power accrues to persons who have the power to punish or to exercise physical force. This is in contrast to "reward power," in which the person wielding influence can provide rewards such as money, status, affection, or food.

Experts also have power. Physicians have power over patients because they have knowledge that the patient requires. They also have access to medication, to hospital facilities, and to a variety of resources with which the patient hopes to alleviate pain, discomfort, and fears. Experts in geology, in psychology, in computer sciences, in landscaping, in dress design, in hair styling, and in evading taxes all have power over some people.

The wielding of certain kinds of power is seen as appropriate; other uses of power are seen as unfair. Although to some extent such perceptions are based on whether the perceiver agrees with the values of the person holding the power, the way the power is used is also a factor. You might dislike coercive power intensely, but you are likely to excuse its use—if not unduly cruel or blatant—for a cause you approve of. Many who disapprove of coercion will excuse the spanking of children as an unfortunate but necessary expedient. On the other hand, you might interpret the use of reward power as, in fact, coercive, if you were opposed to the values of the person in power. If a revolutionary group kidnapped local government leaders and demanded in ransom enough money to build a hospital, you might see the revolutionaries as using coercive power if you disapproved of their cause but as using reward power if you approved.

Two additional kinds of power are referent power and legitimate power. Referent power accrues to a person with whom others identify, or whom others use as a basis for self-evaluation. Legitimate power denotes the influence of a person whose role in the power structure is seen as legitimate and who is therefore seen as worthy of having power. One example is the familiar claim of military personnel that their treatment (or mistreatment) of prisoners is justified because it is ordered by legitimate power figures (Raven, 1965).

The concept of power has come up in various contexts in this book: power as it relates to obedience, to conformity, to social pressure, to persuasion, to international relations, to legal issues, to sex roles and sex relationships. In each instance, the social implications of power are immense.

☐ What kinds of power do you like to wield? Do you believe that you're able to evaluate your own use of power objectively? In what ways might you be blind to your abuse of power? ☐

## A FEW CONCLUDING COMMENTS

In this chapter we discussed the socialization process as it applies to familiar kinds of behavior. Aggressiveness and dependence were selected for this discussion because they involve extremely significant issues that lead to a great deal of writing and commentary in our society. Other personal qualities, however, are undoubtedly equally deserving of attention. For example, the concept of shyness has received considerable attention recently. Altruism—the tendency to give to others without anticipating or desiring an equivalent material return—has also received growing attention from psychologists. And there are other possibilities that have continued to elude the scrutiny of most behavioral scientists: jealousy, lovingness, heroism, argumentativeness, greed. You can add to the list.

# REFERENCES

Berkowitz, L. Impulse, aggression and the gun. *Psychology Today,* September 1968, 19–22.

Berkowitz, L. The contagion of violence: An S-R mediational analysis of some effects of observed aggression. In W. I. Arnold & M. M. Page (Eds.), *Nebraska Symposium on Motivation.* Lincoln, Nebraska: University of Nebraska Press, 1970.

Feshbach, S. Dynamics and morality of violence and aggression: Some psychological considerations. *American Psychologist,* 1971, *26,* 281–292.

Goldfarb, A. The psychodynamics of dependency and the search for aid. In R. A. Kalish (Ed.), *The dependencies of old people.* Ann Arbor, Mich.: Institute of Gerontology, 1969.

Hanratty, M. A., Liebert, R. M., Morris, L. W., & Fernandez, L. C. Imitation of film-mediated aggression against live and inanimate victims. *Proceedings of the 77th American Psychological Association Convention,* 1969, 457–458.

Mussen, P. H., Conger, J. J., & Kagan, J. *Child development and personality* (4th ed.). New York: Harper & Row, 1974.

Raven, B. H. Social influence and power. In I. D. Steiner & M. Fishbein (Eds.), *Current studies in social psychology.* New York: Holt, Rinehart & Winston, 1965.

Whiting, J. W. M., & Child, I. L. *Child training and personality: A cross-cultural study.* New Haven: Yale University Press, 1953.

Wolfgang, M. E. Violence and human behavior. In M. Wertheimer & Associates (Eds.), *Confrontation: Psychology and the problems of today.* Glenview, Ill.: Scott, Foresman, 1970.

# CHAPTER 14

## ENRICHMENT AND DEPRIVATION

Some communities, and some parents within all communities, provide experiences for their children during the socialization process that enable the children to develop great depth and breadth of interests and abilities. These experiences are determined by the values of the parents; some children will learn more about athletics, others will be exposed to the creative arts, others to outdoor living, math and science, social studies and social issues, or mechanical and motor skills. Sometimes the individual parents or the community resources will enable children to have both the breadth of exposure to all these experiences and the depth of developing substantial skill in one or more. These experiences are referred to as *enrichment*, because they go beyond the normal experiences provided for children. The assumption is that these children will be more successful, as the socializing agents define success, because of this enrichment. Some parents encourage enrichment because they feel their children will learn job-related skills; for others, enrichment is a way to help children fulfill the demands of a social role; for still others, enrichment will enable children to enjoy more of what life might offer.

Other communities, and some parents within all communities, provide insufficient learning experiences for their children. The reasons are multiple; they include inadequate finances, lack of awareness, time limitations, great involvement in other matters, and values and resulting priorities that place the focus of effort elsewhere. These children are probably less likely to fulfill the society's definition of success.

Although most discussion of enrichment and deprivation focuses on children, we know from clinical reports of institutionalization, solitary confinement, and other forms of social isolation that the need for stimulating learning experiences does not disappear at the end of childhood. Monotony and lack of stimulation lessen the likelihood of success, as that term is ordinarily defined at any age.

The terms *deprived person* and *disadvantaged person* are widely used today to refer to individuals whose personal history includes some deficit that has left them functioning at a level below their potential capability. The assumption is that this deficit resulted from conditions over which the deprived persons had little or no control. The concept of deprivation covers a multiplicity of meanings; we have selected as the most salient the categories of sensory deprivation, nutritional deprivation, parental deprivation, and cultural deprivation.

How deprived must a person be to suffer "deprivation"? Birren and Hess (1968) suggest that this term be used to anchor one end of a continuum. In their scheme, *deprivation* refers to receiving only the minimum necessary for survival. *Satiety* describes the other end of the continuum—the optimum amount of stimulation, nutrition, or whatever, for the individual (note that *optimum* is different from *greatest*). And *sufficiency* is the term applied to whatever is normal or expected for the society. Presumably, enrichment or satiety helps individuals to enjoy life more and deal more effectively with it; deprivation closes people off from the enjoyment of life and reduces their capacity for coping with it; and sufficiency means that they stay about where they have been.

# SENSORY DEPRIVATION AND ENRICHMENT

The senses are our windows to the world. Through our senses, we see, hear, feel, touch, and taste our environment, learning through experience to predict certain consequences when certain patterns of stimuli are perceived. We must process this multiplicity of incoming information in order to function effectively—or, for that matter, to function at all. In order to survive, we must receive and integrate information from the specialized nerve endings in the various sense organs.

When one of these windows is closed, our knowledge of the world is reduced commensurately, and we must find some way to compensate. Such partial deprivation occurs to people with extensive loss in vision or hearing. Given the opportunity, these persons can still receive enough kinds of stimulation to remain alert and involved. Experimental studies of sensory deprivation have produced environments with little or no visual, auditory, or tactual stimulation permitted. After two or three days broken only by eating, using the toilet, and responding to a few questions, the subjects typically exhibit general disorganization, inability to think or concentrate, anxiety, bodily complaints, confusion regarding time and space, and hallucinations (reported in Heron, 1957). Brain changes, such as reduced activity in the alpha range, have also been found.

Studies with animals may have implications for humans as well. Although much more research must be done to confirm the findings, some studies have suggested that the brains of rats raised in isolation and kept in an impoverished environment differ anatomically and chemically from normal rat brains (Krech, 1968).

Often occurring in concert with sensory deprivation, although not identical with it, is social isolation. This occurs when an individual is removed from social interactions with other people. Its importance is signalled by its use as a punishment: in prisons, inmates may be put in solitary confinement; in schools, children are told to stand in the corner or leave the classroom; in the community, interactions with the offender are avoided. Although most of us find times when we desire temporary social isolation, extended exposure to it is distressing and potentially harmful.

Brain changes, hallucinations, disorientation in regard to time and place, and somatic complaints have followed sensory deprivations—some of them not particularly extreme—in controlled settings. Does anything comparable occur in a real-life setting? Some research, although not well controlled, suggests that young children living in institutions without much sensory stimulation have a higher rate of illness and death than do children living in their own homes (Spitz, 1949). "When there is little inducement to sensory exploration of the environment, one may expect poor growth and retarded mental development" (Casler, 1968, p. 242).

Sensory deprivation should not be immediately associated with socioeconomic disadvantages. One of the common assumptions in programmed interventions to help low-income underachievers to progress faster in school is that they have lacked adequate sensory stimulation. This is a questionable assumption. Anyone who has visited a ghetto neighborhood is not likely to look for limited sensory stimulation on a second visit. Although it is true that innumerable individual instances of lack of sensory input can be found, such examples are obviously present in middle-income neighborhoods as well. The rural or urban poor may be disadvantaged in many ways, but sensory deprivation is not likely to be one of their disadvantages, even if the kinds of sensory stimulation they are exposed to may be alien by middle-class standards. Sights, sounds, and smells abound in these environments in highly stimulating fashion. That the babies of the poor do not have mobiles swaying over their cribs, that the children are not exposed to the conversations or artwork or magazines of the middle class, are not evidence of sensory deprivation.

Can sensory enrichment compensate for either sensory deprivation or social isolation? The answer is affirmative—at least for rats, whose brains have gained in weight and changed in chemistry when exposed to an enriched environment (Rosenzweig & Bennett, 1972). How about people? Those persons subjected to experimentally controlled environments or to hospital environments do not continue to hallucinate when they return to normal environments. The work done with low-income children has included not only sensory enrichment but a variety of other kinds of enrichment, so we cannot determine whether changes resulted from a more stimulating sensory experience or from a combination of experiences. We would assume the latter, but we still do not know how much sensory deprivation is required in a real-life setting before sensory enrichment can no longer bring the person back to the previous level of functioning without the added input of other forms of enrichment.

# NUTRITIONAL DEPRIVATION

The need for good nutrition begins during the fetal period and extends throughout the life span. When a pregnant woman does not receive adequate nutrition, she endangers the health of her unborn child as well as her own. Severe malnutrition in the expectant mother not only increases the probability of birth complications and illness but appears to increase the chances of later illness and perhaps mental retardation for the infant (Mussen, Conger, & Kagan, 1974).

Evidence has accumulated that protein/calorie malnourishment during the first year of life, if very severe, can retard subsequent mental development in an *irreversible* fashion (Ricciuti, 1970). The same author says "There has been ample research evidence . . . that children's physical and biological development may be seriously and even permanently impaired by the combination of malnutrition, infection, and parasitic disease which is endemic in various poor populations" (p. 238).

Malnourished individuals, regardless of age, display a number of symptoms of poor mental and physical health, including fatigue, anxiety, inability to concentrate, confusion, and disorientation (Coleman, 1972). These conditions are normally reversible, however, if the person's diet improves. To illustrate, consider the following story a middle-aged physician told about himself:

> When I was young, I served as medical consultant with a handful of nursing homes—they call themselves convalescent-care facilities now. On several occasions, an elderly patient was brought in by the children with claims that father or mother was confused and disoriented. Sometimes the family lawyer would also testify to this, but when I saw the patient, he always seemed fine to me. I don't mean that he was in perfect health, but there were rarely signs of confusion. I was certain that this old man or that old lady was being railroaded into an institution by ungrateful children, and I made it pretty uncomfortable for those middle-aged brats. It wasn't until a good decade later that I learned more about nutrition, and I realized that lots of old people, even those with adequate income, are malnourished because of their diet and the erratic way they eat. One or two good meals, though, and they would be functioning pretty much like normal. At those nursing homes, I usually didn't see them until they had been there a day or so. So what I—and lots of others of us then—took for a nasty conspiracy of vicious children and greedy lawyers turned out to be simple malnourishment.[1]

The degree of satiety can be extended to the point of over-stimulation, when an overabundance of sensory input leaves the individual unable to cope with all the stimuli simultaneously. Some people experience this when attending a rock concert and light show; others find it when surrounded by a group of healthy, playful kindergarteners. The counterpart for nutrition would be overeating. "Optimum levels of food intake" is a chapter for another book, however.

# PARENTAL DEPRIVATION AND ENRICHMENT

The parent/child relationship is so vital to the socialization process, at least in most societies, that an inadequate parent/child relationship is normally considered highly detrimental to the proper maturation of the child, and the community is likely to intervene in some way to take over the missing parental role. *Parental deprivation* has overlapping but different meanings. It can mean the lack of *parents* (one or both parents are missing because of death, divorce, chronic illness, institutionalization, work demands, or other form of separation), or it can mean the lack of "parenting" (the child receives inadequate mothering and fathering). The implications for socialization are quite different when these two circumstances coincide than

---

[1]Recreated from a presentation by Maurice Linden, M.D.

when substitutes are provided for missing parents or when the child's own parents provide a low level of care but remain physically on the scene.

Descriptions of what children miss under conditions of parental deprivation can be specified. Essentially, the children are deprived of attention, physical affection and care, and some of the visual, auditory, and tactual stimulation that comes with an adequate parent/child relationship.

Children who were lacking in the normal visual and auditory stimulation of toys, of the movement and conversation of adults, and of the experience of being cuddled, talked to, and played with have been found to behave in abnormal fashion. Their physical development was slow, they showed little facial expression, their play was repetitive, they would respond inappropriately when people approached them. And some even became ill and died, apparently having developed less resistance to illness and disease, a condition termed *marasmus* (from the Greek *marainein*, "to waste away").

Bowlby (1969) described three stages that he had observed in young children separated from their mothers for extended periods: protest, despair, and apathy. In the latter two stages, children created little trouble for their caretakers, and their apathy was sometimes misinterpreted as a type of passive adjustment.

(Among the institutionalized elderly, an amazing similarity can be found. Gerontologists believe that behavior we describe as "senile" is only in part the result of organic brain changes. In part, these specialists feel, what passes for "senile" behavior is actually a normal response to the isolation and loneliness and lack of stimulation that many older persons find in their living conditions, especially in some of the less adequate institutions.)

Probably the only long-term follow-up study of enrichment of the affectional environment was published almost 40 years ago (see Skeels & Dye, 1939, in Jessor & Richardson, 1968). A small group of children who showed slow mental development were transferred from an orphanage to an institution for the retarded, where they were given a great deal of individual care and affection by some of the older retardates. Thirty years later, most of these children had been adopted, had been living in the community, and had become parents of reasonably normal children. In contrast, a control group who had remained in the orphanage, where care was impersonal and limited, still required some form of institutional support. Although this study lacked methodological refinement and adequate controls, several implications are clear. First, enriched environments can enable some apparently retarded children to cope with community living; second, the definition of enrichment is a highly relative matter; and third, people don't need university educations or special training to provide enrichment in a human relationship. What they do need is a capacity to give love and attention.

# CULTURAL DEPRIVATION AND ENRICHMENT

When the home environment and the neighborhood lack sufficient intellectual stimulation and encouragement to enable the children to succeed in our school system, our work system, or our bureaucracy, the children (or adults) are termed *culturally deprived* or *culturally disadvantaged*.

The circumstances of the culturally deprived have recently become impossible for the rest of the society to ignore. Several changes have taken place to bring this about. First, school integration and other forms of integration have brought culturally disadvantaged children, often of minority status, into middle-class schools; second, government agencies have learned that finding appropriate jobs for welfare recipients is a difficult task, and welfare budgets have continued to climb; third, criminal violence, according to available data, is increasing, with more robberies and attacks directed against the non-poor; fourth, the impoverished, especially the minority poor, have recently found some political voice; fifth, increasing numbers of people, primarily young, appear willing to take the side of the culturally disadvantaged for moral reasons and against their own financial best interests. You can probably think of other reasons, but the point is that the culturally disadvantaged have become more visible and have begun to receive attention and services.

As described in the professional literature, the culturally disadvantaged have:

1. limited opportunity to explore and to experience the world;
2. inadequate adult models at home and in the community after which they might pattern themselves, a situation often made worse by the absence of one parent;
3. a lack of creative toys and stimulating (or any) reading materials;
4. exposure to a milieu that places low value upon intellectual promise and performance as a basis for status and acceptance;
5. little encouragement to think of education as leading to what is defined by the group as success;
6. the belief that the present system allows few opportunities for status improvement by fair means (Jessor & Richardson, 1968).

Disadvantaged children come to school with less ability to function (but not necessarily with less potential), with limited motivation, and with reduced awareness of how to succeed in an academic setting.

> The net result is that the students are labelled uneducable and treated as such. Little is expected of them and little is offered. Comparatively speaking, such students "get dumber" as they grow older. By fifth grade they are three years behind. This, in turn, adds to lowering of self-expectation and generates hostility to the school, teachers, and the whole business of learning. This is probably the dynamics which turns those children who in kindergarten are described as curious, cute, affectionate, warm, independently dependent, and mischievous, into the ones described in the fourth grade as alienated, withdrawn, angry, passive, and apathetic [Deutsch, quoted in Taba, 1971, p. 140].

The biases of teachers are often reflected in their treatment of their students, and it has been shown that children known to be culturally deprived have less expected of them and, therefore, accomplish less. Their own resulting performance and behavior serve to confirm the teacher's initial biases and to reinforce this behavior. Comparable situations undoubtedly occur on the job, in the military, with friends, and so forth.

Many schools have established enrichment programs, ranging from the well-known Headstart programs directed at preschool children and their parents to innovative programs at the high school and college levels. Long-range results from these programs are not yet available, and the short-range results are contradictory. Some studies have shown that children in enrichment programs slip back to their previous status unless provided continuous exposure to some form of extra attention; other studies suggest that progress does occur; still other studies pessimistically deny any meaningful changes.

# MODELS OF DEPRIVATION

What causes deprivation? Birren and Hess (1968) suggested 11 alternative explanatory models:

A. Based on the malnutrition model.

1. *Economic deprivation.* The basic reason for many kinds of deprivation is lack of money, not lack of awareness, capability, or motivation. According to this view, given adequate funding the disadvantaged would function at a level comparable to that of the majority in a reasonable length of time.

2. *Lack of exposure to appropriate stimulation.* Deprived persons have not had exposure to proper preparation for formal learning at home and have not been adequately stimulated by the environment.

3. *Lack of proper reinforcement.* Nothing in the life of deprived persons rewards the kinds of behavior that lead to success.

4. *Lack of stimulation necessary to produce cognitive maturation.*

Based on the research showing enrichment to affect brain chemistry, this view assumes that deprivation is the outcome of inadequate "maturation of the neural structures . . . important for later cognitive development and learning" (p. 93).

B. Based on the cultural-disparity model.

5. *Cultural pluralism.* Ethnic differences and segregation have led to types of speech, manners, and values that are downgraded by the majority society, exacerbating existing prejudice and discrimination.

6. *Socialized behavior is not rewarded by the dominant society.*

7. *Inadequate social institutions.* This view may blame the middle class in general for its failure to work effectively with the disadvantaged. More specifically, the fault is seen as being with the school and the teachers, for not being sensitive to the needs and values of the disadvantaged children, or with economic institutions or legal institutions.

C. Based on the social-structural model.

8. *Competition for scarce resources.*

9. *Lack of alternatives for action.* The deprived lack power and prestige and thus have limited the potential for action (or even awareness of how to promote action) for upward mobility.

10. *Discrimination against ethnic and income groups.*

D. Based on miscellaneous models.

11. *Environmental trauma.* Young children of disadvantaged groups are treated so destructively by their social milieu that they are irreversibly damaged in a psychosocial sense and are subsequently incapable of moving beyond their present status.

Perhaps all 11 of Birren and Hess' deprivation models are necessary to understand the phenomenon of deprivation; perhaps only one or a few are needed. Your beliefs concerning which factors are most important will affect your views on what constitutes an effective intervention program, on how federal and local money should be spent, on whether change is possible or whether entrenched interests are likely to undermine it, and on how you as an individual can spend your time and energy for greatest effect.

# "COMPARED TO WHOM?" AND OTHER ISSUES

Q. "How's your wife?" A. "Compared to whom?"

An oldie, but *apropos.* Deprived? Enriched? Compared to whom? And, a step further, according to what criteria? Appropriate parental behavior is in the eye of the beholder. To one person, cultural deprivation would be to exist on a musical diet of folk rock; another person might consider this diet to be enrichment. What older people perceive as a confusing multiplicity of incoming stimuli attacking several senses simultaneously, younger people might perceive as an exciting sound-and-light show.

Although we have distinguished four types of deprivation, the interaction among them is obvious. Parental deprivation and cultural deprivation are likely to be found in the same home; nutritional deprivation is more common among low-income persons, and these persons are also more likely to lack the resources to provide satiety in parent/child relationships and in cultural stimulation. Sensory deprivation, although more difficult to relate to the other forms of deprivation, probably occurs more frequently, at least in mild form, where other stimulation is lacking.

Several important questions remain unanswered.

First, are these deficits ever irreversible? If so, when do they become irreversible? Is there a critical age at which, or by which, something must happen in order for the remainder of the life span to unfold at its proper rate? For example, assume that parents knew at the birth of their child that the child would need an operation within the following two years that would require isolation from the parents for six weeks. What would be the least destructive period for the child to have the surgery? What if the operation would lead to six weeks of deafness or blindness?

Certain nutritional deficits undoubtedly lead to lowered resistance to disease and, most probably, to brain damage, both outcomes often being irreversible. But, by and large, we have little evidence regarding the long-range psychosocial impact of other kinds of deprivation, assuming that conditions of sufficiency later prevail.

Second, is there a culture of poverty into which children are effectively socialized, so that only a relatively few can later be successful in coping with the broader society? Can values, expectations, manners, and behavioral modes that were internalized in the very early years be unlearned later on? If so, can individuals learn new values, expectations, manners, and behavioral modes—and feel comfortable in using them? Is leaving the culture of poverty (if such there be) comparable to migrating from one country to another? Are we helping to create a culture of poverty by talking about a culture of poverty?

Answers to these questions are speculative at best. We do know that a certain proportion of the persons reared in what we have termed "a culture of poverty" do indeed leave. Those who leave do generally have a greater awareness of self, a more positive self-image, than those who remain.

Third, is what the middle-class researcher, the middle-class educator, and the middle-class writer call *deprivation* really just the manifestation of an integrated set of social values and expectations, as satisfying and rewarding in its own right for those abiding by it as the middle-class norm is for its adherents? Both children and adults who display little imaginative ability also indicate more limited ability to plan, to delay gratification, to control impulsive expression of anger and aggression, and to control restless motor behavior (Jessor & Richardson, 1968). One who looks at this finding from a middle-class view may respond "How unfortunate we should do whatever we can to help these people overcome their deficits." But is there another way to look at these characteristics? Is it possible to take the position that imagination may not be so important, that the ability to plan ends in fruitless effort, that delaying gratification merely means one enjoys life less, that controlling anger and aggression is a sign of weakness, and that controlling restlessness amounts to restricting one's natural and vital inclinations? Should we turn the microscope around so the eye at the other end is looking at middle-class values? In this regard, Cole and Bruner (1971) suggest that group differences in cognitive abilities really do not exist; rather, each group socializes its members to its language and its values. Since low-income children, especially those of discriminated-against minority groups, have never been part of the broader culture, they are not deprived in terms of their own culture, but only in terms of the outside culture. For example, they have an excellent language that communicates extremely well with those who understand it, but because it does not correspond perfectly with standard English, these persons are believed to lack appropriate language skills.

Both language and interpersonal competence require an awareness of the expectations of the other person. To interact successfully with another person, an individual must (1) be able to take the role of the other and predict correctly the effect that various acts will have upon the other's definition of the situation; (2) possess a large and varied repertoire of alternate lines of behavior; and (3) possess the inner resources needed to behave effectively (Jessor & Richardson, 1968). To meet these requirements, the individual must have a broad and deep understanding of the culture within which the other person is functioning. Without postulating the existence of a culture of poverty, one can argue that the living styles of different social-class groups are often sufficiently different to make this understanding extremely difficult.

Fourth, if these deficits (itself a loaded word) *can* be reversed, and if they *should* be reversed (both highly controversial "ifs"), what is the best method of changing them? To what set of standards should "deprived" persons be socialized? Who should decide upon these standards? Using what guidelines? And who should carry out the resocializing procedures? Obviously we are again pointing out some of the issues involved in planned interventions, a concern that has come up repeatedly in this book, as it does in real life.

Your reactions to this chapter will depend largely upon your beliefs about the nature of humanity and human behavior. You might even grimace when you read the words *deprivation* and *disadvantaged*, since both terms obviously assume that some outside set of forces has deprived certain individuals of something or put them at a disadvantage. You may believe that these persons could lift themselves up by the bootstraps if they wished, or that they are fated to remain as they are, or that only carefully and creatively engineered interventions could possibly lead to change.

You may, of course, believe that the truly disadvantaged are those who must talk, write, and study about others whom they seem to patronize, who must make money from selling their expertise on the poor, who find pleasure in locating emotionally healthy, "natural" people and trying to subvert them by introducing to them the values and goals of a sick society. We may not agree with you, but, as one sage stated so acutely, "If we all thought alike, everyone would want to make love to my wife."

# REFERENCES

Birren, J. E., & Hess, R. D. Influences of biological, psychological, and social deprivation upon learning and performances. In *Perspectives on human deprivation: Biological, psychological, and sociological.* Washington, D.C.: U.S. Department of Health, Education and Welfare, 1968.

Bowlby, J. *Attachment and loss. Vol. I: Attachment.* New York: Basic Books, 1969.

Casler, L. Maternal deprivation: A critical review of the literature. In *Perspectives on human deprivation: Biological, psychological, and social.* Washington, D.C.: U.S. Department of Health, Education & Welfare, 1968.

Cole, M., & Bruner, J. S. Cultural differences and inferences about psychological processes. *American Psychologist,* 1971, *26,* 867–876.

Coleman, J. C. *Abnormal psychology and modern life* (4th ed.). Glenview, Ill.: Scott, Foresman, 1972.

Heron, W. The pathology of boredom. *Scientific American,* 1957, *196,* 52–56.

Jessor, R., & Richardson, S. Psychosocial deprivation and personality development. In *Perspectives on human deprivation: Biological, psychological, and sociological.* Washington, D.C.: U.S. Department of Health, Education and Welfare, 1968.

Krech, D. The chemistry of learning. *Saturday Review,* January 20, 1968, pp. 48–50.

Mussen, P. H., Conger, J. J., & Kagan, J. *Child development and personality* (4th ed.). New York: Harper & Row, 1974.

Ricciuti, H. N. Malnutrition, learning, and intellectual development: Research and remediation. In F. F. Korten, S. W. Cook, & J. I. Lacey (Eds.), *Psychology and the problems of society.* Washington, D.C.: American Psychological Association, 1970.

Rosenzweig, M. R., & Bennett, E. L. Cerebral changes in rats exposed individually in an enriched environment. *Journal of Comparative and Physiological Psychology,* 1972, *80,* 304–313.

Spitz, R. A. The role of ecological factors in emotional development in infancy. *Child Development*, 1949, *20*, 145–156.

Taba, H. Cultural deprivation as factors in school learning. In E. B. McNeil (Ed.), *Readings in human socialization*. Monterey, Calif.: Brooks/Cole, 1971.

# CHAPTER 15

## FILIAL MATURITY

Perhaps you are the parent of a child; if not, perhaps you will someday be the parent of a child. In any event there is not the slightest doubt that you are the child of parents. Your parents may be living together or apart, happily or unhappily; you may be living with both of them, with one of them, or with neither of them; they may be living or no longer living; one or both of your biological parents may even be unknown to you, and your rearing may have occurred in the home of adoptive parents or in an institution. Your knowledge, awareness, and memories of your parents may be vivid or vague, pleasant or unpleasant, or—more probably—a mixture of these. But whoever your parents are, whatever your relationship with them, and however you may fantasize them, they are highly significant individuals in your life.

So important is the parent/child relationship that thousands of books and articles are written about it each year, virtually all of them concerning infants, school-age children, or college-age youth. Only a minuscule portion of the parent/child literature discusses the adult child, and much of this writing creates villains. That is, many discussions of adult children fall into one of two categories: either they describe the social and emotional difficulties of adults, often adults in psychotherapy, and lay the causes for these difficulties at the door of the parents, *or* they discuss the plight of elderly parents, with the implication that a major basis for their problems is the negligence and selfishness of their adult children. We hope to be able to discuss older-parent/adult-child relationships without turning either generation into a scapegoat for the difficulties of the other. However, since most of our readers—like ourselves—are presently more involved with *being* adult children than with relating to their own adult children, we will attempt to view the material through the eyes of the generation of adult children.

# THE AGING PARENT
# AND THE AGING CHILD

The dynamic nature of the parent/child relationship is well recognized during its early years, when the child is an infant or even a teenager. Little regard is given to the dynamics of this relationship after the child reaches maturity, however, although the relationship is just as changeable in these years as it is earlier. The interactions between children and parents do not become static just because the children have left home or married or become 39 years old.

Numerous factors contribute to this changing relationship. Often, many of the earlier tensions arising from the attempts of children to gain autonomy from their parents are resolved once the children are satisfied that autonomy has been achieved and that this is recognized and accepted by their parents. Parents, of course, are sometimes reluctant to permit their children to have this autonomy and continue to maintain some form of control over their adult offspring. On the other hand, many adult children have developed an image of their parents as wishing to retain control when, in actuality, their parents are more than willing to develop an egalitarian relationship with them. In other words, both generations frequently respond to outdated images of the other generation's needs and expectations. When these images are brought into accord with reality, new and more appropriate relationships can develop.

## *VARIABILITY IN AGE DIFFERENCES*
## *BETWEEN PARENTS AND CHILDREN*

As we write this, our own children range in age from nursery-school age to college. Some of our age peers have children who are in college or newly married, and a few are just beginning their families. The variability in age differences between parents and their children is virtually unexplored in the academic literature, but it must make a meaningful difference in parent/child relationships. We can only speculate on what that difference might be. The relationship of a 40-

year-old man with his 22-year-old son is obviously different from that of a 40-year-old man with his 9-year-old son or that of a 60-year-old man with his 22-year-old son. A woman whose children have all left home by the time she is 37 will not have the same relationships with them as she would if she were 57 before they were old enough to be on their own.

In many circumstances, adult children are facing retirement at a time when their own children are in college (with all the financial pressures that brings) or just getting settled in the working world. These adult children must deal simultaneously with one or more elderly parents who are entering a period of high medical expenses and who have health conditions that demand personal attention, with their college-age or teenage children, and with their own imminent retirement. Because of health, income, and age differences, some adult children are in their twenties or early thirties when they must cope with parents whose aging processes are causing problems; other adult children don't encounter these problems until their sixties.

Consider, for example, Ms. A. and Mr. B. Ms. A. was 62 when her 84-year-old mother suffered a heart attack and was placed in a convalescent-care facility because she was confused and depressed as well as in need of nursing care. Mr. B. was only 29 when his 69-year-old father had a stroke and was placed in the same nursing home. Mr. B. was just beginning his work life, had small children who made major demands on his time and emotional energies, and felt his primary responsibilities were to his wife and children. Ms. A. had just retired and begun to receive social security. She was therefore living on a suddenly reduced income. Although she wanted to travel with her husband, she felt her primary responsibilities were to her mother, especially since the intense demands of her own children had long since been exchanged for occasional dinners and infrequent babysitting with her grandchildren. And neither Ms. A. nor Mr. B. offers the same picture as Mr. and Mrs. C., who were both in their mid-forties and actively pursuing careers when they suddenly found that each of them had an elderly parent in need of attention.

## FILIAL RESPONSIBILITY

As Margaret Blenkner has so well stated, "It is becoming increasingly sterile to view the latter two-thirds of life as mere repetition and reenactment of the first third" (1965, p. 56). She proposes the stage of *filial maturity* as representing a healthy transition from adolescent years. Filial maturity occurs when the *filial crisis* is effectively dealt with:

> . . . the filial crisis may be conceived to occur in most individuals in their forties or fifties, when the individual's parents can no longer be looked

to as a rock of support in times of emotional trouble or economic stress but may themselves need their offspring's comfort and support .... Healthy resolution of the filial crisis means leaving behind the rebellion and emancipation of adolescence and early adulthood and turning again to the parent, no longer as a child, but as a mature adult with a new role and a different love, seeing him for the first time as an individual with his own rights, needs, limitations, and a life history that ... made him the person he is long before his child existed [Blenkner, 1965, pp. 57–58].

To this excellent account we would add only that the transition to filial maturity need not be a crisis if people are prepared for it. Such preparation means that the parent/child relationship must be maturing throughout the post-teen years. Hopefully, adult children will not need to wait until they are 45 or 50 to realize that their parents are individuals who have their own rights and who are as much the products of their own eras as the children are the products of theirs.

Primary responsibility in our society is commonly seen as serial rather than reciprocal. In other words, each generation perceives its major responsibility as serving the needs of the next generation. The alternative would be that Generation I took care of Generation II when the former was strong and the latter was weak, and that the care would be reciprocated when the roles were reversed and Generation II was the stronger.

Although it is commonly assumed—with some justice—that the most significant responsibility of adult children is to their spouses and their own children, it is not true that adult children commonly neglect their older parents. In one study, 60% of the older persons surveyed had seen at least one of their children during the previous week (Shanas, 1967). This figure does not take into account older persons who live with their children, so it is an underestimate of the actual figure. When we consider how many elderly have no children, this high percentage begins to approach the remarkable. In Sussman's review of the literature, it becomes obvious that adult children and their parents provide each other with many forms of material and non-material help, including financial aid, help during illness, child care, and so forth. Significantly, elderly parents are more likely to give money, advice, and valuable gifts (as well as child care), while help during illness is provided relatively equally by the generations (Sussman, 1976).

Obviously, as the family members age, the direction of support undoubtedly shifts, so that adult children with very old parents are no longer likely to receive financial aid (although they may give it), no longer in need of child care (although they may occasionally have to provide physical care for their parents), and probably no longer willing to accept advice.

# IMPEDIMENTS TO FILIAL RESPONSIBILITY

Older parents with adult children have invested from a third to a half of their lives in rearing their children and enabling them to become independent. They have developed roles in relationship to these children in which they are nurturant, competent, powerful, and authoritative. As these parents become elderly, to the point that they are no longer capable of fully mastering their environment, the role of filial maturity now calls for the adult child to become nurturant, competent, powerful, and authoritative. Some elderly can accept this new interaction without difficulty, but others find it extremely troublesome and are essentially unable to adjust to having their children—who had always known them as strong—now see them as in need of nurture and help and advice.

Adult children may also find this role change difficult. The power and responsibility that come with this change are uncomfortable and perhaps even embarrassing. Adults can deal with the dependency needs of their children, but they may become irritated when their parents also express dependency needs. When their mothers or fathers repeat an anecdote for the seventh time, or make several foolish errors in driving, or insist that today's youth are decadent, or have little to talk about other than their own ills, these middle-aged men and women often find themselves with much less patience than they would have if the parents of a friend indulged in the same behavior.

There are other reasons that filial responsibilities are not met. Parents and their children do not always like each other. Inevitably, there are selfish children who refuse to be concerned about their parents. And many parents who have spent a lifetime neglecting their children find that, when they themselves are old, their children neglect them in turn. Although guilt and shame still attach to the neglect of older parents, neither social pressures nor legal sanctions are sufficient in our society to coerce unwilling children into providing emotional, physical, or financial support for their parents.

Another barrier to the development of a healthy older-parent/adult-child relationship is the difference in the issues that are at stake in their personal development. Bengtson and Kuypers (1971) point out that middle-aged parents, for example, are at a point in their lives when they are concerned with "issues centering around the meaning, the justification, and ... the validation of their life and the commitments they have made to it. This is especially true in times of rapid social change when previously assumed cultural values are called into question" (p. 256). Young adults, however, are more concerned with "establishing their personal life styles, in forming their attitudes toward major issues and institutions" (p. 257). Thus, middle-aged parents wish to believe that the next generation will carry on their values and thus validate their existence; they will minimize the differences between the views of their generation and those of their successors. Young adults want to establish themselves and consequently tend to maximize the differences between generations.

The results of a study conducted by Bengtson and Kuypers support their hypotheses. Young adults—university students in this instance—were much more likely than their parents to see the major bases for generational differences as related to values and morality (22% versus 9%) and politics and social relations (13% versus 8%). Their parents tended to believe that major sources of disagreement were personal habits and traits (22% versus 7%); a sizable proportion denied that significant differences existed (16% versus 7%). Bengtson and Kuypers conclude:

> It is as if the parents were saying, "Yes, there are differences between the generations, but these are not intrinsic; they are simply due to difference in life status and maturity." The students, by contrast, are saying, "The contrasts we see are in values and basic orientations to life. There are differences and they are important" [1971, p. 253].

Some adult children are never fully capable of establishing themselves and confirming their own validity. They therefore have difficulty in attaining filial maturity. Perhaps their values are unsettled because there is now a *new* younger generation that is challenging them; perhaps their shaky self-esteem or their relationships with their parents cause them to continue to fight the intergenerational battles long after most of their age peers have stopped.

In spite of these impediments to filial responsibility, most adult children do remain in contact with their parents, respond to their parents' need for help, and feel responsible for their parents' well-being when appropriate. When poor relationships occur, they often represent the culmination of many years of poor relationships, rather than the irresponsible or neglectful nature of the children.

## SOME ISSUES

What, then, do adult children owe their parents? To what extent should society, through legal and social pressures, demand filial responsibility? To what extent should the adequacy of the parenting they received determine the children's sense of filial responsibility? What values are implied by these questions and the answers we give to them?

The meaning of responsibility toward parents changes over time. With young adults whose parents are in their fifties and sixties, the task is to develop, if possible, a mutually satisfying relationship that incorporates new family members (spouse, children, in-laws) and permits appropriate interdependence. As parents become elderly, different kinds of responsibilities emerge, largely related to the increased limitations of the parents and the greater competencies of the children.

Many issues arise during the years of filial maturity, including the capacity of each generation to recognize changes in the other generation, but it is often difficult to leave old roles behind and to take on new ones. Do "good children" defer to their parents? Should the parents be consulted prior to job changes, marriage or divorce, the purchase of an automobile or an insurance policy? Do responsible adult children provide their parents with financial support? How much? Under what conditions? If aging parents need such personal attention as help with the shopping or transportation to the physician's office or the hairdresser's, how much and under what circumstances do "good children" help in these ways? Is it appropriate to argue with parents? To become angry or yell at them? To ignore them for an extended period?

A very common statement uttered by parents of all ages, but particularly by those who are older, is "I do not want to be a burden on my children." This kind of statement is not the self-deprecating comment of elderly people afraid of becoming a nuisance but rather an affirmative statement by persons who wish to retain autonomy and mastery as long as possible, perhaps even to the time of terminal illness. Given the opportunity, the functional capacity, and the income, most older persons would rather live by themselves than with their children or in institutional settings.

Despite the wish of most older persons to be independent, adult children are sometimes called upon to provide such extensive help as caring for older parents during times of serious medical problems. Do the obligations of "good children" extend to this? What if a parent is incontinent: do "good children" change the bedding and see that mother or father has clean pajamas in the morning? There is an obvious irony in this last issue. After all, your parents changed your diapers several times a day for many months, perhaps for a couple of years or more, yet the task of reciprocating this service strikes many adult children as difficult or virtually impossible.

Sometimes the task of caring for older parents falls unequally on the adult children in the family. Sometimes the more well-to-do child provides money, while the less well-to-do provides services. Instances in which an unmarried child remains with the parents as they age are not unusual. In any event, the division of responsibility can be a troublesome issue.

Consider the following typical example of the problems that arise in such circumstances. A middle-aged couple had provided a home for the wife's mother during their entire 18-year marriage. When the older woman became confused and forgetful, sometimes wandering off and getting lost, the couple decided that she needed to be placed in a convalescent facility. Both husband and wife worked full-time, and they felt that the cost of hiring full-time home care during their absence would be prohibitive. The wife's brother, however, became furious and insisted that his mother return to his sister's home, even though he himself had never encouraged her to stay with him for more than a few days. This brother enjoyed a substantial family income, much larger than that of his sister, but he had three children rapidly approaching college age, while the sister and her husband had none.

Six months after the mother entered the institution, the two families still were not speaking to each other. Each had feelings of guilt, and each had a basis for laying the blame on the other. How can responsibility be apportioned in a situation like this? What if there had been another brother or sister who was a struggling painter wandering around Europe, or a mountain climber intent on conquering Everest?

## MODELS FROM THE PAST/
## MODELS FOR THE FUTURE

One often hears the complaint that "young people today just don't respect their parents the way children used to." Behind this complaint is the assumption that the elderly of past generations were treated with veneration, whereas today's older people are relegated to institutions by heartless offspring and stingy taxpayers. In fact, the magnitude of the problems of the elderly may be greater than ever before simply because there are more elderly than ever before. The belief that the elderly of times past were given much better treatment than the elderly of today may well originate in a tendency to romanticize and idealize the past while being pessimistic and antagonistic concerning the present.

The truth is that we know relatively little about the circumstances of old people as recently as at the turn of the century. Certainly those who owned property, perhaps a farm or a store or a home of moderate size, received fairly good treatment from their children. Adult children would either live with their parents, often in the home previously owned by the parents, or else make certain that some other form of care was provided when the elderly became dependent. But there were reasons for this that are often forgotten. For example, the kinds of loans for buying houses that have been so readily available in the recent past were then beyond the reach of all but the wealthiest of younger persons. For most people ownership was out of the question until middle age. Nor did formal education enable large numbers of young people to earn substantial incomes, as has been the case in recent decades. Relatively few young people today are strongly influenced by the possibility that their parents might hold back their inheritance, but such a threat could make a real difference 75 years ago. And, since sons tended to follow fathers into jobs—for example, on the farm, in the mine, in the store—the fathers retained a greater measure of power.

What we are suggesting is that some changes in adult children's attitudes toward their parents may have been caused in large part by changing financial power. You may feel this to be an unduly cynical analysis, but we do believe that behavioral scientists are so geared to seeking psychological bases for change that they frequently ignore the role of such material considerations as money and power. Although we certainly would not assume that money and power entirely account for children's attitudes toward their parents, respect for the elderly does appear greatest where their control of finances is greatest.

## THE CHANGING ROLE OF INSTITUTIONS

In recent times, public and private institutions have increasingly replaced the family as the primary providers of care for the elderly. Just a few generations ago, older people who were unable to work would live off their savings, receive help from their families, or be compelled to find some charitable organization to support them. Today many (but by no means all) older persons receive money from company pension programs, private health-insurance agencies, and annuity programs established in the middle years. Supplementing the private sector are Social Security payments, Medicare reimbursements, and the possibility of survivor benefits. A circle has been established in which support from public and private institutions encourages the withdrawal of family support, which, in turn, requires new levels of support from institutions. Simultaneously, the demands for support are expanding to include not only subsistence but health care, housing costs, food supplements, home-care services, and so forth.

## THE CHANGING ROLE OF INDIVIDUALS

It may be that the satisfaction felt by previous generations of adult children in caring for their elderly parents has been romanticized, but it is true that children did provide the care in many, perhaps most, instances. Often three or four generations lived in the same household, interrelating with one another. That there were tensions and anger is obvious; that there were also love and warmth is also obvious.

Clearly, societal changes have altered this pattern. How will *you* respond to *your* parents when they need *your* financial, physical, social, or emotional support? Will your response be in any sense a reflection of what you perceived your parents doing for your grandparents? If you display concern for the well-being of your parents, if you offer them a caring and warm relationship, will that predispose your children to relate to you in a similar fashion? To our knowledge there is no research on this question. Although common sense might suggest an affirmative response, the vast array of other factors impinging on parent/child relationships may well outweigh the effects of children's perceptions of the relationships between prior generations. At this point we simply don't know.

# AS PARENTS GROW OLDER

What does it mean to grow old? Or, to put the question in the context of an adult child viewing an aging parent, what does it mean to have a parent grow old?

This question has many facets, each of which needs to be considered independently. For example, what does it mean *financially* to grow old? What does it mean *medically* to grow old? What does it mean *socially* to grow old? What does it mean *psychologically* to grow old? And there are other approaches as well. Moreover, individual differences in development among older adults are at least as great as for any other age group. Each community also exerts a major influence on the meaning of growing old through its social and economic structure, its value systems, its family orientations, and its personal, social, and medical-care systems.

While recognizing individual, regional, and subcultural differences, we will attempt to delineate what we see as some of the more significant concerns for adult children in regard to their aging parents. The discussion cannot possibly be exhaustive, especially in view of the lack of research into the dynamics of the adult-child/older-parent relationship. Instead, it must be looked upon as exploratory.

## *FINANCES*

In 1975, the median income for married couples when the major breadwinner was over age 65 was $7000; the median income for single persons over age 65 was about $3300. Although they were supplemented by help from children in some instances, these amounts represented slightly over half of what comparable family units under

65 had to live on. Many low-income older persons had always been in low-income brackets, but others had faced a severe and rather sudden reduction in disposable income upon retirement. Only a modest minority of elderly families (20%) had an income in excess of $15,000 a year (Brotman, 1977).

At the same time that older persons' income diminishes, credit becomes more difficult to obtain, and there is little chance that the future will bring any substantial increase in available funds. When these limitations are made worse by inflation, the elderly are required to revise their bases for allocating money, sometimes drastically. Money once spent for an automobile, new clothes, or entertainment now must be spent for food, property taxes, and medical care.

Although financial stresses are greatest for those with extremely limited income, the frustration and anxiety of persons who have always enjoyed a moderate income and must now cope with reduced funds also lead to a high level of stress. Nor are the effects restricted to those whose retirement has already produced income reduction, since older persons still working begin to plan for their forthcoming retirement before they actually leave work.

When young and middle-aged adults are trying to improve their own living conditions, to plan for the future education of their children, and to supplement the income of their aging parents all at the same time, compromises often must be made. Older people often prefer having less money themselves to becoming the source of financial tensions for their children. Rather than accept an extra bit of money each month, they are likely to encourage their children to establish a college fund for the grandchildren.

Many people turn to the government for additional financial support for older people, but the governmental decision makers have to weigh such demands against competing demands for many other services—education, police protection, military strength, protection of the environment, libraries, transportation systems, general health services, and so on. It often seems as if the needs of people are infinite and the available money is finite, so that there is no possible way that all persons and all groups can receive what they feel to be their fair share.

## HEALTH

As people age, the likelihood that they will require medical care becomes greater. Health problems are distressing for many reasons. Their costs in time and money can be extensive; they may restrict activities or mobility; they often involve pain and discomfort; and—for older people in particular—they may provide an unpleasant reminder that life is finite.

Older people often adjust amazingly well to chronic health problems that initially appear horrendous. Though they may have had a major coronary or be suffering a progressive loss of vision, older people frequently make the decision that they must gain as much satisfaction as possible from their remaining time and manage to ignore the destructive aspects of their illnesses. Emotional support from those they love undoubtedly contributes significantly to their capability to cope with their conditions. Seeing meaning in both their past life and their future existence also contributes to their psychological well-being.

At times, particularly for the very old, the services of a personal caretaker is required, either because of physical limitations or because of confusion and forgetfulness. This care can sometimes be best provided in the home of the elderly person, perhaps through a hired person or perhaps through the services of family members, friends, or neighbors. On other occasions, the older person must move to the home of a relative or to an institution.

Sometimes the physical conditions of older people improve, either through health care or simply through time. At other times, the most that can be done is to keep them from getting worse or to slow the rate at which they do get worse. Good medical care and good nutrition are extremely helpful in improving physical health, but the role of psychological factors should not be underestimated. For an older person the knowledge of being wanted, loved, and needed can be a very important medicine. As we observed earlier, however, adult children have their own lives to lead, and the personal care of older parents must compete with other responsibilities, gaining very high priority in some instances and having much lower priority in others. Although we may like to think that such priorities are established on a rational basis, personal values and personality interactions are very much at the heart of these decisions.

## SOCIAL ROLES/SOCIAL INTERACTIONS

With advancing age come changes in social roles and social interactions. As parents see their children develop from highly dependent infants to self-sufficient adults, they normally feel great satisfaction, especially if the children become the kind of adults that the parents respect. The "empty nest," although distressing for some parents, is often viewed with relief: now that the children are grown and on their own, the parents, realizing that they, too, have a new autonomy, are able to participate in activities and do things that child care had previously prohibited. Soon thereafter, many parents become grandparents. Although this role is not without its conflicts and stress, it does permit many people to have a relaxed relationship with young children they can love—and to leave when they wish to go on to something else.

Work roles change also—almost always for men and increasingly for women as well. As people become older, they must confront the realization that they may never in their careers achieve the heights to which they had aspired earlier. The supervisory position will never be attained; the book will always be unwritten; the store will always be small. At the same time, older people often can look back on a lifetime of work-related accomplishments, whether these accomplishments were in terms of children taught, legal briefs filed, insurance sold, television sets repaired, or tires changed and engines fixed. We don't wish to romanticize work; countless workers do consider their jobs to be tedious and unpleasant. Our point is that in the later years people begin to think both about their failures and unrealized hopes and about their successes and achievements. There is pain in this process, but there is pleasure as well.

By the time retirement comes, many people have already begun the process of disengaging from their work setting and are looking ahead to new activities. For some, however, retirement can be difficult and even destructive, not so much because they loved their work as because work provided status, filled time, was financially remunerative, offered a source of friends and social interactions, perhaps even gave meaning to life. Some people identify themselves in terms of their work: asked the question "Who are you?" they will answer "a stockbroker," "a nurse," "a gardener," "a teacher." Being retired means that these responses are no longer appropriate. The statement "I'm retired" or "I'm a retired salesman" just isn't the same. Retirement can thus entail the loss of an important feeling of identity, of self.

Some older persons do move into an active retirement or at least continue to function as actively as they have always functioned. They may become involved with gardening (feeling responsible for living and growing things can be an extremely significant experience), with travel, with reading, with community or political activities. Such people utilize their increased time flexibility to good advantage. Others feel that the community is withdrawing from them, and they withdraw or disengage from the community in return. They cannot organize time to their own satisfaction—they can neither enjoy doing nothing nor marshal their energies to do something.

Adult children often become distressed when their parents retire, sometimes with good cause. These children may urge their parents to "become active," even though such exhortations are notoriously unsuccessful. They may try to involve their parents in their own lives, broadening the boundaries of their own nuclear families to embrace the older generation. Yet the fact is that most retired persons can take care of themselves perfectly well—they've been doing just that for decades—and the most important thing their children can do is to be responsive, to be caring, and to treat them as mature adults. It is amazing and ironic how capable adult children are of reacting to their parents as though they were children, simply because their parents have not remained aware of contemporary political issues or have become somewhat forgetful about medical appointments or have developed a hearing impairment.

Other social roles also change with retirement. As people move through their middle adult years, they are likely to acquire positions of power in the community, in their religious and social groups, and in their work. Once in their sixties, however, their power usually wanes; relatively few 70-year-olds occupy leadership roles.

## ATTITUDES AND VALUES

Since attitudes and values are closely related to roles, there are considerable differences in the social, political, and religious values of different age groups. An interesting issue is the extent to which these age-related differences are a function of the process of becoming older and, perhaps, nearer to death, and the extent to which they arise from differential learning experiences in the very early years of life. If, for example, older people today tend to express more traditional religious views than their children, is it because people naturally become more religious as they get older? Or do people in their seventies differ from those in their fifties or thirties because they received their basic religious instruction in a different cultural environment? Our guess is that differences in early experience are more significant with respect to religious views than are age-related differences. Nevertheless, attitudes toward death probably are strongly influenced by how close people think they are to dying, as well as how many times they have lived through the deaths of loved ones. Similarly, the increased tenderness and passivity of men and the increased overt aggressiveness of women that Gutmann (1969) found occurring with age in several cultures may be more a result of almost universal conditions than of culturally determined learning.

## PSYCHOLOGICAL ASPECTS OF AGING

Do people become more cautious when they get old? More rigid? What happens to memory, learning, and psychomotor responses? How is the self-concept affected? Despite the substantial academic literature concerning these questions, the answers remain unclear. We know, for example, that the research on caution and rigidity and on self-concept does not disclose a clear-cut, age-related pattern of change with respect to these qualities.

When we look at memory, learning, and psychomotor responses, the results are consistent, but their interpretation is still unclear. If we measure memory, learning, or psychomotor responses in 50-year-olds, 60-year-olds, and 70-year-olds, we will find considerable differences between the age groups. However, if we follow a group of 60-year-olds for a ten-year period, we observe that the changes over time are much less than the differences between our original sampling of 60- and 70-year-olds. Perhaps educational levels, quality of health care, and differing values and attitudes contribute more to these age-related differences than does the process of aging itself. That is, we might find that 50-year-olds differed systematically from 60-year-olds, and that 60-year-olds differed systematically from 80-year-olds, if we examined what happened to all three age groups between the ages of 30 and 39.

One danger in relating to older people is to assume that age inevitably brings with it such unfortuate consequences as poverty, poor health, forced retirement, reduced cognitive powers, loneliness, and others. Although these characteristics are often attributed globally to the elderly, they actually pertain only to a portion of older persons. Most people over 65 are in good health (95% live outside of institutions), are adjusting well to retirement, are not lonely, and retain good cognitive powers. Relatively few are affluent, but even in this regard most elderly persons seem to cope effectively. The elderly are a remarkably alert and resilient segment of the population; they cope well with problems and limitations that younger people see as highly distressing.

## THE ELDERLY OF THE FUTURE

Each year, the average educational level of persons over 65 goes up a little. Around the end of this century, the number of years of formal schooling of the elderly will equal that of the rest of the population. Given some of the present downward trends in college education, the future may find younger persons more lacking in formal education than their elders, instead of the other way around. Partly as a result of this change, older people are becoming less docile and submissive, more demanding and angry. Moreover, with the reduction in the birth rate that began in the late 1960s, older people are becoming an increasingly large proportion of the population. Although life expectancy has gone up very little during the past several years, a significant reduction in deaths from any one of the three major chronic diseases—heart, stroke, and cancer—could easily increase the average life expectancy by four or five years. Significant reduction of all three diseases could mean an additional ten or more years of life.

There is also the possibility that the process of aging itself will come under control. If biomedical sciences find a way to retard the aging process in younger persons so that an extra decade or so of healthy, vigorous life might be added to the usual life span, the social, psychological, political, and financial consequences would be incredibly immense. According to many biogerontologists, such a development could well take place around the end of this century. Whether our society or any society will be prepared for the event is another matter.

□ The odds are high that you will be elderly someday. How might your values be different at that time? Do you think you will consider yourself elderly when you are 65? What sort of life do you envision for yourself at that time? There is a danger in responding too quickly to these questions, because it is very difficult to understand ourselves at an age we have never experienced. You might interview some older people to find out how they feel about retirement, leisure, money, health, death, sex, family relationships, and religion. Then try to project yourself into their age group. □

# REFERENCES

Bengtson, V. L., & Kuypers, J. A. Generational differences and the developmental state. *Aging and Human Development*, 1971, *2*, 249–260.
Blenkner, M. Social work and family relationships in later life, with some thoughts on filial maturity. In E. Shanas & G. F. Streib (Eds.), *Social structure and the family: Generational relations*. Englewood Cliffs, N.J.: Prentice-Hall, 1965.
Brotman, H. B. Income and poverty in the older population in 1975. *The Gerontologist*, 1977, *17*, 23–26.
Gutmann, D. I. The country of old men: Cultural studies in the psychology of later life. *Occasional Papers in Gerontology #5*. Institute of Gerontology, University of Michigan/Wayne State University, 1969.
Shanas, E. Family help patterns and social class in three countries. *Journal of Marriage and the Family*, 1967, *29*, 257–266.
Sussman, M. B. The family life of old people,. In R. H. Binstock & E. Shanas (Eds.), *Handbook of aging and the social sciences*. New York: Van Nostrand Reinhold, 1976.

מבוא

# PART FOUR
## MENTAL HEALTH AND HUMAN VALUES

# CHAPTER 16

## STRESS: ITS NATURE
## AND DEVELOPMENT

Every day we are exposed to advertisements—on the radio, on television, in newspapers and magazines—reminding us of the immense stress we are suffering. The advertisers, of course, have the remedy. Because, the commercial tells us, we worked hard or our children yell a lot or our bosses are grumpy, we must be suffering terribly. Fortunately, all we need to be healthy, vigorous, sexy, and capable is one or two little pills.

We are not concerned here with the validity of these messages but with the assumptions the advertisers seem to be making about people—assumptions that, obviously, enough people accept to keep drug manufacturers solvent. If advertisers are selling happy, stress-free living through pills, then they are implicitly selling a biomedical model of human behavior. They are implying that altering the biochemical basis of your behavior will produce a reduction of tension and, therefore, a change for the better in your feelings. Usually the subliminal message is that this change will bring happiness or success. This is a fairly strong deterministic view, since it replaces our own control of our feelings and behavior with a chemical compound.

☐ What implications does this trend have for the future? If you take a pill to reduce feelings of tension, another to dampen your "highs," and a third to pull you up from the valleys of depression, will you eventually take a pill to make you more aggressive when you demand a salary raise, a better examination grade, or improved political leadership? Will the overly talkative take a shut-up pill when they wish to act subservient? Will the frightened take a self-confidence pill when they want the courage to impress others? Such pills are not merely the stuff of science fiction; drugs that affect fear in animals are already under study (Kumar, Stolerman, & Steinberg, 1970). □

The ability to cope effectively with a great variety of stressful occurrences is, of course, necessary to the enjoyment of life, and perhaps even to survival. We do encounter stress all the time, and we each respond to it in our own fashion, depending upon the nature of the stressful circumstances and our own unique life history and present situation. We may deal ineffectively with stress, traveling down the road to further ill effects such as withdrawal, undue aggressiveness, confusion, conformity, socially disapproved behavior, or emotionally disturbed behavior. Or we may do a reasonably good job of handling most stress, perhaps even turning it into a growth experience.

"Growth through stress" can happen when the stress requires that we confront our values and style of life, seeing these in a new and healthier perspective; when the stress demands so much effort, capability, endurance, and personal or intellectual strength that our ability to cope successfully is sufficient to improve our self-esteem; when the stress makes us realize that the old way of doing things is no longer good enough and that we must seek better ways. As we learn that living with some stress may be necessary, the problem becomes one of keeping the inevitable from becoming overwhelming.

## STRESS: DEFINED AND OUTLINED

*Stress* is one of those terms that has two meanings similar enough to cause confusion and different enough to require discrimination. In essence, stress is both cause and effect. *Stress* can mean the force, pressure, or threat that produces unpleasant feelings of tension or strain (meaning #1); it also can be a synonym for the terms *tension* and *strain* (meaning #2). Thus stress (#1) causes stress (#2). For the sake of simplicity, we will use the term only for meaning #1; for meaning #2, we will use the synonym *tension*.

Stress can be ranged on a number of continua. For example, stress ranges from chronic (ongoing, relatively continuous) to acute (beginning suddenly and terminating within a short time); from avoidable to unavoidable; from predictable to unpredictable; from reversible to irreversible; from incapacitating to annoying; from stultifying to growth-producing.

Further, stress can be either physiological or psychological. Similarly, its effects (tension) can also be either physiological or psychological. Physiological and psychological manifestations of stress interact dynamically with each other and can also be seen as points on a continuum. The following chart depicts some examples.

| | Symptoms of Psychological Tension | Symptoms of Physiological Tension |
|---|---|---|
| *Psychological Stress* | 1. Frustration over not being promoted leads to inability to concentrate.<br>2. Death of a parent leads to period of depression. | 1. Conflict regarding whether or not to get married leads to sleepless nights and bad digestion.<br>2. Anxiety over serious illness of child leads to psychosomatic stomach cramps. |
| *Physiological Stress* | 1. Lack of sleep leads to irritability.<br>2. Required extra effort for handicapped person causes chronic somatopsychic feelings of tension. | 1. Severe headaches lead to psychosomatic skin symptoms.<br>2. Breathing difficulty leads to fear and resulting physiological symptoms. |

## WHAT FACTORS ARE STRESSFUL?

Almost anything one can name would be stressful for someone. Although you may readily see why failure would be stressful, for example, success can also be stressful; for some people, under some circumstances, success might well be more stressful than failure. Success in work leads to more responsibility; success in love leads to involving relationships; success in school leads to higher expectations of oneself. All can produce stress.

Other common stresses come to mind. Family relationships often eventuate in stressful situations, such as being in love, displaying affection, competing with brothers and sisters, trying to gain independence, establishing identity apart from one's parents, relating sexually to a spouse, and being responsible for the physical and mental health of children. Purely physical factors can be stressful: pain, illness, disability, or the potential loss of self through death. Social institutions can present stresses: financial pressures, desire for social status and prestige, job expectations, demands from religious groups for certain behaviors and attitudes, academic pressures. Stresses also reside in the ways people perceive themselves: fears about personal adequacy, inability to accept themselves as worthwhile individuals, feelings of sex-role inadequacy, anxiety about body image. As a final cluster of stressful factors, we might list social and sexual relationships, loss through separation, divorce, or death, and difficulty in relating to authority figures.

Conflict is a common kind of stressful situation. You may want to attain two goals that turn out to be mutually exclusive; you may find all the possibilities open to you distasteful; or, to do something you want to do, you may be forced to do something you don't want to do. Examples are probably helpful. (1) You may find that you can't *both* earn more money by working longer hours *and* enhance your personal growth through a program of reading or painting or sports. (2) You may find yourself having to choose between inadequate, overpriced housing that is conveniently located and somewhat better, reasonably priced housing that is badly located for your purposes. (3) You may anticipate an enriched relationship through marriage at the price of the loss of certain kinds of freedom.

## STAGES OF STRESS AND TENSION

In an effort to clarify the meaning of stress and tension, as well as some related concepts, we will outline a five-stage sequence in the functioning of stress. These stages chart a general trend rather than an inevitable or rigid progression.

*Stage One: Awareness.* In a psychological sense, stress cannot occur unless we perceive some circumstance as stressful. This perception need not be conscious. Thus, the first stage in stress is becoming cognizant, consciously or unconsciously, that stressful events are in the wind. The alarm stage, described by Selye (1956) as the first step in the General Adaptation Syndrome, is an outgrowth of this initial awareness. Although Selye's frame of reference was physiological stress, such as illness, his writings are readily applicable to all forms of stress. During the awareness stage, we ready ourselves and mobilize our resources for coping with what is to come.

Inadequate opportunity for this preparation—for example, an awareness stage with a duration of only a few seconds—can leave us confused and disorganized when the impact of the stressful situation is felt. Suddenly hearing of the death of a loved one, being unexpectedly fired from a job, getting a blowout while driving at high speeds on a crowded freeway: these events leave no time for anticipation. On the other hand, if the awareness stage is unduly long, as when a dying person lingers far beyond our expectations, the stressful component may dissipate before the beginning of the second stage. It may also happen that such a prolonged awareness stage proves to be more stressful than the anticipated event.

*Stage Two: Initial Reaction.* At some point, often undefined, the major impact of the stress is felt. Selye describes the resistance that the organism generates in fighting off the destructive elements of physiological stress. The stage of anticipating and, perhaps, role-playing ways of handling the future stress is over; now we are required to respond to the ongoing circumstances. There may be some overt emotional expression, such as crying, cursing, laughing, or vomiting, and there is inevitably some form of covert emotional expression, such as acceptance or denial, embarrassment, anger, or fear. Unconscious reactions are not uncommon. These responses may be a continuation of the feelings and behavior begun in Stage One. At times, however, we feel or behave in ways quite different from those we had expected and planned for.

Our immediate reaction to emotion-arousing stimuli is often one of enhanced effectiveness. Increased alertness, strength, recall, or speed are not uncommon. Biochemical explanations for these responses are available. However, overwhelming stress can also lead to reduced alertness, feelings of numbness, reduced effectiveness of sensory and motor responses, narrowed attention span, loss of memory, confusion, and "suspension of affective awareness" (Weiss & Payson, 1967).

*Stage Three: Subsequent Response.* In time, the initial impact subsides, but the stress continues. In Selye's terms, resistance will also continue, although exhaustion will begin to set in if this stage lasts too long. Selye describes exhaustion as the depletion of those capacities used in fighting the stress.

Clearly our behavior an hour after hearing of our loved one's death, after being fired, or after getting the blowout is different from our immediate response. The stressful circumstance still exists, but some initial coping has been accomplished, and movement toward regaining equilibrium is likely to occur. This movement can be deceiving, since some kinds of stress are so overpowering that we cannot take it on all at once. When this happens, we seem to try to digest it a piece at a time. People's responses to news of a personal tragedy often follow this path. Given unexpected, tragic news, individuals may be able to deal with their powerful feelings only through a succession of behavior patterns that may strike observers as incongruent with the event. First they may seem very calm; then they may talk very rationally; eventually they may cry a little or a lot, become very quiet, or decide to go to a movie or to return to work. The full and overwhelming impact of the stress is so great that the implications take time to be grasped. (See Kübler-Ross [1969] for a discussion of the five stages she has observed people go through in dealing with the knowledge of their own impending death. Her five stages fall mainly under our second, third, and fourth stages.)

From the first glimmer of future stress, we try to cope with what is to come, seeking to reduce its destructiveness. Our response may be overt, such as walking away from an unpleasant encounter; it may be covert, such as planning alternative programs after losing the job; it may be unconscious, such as rationalizing our failure. Sometimes our interventions in alleviating our own tension are aided by friends or other sources of support; sometimes others intervene on our behalf when we appear incapable. If Selye's exhaustion stage or its psychological equivalent has begun, then our own efforts at intervening may be ineffectual. Time or outside help are required before effective coping is possible.

**Stage Four: Outcome.** If the stress is too lengthy and too intense, exhaustion is complete, and we must seek outside resources. If the stressful situation begins to recede in perceived intensity, we can return to our previous level of functioning. Obviously, most instances of stress are not incapacitating; usually they do not even demand more than passing attention. For such occurrences, this entire sequence involves only a small portion of our time and energy.

**Stage Five: Post-Traumatic Response.** Weiss and Payson (1967) define a fifth stage, which occurs "when the sense of self has been maximally reconstituted." Usually we have by now overcome all effects of the stress, except some recollections; all our functioning has overtly returned to whatever was normal for us before the onset of the stress. In some extreme instances, however, the post-traumatic response retains enough of the effects of the stressful circumstances themselves that full recovery does not occur. Victims of Nazi concentration camps will always carry with them the post-traumatic scars of their psychological injuries; other victims of intense tragedies may similarly be marked in ways that can be compensated for only with extreme difficulty—or not at all.

Most of this discussion has referred to acute stress. Chronic stress follows a somewhat different pathway. Perhaps it develops slowly from an increasingly impossible job or marriage situation. Or it may come about through a chronic illness that has disrupted previous life patterns and is likely to continue for months or years. Or it may be the cumulative effect of being the only Black worker in an otherwise all-White organization or a woman competing with men in a traditionally male setting. You can easily translate our description of the five stages to cover chronic problems.

# THE IMPACT OF STRESS

The impact of stress can be felt in several ways. Stress can cause frustration, the feeling that you cannot obtain something that you wish to obtain. A barrier is in your way. The barrier might be realistic: you don't punch your boss (or instructor) because you would risk a variety of sanctions. The barrier might be unrealistic: you don't try for a certain job (or date or college) because you believe without good reason that you will be rejected.

Stress can also lead to fear, anxiety, or guilt. *Fear* is a realistic feeling or awareness that you might suffer harm—the loss of your job, your spouse, your health, your leadership role. *Anxiety* is closely related to fear, but the source of the harm is much more vague. You fear the loss of your job, but you don't have any apparent reason to; you feel uncomfortable about your academic performance, although your grades are exemplary. *Guilt* is feeling responsible for having violated your own precepts of good and bad.

## *INDIVIDUAL DIFFERENCES IN PERCEPTION OF STRESS*

Although a stressful situation may be objectively the same for everyone involved, subjectively it will differ. Your values, your personality, your self-concept, your feelings about people in general and certain people in particular, your feelings about the nature of humanity and the nature of the world: all these considerations will enter into your interpretation of potential stress. And so will your age, your race, your religion, your sex, your physical appearance. Earlier in this chapter, we gave as an example of conflict a choice of a place to live. The issue at hand is that the conflict-inducing stress will only occur for those whose values make it a conflict. For many the choice would be clear: the convenient location would be selected because it was the only apartment that permitted access to needed local transportation, because cost was not a matter of major concern, because they would enjoy fixing up the apartment so that it would be more pleasant. Others would make the opposite decision just as readily. None of these people would suffer more than a slight amount of conflict or stress.

Individual differences would also exist in the examples we gave of frustration. Some people never really work up enough anger to want to punch someone; some do not fear rejection enough to refrain from going after what they want.

To select a simple but highly differentiating example of frustration: getting on and off most city buses requires that you navigate an extremely high step. Perhaps you've never noticed, but watch what happens when the step is approached by an elderly person, a woman in a tight skirt, a pregnant woman, an obese man, or a child on crutches.

There are sources of stress in the world that you've never noticed—perhaps never needed to notice. Traveling in a country where you can neither speak the language nor read the signs; living in such poverty that you fear your children will be bitten by rats; learning that you are the future parent of a child, while having contempt for the other parent; being told that recent tests indicate you may have cancer but that a more thorough examination is necessary.

Individual differences in perception of stress, then, are partly the result of values and personality, partly the result of roles and physical characteristics, and partly the result of the objective situation. All these factors interact to produce the amount of stress perceived by each individual.

## RESPONSES TO STRESS

Regardless of its origins, stress causes changes in both the psyche and the soma, in both feelings, thoughts, and behavior and body physiology and biochemistry. The biochemical and behavioral responses act in concert, rather than individually, but the differentiation between them is useful in spite of its oversimplification.

Bodily reactions to stress are familiar; even the terms *tension* and *strain* conjure images of physical changes. These changes include increased heart activity, rapid breathing, increased perspiration, changes in the circulatory and digestive systems, altered flow of adrenalin and noradrenalin, reduced salivary activity, and so forth. In other words, your heart beats faster, your hands sweat, your breath comes quickly, your stomach is in knots, your head pounds, and your mouth is dry. Perhaps your hands feel tense; perhaps your teeth clench; perhaps your fingers move back and forth or close into a fist. Perhaps you lose control of your bowels or vomit or feel dizzy. If the stress is chronic, the physical reactions will be ongoing for extended periods and may have a harmful effect upon the organism.

Behavioral changes due to stress are also well-known. We have already discussed the defense mechanisms in the context of dynamic changes that occur in the services of maintaining a stable and self-esteemed self-concept. Other reactions include confusion, disorganization, rigidity, and withdrawal, as well as the growth responses discussed earlier. To this list we can add the behavioral disorders—neuroses, psychoses, and personality disorders (alcoholism, drug addiction, suicide, compulsive gambling).

# INDIVIDUAL DIFFERENCES
# IN RESPONSE TO STRESS

Does everyone respond to stress in the same way? Obviously not: our responses to stress are as unique as we are. Other questions we can ask about responses to stress have less obvious answers. We will consider three: (1) Can we socialize children to cope more effectively with a variety of kinds of stress? (2) Are some people consistently more capable of dealing with stress than others? (3) Do people develop consistent patterns of response to stress that they employ in many different stressful situations, or do they respond so differently to each new occurrence that their behavior is virtually unpredictable?

Present knowledge does afford reasonably adequate answers to each of these questions. To enable children to cope more effectively with present and future stress, we apparently need to attend to their early development. Many believe that helping children to feel secure, loved, and accepted in the early years will help them to develop healthy self-concepts and a sense of stability, so that later stress is not as destructive as it otherwise might be. However, parents who overprotect, overindulge, or overvalue children may be as harmful as those who ignore, neglect, or deprecate children. (Often, overindulgence is actually a sign of strong, unrecognized feelings of hostility.)

One way parents can help their children to cope with stress is to let them explore their environment and deal with stress as they encounter it. This is an easy statement to make, but putting it into practice can cause conflicts of values for parents. For example, how much risk do you feel you can take with your children's safety or your property in order to encourage your children to explore, to stimulate their curiosity, to encourage them to be inventive and creative? To get down to cases:

- Rachel, age 4, picks up the milk glass by the edge to move it to where she can grab it with both hands; the glass careens and the milk sloshes, but she doesn't lose a drop or crack the glass—yet.
- The model airplane is the first that Dan, at 7, has ever had, and he wants to work on it by himself.
- The ice skating rink is in the middle of a rough section of town, but Leah, age 10, wants to walk home from there with her friend at twilight.

What happens to the child when the parent insists upon moving the glass, supervising the model construction, picking up the child by car? We can at least speculate that not only would the immediate situation create tension but the child would defer to the parent or other authority in subsequent situations that might arouse stress.

The second question—whether some people can consistently

deal more effectively with stress than others—must be answered in the affirmative. All our experience tells us that certain individuals manage to retain their composure, think quickly, and use good judgment under numerous stressful conditions, while others just seem to fall apart. Nonetheless, we should not overlook the unique situational components. Consider the following two examples of the interaction of personality and situation:

> A, age 64, has worked his way up to superintendent of schools for a medium-sized city. He has weathered the Depression and World War II (in which he lost an eye), completed college in the postwar years while working full-time, taken the hard road to his present position, and coped with militant students and an aggressive teachers' union. He thrives on work, but in three months he will reach mandatory retirement age. Arthritis is making it increasingly difficult for him to do anything with his hands, including driving and gardening. Is his past history of success in dealing with stress prognostic of future success? Or will he find his enforced retirement more difficult to deal with than his more passive age cohorts find theirs?

> J, age 29, has spent over half his life in custodial and penal institutions. More by chance than by design, he has never killed anyone, although he has consistently dealt with frustration by aggressive and often violent action. An extremely bright, verbally capable person, he now has a good job with considerable responsibility. Given security, a modest income, and friends who do not perceive violence as a requirement for masculinity, he has developed socially acceptable methods of responding to frustration.

Our third question was whether people develop fairly consistent patterns of response to stress. Research has shown that a given individual is likely to exhibit moderately similar physiological responses to stress, regardless of the cause of the stress. Evidence is available that each individual's psychological and social responses to stress also show some consistency. For example, some people tend to respond to frustration by directing their anger (or other feelings) outward; others direct their feelings inward, often turning aggression against themselves; still others attempt to deny that the frustration has produced strong feelings. What do your own experiences suggest?

## CULTURAL DIFFERENCES IN RESPONSES TO STRESS

Immense differences exist between countries in rates of suicide, alcoholism, divorce, homicide, and mental illness. To some degree, we can accept this disparity as reflecting cultural differences in responses to stress. However, these data also reflect international differences in the definitions of these occurrences, in the adequacy of record-keeping, in laws, in age distributions, in the accessibility of alcohol or guns, and in the degree to which family and community members hide cases of social pathology.

Some clear cultural differences in responses to stress can be found. For example, Caudill (1959) described a syndrome that is especially common in Japan. (The symptoms are found in other cultures, but are not normally considered to be a distinctive syndrome.) The syndrome, termed *anthrophobia* (fear of people), "is manifested by feelings of inadequacy, fear of meeting people, flushing, stuttering, and other signs of anxiety" (p. 237). In parts of Asia and Africa, running amok is a recognized psychiatric manifestation rarely found in North America or Europe (Weiss & Payson, 1967).

Even within the United States and Canada, social-class differences in the expression of stress-induced anger have been noted, with middle-class persons much more likely to react with verbal aggression, whereas lower-status individuals may display physical aggression. Such examples could easily be multiplied.

☐ Some provocative value questions arise. In socializing low-income children, do teachers and others have the right (or even the responsibility) to do their best to produce nonphysical responses to stress, even if the children live in a neighborhood where their peers respect fists more than words? Should middle-class parents encourage their children to learn to fight—and, more important, to be willing to fight—on the assumption that verbal aggression is insufficient to cope with many situations?

The question, of course, is much broader than whether to fight or to talk. The issue is the proper task of the socializing agents when their own values support one mode of dealing with stress, while the persons they are socializing live in a community that rewards other modes.

People of some nations and ethnic groups readily express feelings of anger, joy, and sorrow. They shout and swear, they laugh and hug each other, they cry. Are these responses to stress more indicative of emotional health and stability than "staying cool"? Or, if society has other values, should socializing agents encourage these persons to identify with less emotive models and to avoid strong expressions of feeling? ☐

# WHEN STRESS OVERWHELMS

Situations arise for us all when stress appears so great that we feel overwhelmed. The frustration of a lost love or a lost parent, the conflict between integrity and greed, the anxiety of an uncertain future, the impending threat of encountering violence: each can lead us to feel that we cannot continue, that we must find release, support, rest, freedom. Eventually we weather the storm—we recover from the loss, make our decision, meet the future, emerge through the violence—and we do continue, perhaps the better for the experience and perhaps not.

Occasionally some of us don't make it through. The stress is sufficiently intense and of sufficient duration that our various defense mechanisms and other self-protective devices no longer enable us to maintain an adequate self-concept. In order to continue to perceive ourselves as reasonably consistent, esteemed, and worthy, we may distort reality. Perceptions of the world, of other people, and of the self become chaotic, at variance with the real world. When perceptions become distorted, behavior disturbances follow.

The symptoms of these disturbances are numerous. They include depression, inappropriate worry and fear, suspicion, inadequate emotional control, overly strict emotional control, extensive fantasy, rigidity, organic symptoms, extreme hostility, ineffectual behavior, unhappiness, chronic feelings of tension, and inadequate interpersonal relations. Obviously each of these symptoms represents a continuum, extending from *slightly disturbed* to *extremely disturbed*. Each can also be represented on a continuum of frequency, from *only occasionally* through *often* to *almost always*.

When an individual's behavior appears to be highly disturbed, the person is considered to be neurotic or perhaps even psychotic. Differences between these two major classifications of emotional disturbances are not always clear-cut, but the following may serve as an acceptable guide:

1. Psychosis is more severe than neurosis and implies greater personality disorganization.
2. Psychotics are often dangerous to themselves or to others and may destroy property; neurotics are rarely dangerous in these ways.
3. Psychotics usually need hospitalization both for care and for protection; neurotics can function without institutional arrangements.
4. Psychotics rarely recognize that they are emotionally ill, but neurotics are often aware of their symptoms, although they appear incapable of changing their neurotic behavior.
5. Psychotics may display intellectual deterioration, but neurotics can function at or near their normal intellectual level.
6. Psychotics are out of touch with reality in some way; neurotics can differentiate the real from the non-real, although they are unable to control those aspects of their own behavior affected by their neuroses.
7. Neurotics are much more likely to respond to psychotherapy than are psychotics.
8. Psychotics often exhibit delusions (false beliefs) and hallucinations (false perceptions); neurotics do not.

A great deal of time and effort is devoted to reducing stress, but the reduction of stress is not always the most important point. Sometimes coping with existing stress is more significant; sometimes learning from stress is the most important matter; sometimes creating stress in exchange for challenge and stimulation is the issue. When stress is overwhelming, these other matters become academic, and it becomes necessary either to reduce the stress or to cope with it, often with help from others, so that it ceases to be overwhelming. But stress need not be regarded simply as a villain, let alone a unitary phenomenon. We need to look at stress in each situation and recognize that our response to it is largely a function of the values that we have internalized.

☐ What price are you willing to pay for reduced stress in your life? To what extent do you avoid challenging situations, the possibility of loss, or the potential for failure in order to reduce stress, even though you also reduce your enjoyment and satisfaction? Can you think of situations in which you preferred to encounter stress rather than avoid it? What was the nature of those situations? ☐

## REFERENCES

Caudill, W. Observations on the cultural context of Japanese psychiatry. In M. K. Opler (Ed.), *Culture and mental health*. New York: Macmillan, 1959.

Kübler-Ross, E. *On death and dying*. New York: Macmillan, 1969.

Kumar, R., Stolerman, I. P., & Steinberg, H. Psychopharmacology. *Annual Review of Psychology*, 1970, *21*, 595–628.

Selye, H. *The stress of life*. New York: McGraw-Hill, 1956.

Weiss, R. J., & Payson, H. E. Gross stress reaction: I. In A. M. Freedman & H. I. Kaplan (Eds.), *Comprehensive textbook of psychiatry*. Baltimore: Williams & Wilkins, 1967.

# CHAPTER 17

## HELP SEEKERS,
## HELP GIVERS, AND HELP

### HELP SEEKERS

*"There are no perfect human beings!"* Abraham Maslow announces with italics and exclamation mark (1970, p. 176). Maslow is not expressing his surprise with this pronouncement but rather the importance of not becoming disillusioned with other people. An accompanying lesson is that we should not become disillusioned with ourselves when we also fall short of perfection. At the same time, the truism that no one is perfect need not turn anyone aside from a continued attempt to grow and to become, to be effective for oneself and in one's own way.

One value that seems to permeate our society is that change is good. A corresponding belief is that, when necessary, we should seek out others who will enable us to change, whether because our stress has become greater than we can effectively handle or because we want outside help in pursuing greater personal growth. This chapter describes some of the more familiar ways in which psychological help is provided; the following chapter discusses the values that are part of seeking such help.

We each have our own resources both for reducing tension and for personal growth, but sometimes these are insufficient without some kind of community support. Until recently community-based supports were primarily devoted to persons with serious problems, often those responding to feelings of overwhelming stress who found that their functioning was seriously impaired. Although major concern still focuses on these individuals, more attention is now being paid to persons who feel that they are all right, but not good enough. In Maslow's terminology, resources are now available not only for those with strong deficiency motivation but also for those whose motivation is primarily growth.

There are similarities in the goals and procedures of all the various mental-health resources, from a telephone-answering service at a Suicide Prevention Center to a highly paid psychoanalyst. The goals of psychotherapy listed by one psychologist are reasonably applicable to all the resources to be discussed in this chapter, although in varying degrees. These goals are:

(a) increased insight into one's problems and behavior,
(b) a better delineation of one's self-identity,
(c) resolution of handicapping or disabling conflicts,
(d) changing of undesirable habits or reaction patterns,
(e) improved interpersonal or other competencies,
(f) the modification of inaccurate assumptions about one's self and one's world, and
(g) the opening of a pathway to a more meaningful and fulfilling existence [Coleman, 1972, p. 663].

It quickly becomes obvious from this list that the purposes of therapy include both deficiency motives and growth motives, from reducing stress to increasing the meaningfulness of life.

Coleman posits a number of events through which psychotherapy normally proceeds. Again, these are relevant not only to therapy but to many of the other kinds of resources.

1. A therapeutic atmosphere and relationship should be created, so that good rapport based on trust and mutual liking can be established.
2. The help seeker should have the opportunity for emotional expression or catharsis, as an aid to becoming free of some self-imposed restrictions and to reduce feelings of tension.
3. Partly as a result of the previous two events, the individual's self-understanding should improve.
4. These events should culminate in some form of personality or, at the very least, behavioral change. This change may be in terms of liking oneself better, making decisions with more confidence, relating to others in a more relaxed fashion, improved concentration, greater work or school achievement, or whatever else is relevant.
5. The relationship must end, so that the individual can function autonomously from the therapist, although it may be advisable for the client to return at intervals for the psychological equivalent of a booster shot [Coleman, 1972].

Help Seekers, Help Givers, and Help/**233**

The telephone conversation with the Suicide Prevention Center may move quickly through all these events, culminating in the decision of the caller to postpone thoughts of suicide or the recognition that feelings of loneliness can be handled. With the psychoanalyst, the same events might take several meetings a week for two or three years, but with the personality and behavioral changes presumably being more significant, longer lasting, and more comprehensive.

To use available resources, an individual must be motivated to seek them out. This motivation may come from within—for example, from a desire to reduce the felt tension, to improve day-to-day effectiveness, or to make greater use of capabilities. Or the motivation may derive from outside pressures—from family members or friends, teachers or employers, prison authorities or mental-hospital staff. Equally important, the resources must be available at a price that is not too high, either financially or in terms of time, effort, threat to the self-concept, or emotional pain and disruption. And, of course, the person must be aware that the resources exist and, in order to obtain maximum benefit, must believe that his or her needs are capable of being served by them.

Help for personal troubles and resources for personal growth have always been available from family members and friends, from community and religious leaders, from oracles and sages and teachers, from reading, from personal experience and personal exploration. The resources available today resemble those of past centuries, except that they may be more professionalized and institutionalized. The religious leader you see for help might have taken several courses in pastoral psychology; the books you read, instead of being general inspirational volumes, may be directed to emotional stress; the sages from whom you seek support may have doctorates signifying that they have been specifically trained to give such support. In spite of such professionalization, most persons probably still seek their major support from family members and friends, particularly when stress is not acute.

## HELP GIVERS

When stress becomes too great, to whom (other than family and friends) do people turn? Most, according to their own reports, turn either to the clergy (42%) or to physicians (29%) (Gurin, Veroff, & Feld, 1960). Even though these data were gathered some 20 years ago, we doubt that appreciable changes have occurred. Why do people under stress approach their pastors and their physicians? Perhaps it is because they have already developed help-seeking relationships with these persons. Since the clergy help with spiritual needs and physicians help with health needs, it is only natural that people would turn to them for help with psychological needs, which are seemingly a combination of the two. Perhaps it is because these professionals are seen as especially knowledgeable persons, or because taking troubles to a pastor or a physician does not imply that one is "crazy," which many people still perceive to be the case with taking one's troubles to mental-health professionals. It may be that spiritual counselors are assumed to be readily available and that their services do not cost money. Or it may be that visiting ministers in their churches is more comfortable than visiting mental-health professionals at their agencies or private offices. The most basic reason may simply be that people perceive the role of the clergy and of physicians to be one of providing counsel for normal persons with problems, whereas they see the role of mental-health professionals as one of giving services only to those with severe mental disturbances.

Because they are so frequently called upon to work with people under stress, pastors and other professionals (physicians, lawyers, teachers) have recognized their need to learn more about human interactions and personality dynamics. They have participated in formal classes, workshops, and other forms of training to improve their skills. In recent years, however, demands for the professionalization of mental-health services have increased rapidly, and formalized requirements for certification have appeared for psychiatrists, psychologists, social workers, marriage counselors, and professionals in related areas. Training and other requirements (for example, supervised experience, passing a qualifying examination) are now often demanded before individuals can offer services to the public for payment. State laws now prevent untrained practitioners from calling themselves psychiatrists or psychologists or from promoting their services through newspapers or the Yellow Pages of the telephone book. As the demand for professional services has increased, the number of persons professionally trained (and often certified or licensed) to provide psychotherapy has also increased dramatically. Nevertheless, the supply of professionals has in many places failed to keep up with demand.

## PARAPROFESSIONALS

Partly because of the shortage of trained psychotherapists, the past decade has seen extensive utilization of paraprofessionals, persons without extensive formal training who have participated in brief training programs and then provided limited counseling and psychotherapeutic services, usually under supervision. The two groups of persons who seem most likely to provide these services are housewives, especially those with some higher education, and college students. Another kind of service has been offered by individuals who have already encountered, and frequently coped successfully with, the kinds of problems being met by the counselees. Thus, persons who have themselves experienced alcoholism, drug addiction, prison, widowhood, severe heart conditions, or compulsive gambling counsel others who are presently dealing with those particular problems.

Paraprofessionals have also been utilized in working with racial and ethnic minorities and with low-income Whites. These counselors are recruited from the communities where they are to do their counseling. Although they normally receive special training, their own personal experiences, insights, and awareness are frequently extremely useful to professional colleagues who are presumably expert in counseling but who may lack adequate knowledge of persons of a different race, religion, sex, age, or social-class background.

Although we normally think of help givers as having received academic training in officially recognized programs, many persons provide personal counseling without ever having gone through such programs. Pediatricians and lawyers, although rigorously trained for their own professions, may never have received a background in helping people under stress, yet their work requires that they do so. Beauticians, barbers, and bartenders are noted for being drawn into personal counseling. Faith healers, fortune-tellers, and astrologers undoubtedly perform more psychotherapy than is generally realized.

## WHO IS QUALIFIED TO PROVIDE HELP?

The issue of who should be permitted to offer psychotherapeutic services is an extremely complex one. Rules and laws that screen out charlatans may technically make lawbreakers of teachers who counsel students or personnel directors who counsel employees. An additional complication is the difficulty of evaluating the effectiveness of psychotherapeutic services. For example, it is difficult to establish through careful research that a trained psychotherapist will do a better job than a skilled fortune-teller or a sympathetic hospital aide. For one thing, persons who seek help from fortune-tellers or hospital aides may well be more attuned to their vocabulary and awarenesses of these help givers than they are to those of highly educated and highly professionalized certified psychotherapists.

# VARIETIES OF HELP

A radio commercial encourages you to take a pill to soothe your nerves, cure your headache, and become a better parent and person (notice both the deficiency-motivation and growth-motivation aspects of the message); Dear Abby and Ann Landers tell you to see a psychiatrist. Whom to believe? Where to go?

The answer is obvious: it depends. It depends on your own needs and personality, on what resources are open to you in terms of time and money, on the urgency you feel, and on your ability to find the appropriate person or group of persons who can minister properly to your needs.

## INDIVIDUAL AND GROUP PSYCHOTHERAPY

Individual counseling or psychotherapy is probably considered the most appropriate approach for persons who live under stress that appears overwhelming. Whether this really is the most effective approach—or, to ask the question in another fashion, for whom this is really the most effective approach—is not definitively known. Future investigations may well show that we need to know about the help seeker's personality, about the source of stress, and about the personalities and styles of potential help givers in order to determine the appropriate therapist in a given set of circumstances.

Most people, when they think of individual psychotherapy, think of a psychiatrist (always a physician), a psychoanalyst (usually a physician), a psychologist (normally with a Ph.D. or at the very least extensive study beyond the bachelor's degree), or a psychiatric social worker (normally with a Master of Social Work degree). All these individuals have had formal coursework and supervised experience. Others enter psychotherapy from family counseling, educational counseling, pastoral psychology, general medicine, industrial training, social group work, or health education.

One-to-one counseling relationships vary on other continua. They may be brief or they may extend for months or even years; they may consist of a single anonymous telephone call to the Hot Line number, or they may develop into a very close therapeutic relationship; they may be with a trained professional, a supervised paraprofessional, or a person whose credentials might be considered dubious (although the effectiveness of such a person might still be more than adequate); they may be governed by the traditional psychoanalytical model, the more contemporary humanistic or existential models, the behavior-modification model, or some integration of these; they may take place in the office of a private practitioner or of a social agency or of a crisis-intervention center.

Working in a one-to-one relationship has advantages over participating in group-therapy sessions, but it also has limitations. In individual counseling help seekers obviously receive 100% of the attention of the help giver; they may feel freer to discuss matters causing discomfort or guilt with only the therapist there to listen; they need not be concerned about the feelings of others but can concentrate on their own concerns. On the other hand, in group therapy participants receive attention from a variety of persons, even though they are the focus of attention for a briefer period of time. Group participants learn how their words and actions are interpreted by other group members, who represent a more diverse sampling and offer a greater range of interpretations than a single therapist would. A further benefit is that learning of the difficulties of others often puts one's own problems into better perspective, while helping others cope with their difficulties may make it easier to cope with one's own difficulties.

## CRISIS INTERVENTION

Most forms of individual and group psychotherapy require weeks, months, or—occasionally—years to achieve their expected goals. Help seekers often need to wait several days or more for an initial appointment for individual therapy, and groups require that enough people be brought together to begin. For those whose financial resources are limited, waiting lists for therapy sessions may extend for weeks or even months.

But the demands of coping with high levels of stress may not permit waiting. When it hurts, it hurts now and will often only hurt worse tomorrow. This is likely to be as true for emotional hurts as it is for physical pain. In recognition of the need for immediate help, crisis-intervention centers where people can receive immediate attention have been developed. For some, crisis intervention ameliorates the immediate difficulties, so that the individual can wait until other forms of psychotherapy become available; for others, once the crisis is dealt with, the need for therapy ceases.

Crisis intervention grew out of the suicide-prevention movement and shares with this movement a dependence on carefully trained volunteers rather than certified professionals. Some crisis centers provide counselors, both volunteer and professional, for persons on a walk-in basis, with help seekers receiving anywhere from one to six contacts over a relatively brief period of time. Virtually all crisis centers maintain a telephone counseling service, frequently termed a "hot line," with specially trained suicide-prevention or crisis-intervention workers to answer calls and attempt to respond appropriately to the callers' needs. Many centers are not set up to handle personal visits, and persons needing such help are referred elsewhere. A major advantage of the crisis-intervention model is the ease with which it can be established, the availability of volunteers, and the low cost of operation.

## ENCOUNTER GROUPS

Although it is impossible to draw a sharp line between action stemming from deficiency motivation and action arising from growth motivation, all the resources so far described are primarily designed to serve persons under stress. Another kind of resource is variously called a sensitivity group, a T-group, or an encounter group. Although inevitably dealing with the emotional and social tensions of the participants, these groups emphasize the potential for human growth and self-actualization, and are part of what is often referred to as the human potential movement.

These groups vary, of course, in their philosophies and techniques. They range from virtual therapy groups to discussion groups. Some groups work on interpersonal skills and function in more traditional ways, whereas others are more concerned with expression of feelings and the emotional concerns of the participants. Still others are more likely to emphasize leadership skills or improving the effectiveness of managers and educational or public administrators. Aronson (1972) comments:

> The single most important distinguishing characteristic of a ... group is the method by which people learn ... people learn by trying things out, by getting in touch with their feelings and by expressing those feelings to other people, either verbally or nonverbally.... [A group] also allows [people] the opportunity of benefiting from learning about how [their] behavior affects other people. If I want to know whether or not people find me to be a manipulative person, I simply behave—and then allow others in the group to tell me how my behavior makes them feel [p. 239].

The kinds of interpretations of behavior that are commonly made in group therapy frequently are absent in encounter groups. There is much less likelihood that some expert will listen to what is said, then interpret to each person the significance of his or her comments. Although the leader does not always refrain from this task, such interpretations are not common in encounter groups; when they do occur, they often emanate from another group member rather than from the leader. Even the term *leader* is often eschewed by those who conduct encounter groups in favor of such terms as *facilitator* or *coordinator*, signifying that they perform their tasks more as equal participants in the group than as authorities standing outside the group. Coleman (1972) remarks:

> The emphasis in encounter groups is on the removal of masks, the free and honest expression of feelings, and the resolution of confrontations and other interactions that emerge within the group. This in turn requires prompt and honest feedback, both negative and positive, from other group members. Usually a good deal of support and affection develops within the group for members [pp. 687–688].

The popular appeal of encounter groups is immense and pervades all social classes (although such groups are more prevalent in middle-class communities). Innumerable persons have set themselves up as leaders, some with academic backgrounds in the behavioral or health sciences, some with training in special courses and with other leaders, and some with no real training at all.

Relatively few carefully planned, well conducted research investigations of encounter-group effectiveness have been reported. In reviewing these studies, Aronson (1972) presents evidence that groups do tend to reduce ethnic prejudice and to increase empathy and interpersonal understanding, as well as to increase hypnotizability (presumably an indication of increased trust, because people who do not trust others are difficult or impossible to hypnotize).

It should be noted that there are hazards for participants in these groups. Some participants (estimates run as high as 10%) become what are termed *casualties*—that is, persons who are more upset, disturbed, or depressed at the end of their participation than at the beginning and whose behavior and functioning remain less adequate several months later (Lieberman et al., 1973).

The competence (or lack thereof) of the leader/facilitator may be one factor in producing such casualties, although training in psychology, psychiatry, or social work is not necessarily sufficient—or even necessary—for group leadership. One organization in the highly volatile community of Berkeley, California that has run hundreds of groups with a casualty rate of almost zero claims that using sensitive, trained nonprofessionals as facilitators is better than using academically trained persons. Part of the in-service training program is instruction to avoid pushing people to say or do or be things they do not want to say or do or be. One of the hazards of encounter-group participation is the immense social pressure arising from the other participants to satisfy *their* expectations. For example, since openness and honesty are group goals, persons wishing to remain private or to keep thoughts to themselves are under tremendous pressure, whereas "open and honest" persons are rewarded by approval and described as courageous.

In many instances, the warmth and acceptance of group participants enable persons who are tight and withdrawn, who are maintaining an unnecessary kind of privacy, to open up and discuss their concerns. Once such people find that the group accepts them—or at least will respond honestly to them—they feel much freer to participate in the group and feel much better about themselves. In one encounter group, for example, a young woman admitted that she had been temporarily hospitalized for depression. The group members, instead of being horrified by her statement, as she had feared, immediately showed great concern and support, enabling her to realize that her hospitalization need not be a terrible and guarded secret. In another group, a young man from a blue-collar family found that the men in his group could embrace each other physically without embarrassment or reluctance, and his own tension about being touched by men disappeared. But both the woman and the man had to be cautious in the ways they permitted their newly learned behavior to generalize. For her to discuss her hospitalization freely with everyone might cause her difficulty in some relationships; for him to embrace his male friends at the factory might cause even more difficulty in some relationships.

Group pressures to function in discomforting ways and the possibility of overgeneralizing from group experience are two hazards of encounter groups. A third is that some encounter groups participate in arrangements that can be distressing to some of their members. For example, nude encounters undoubtedly do strip away attempts to establish false images through clothing and may also reduce some of the self-protecting devices that people use unnecessarily, but they can also be extremely disruptive for those whose upbringing makes nudity particularly distasteful or arousing. Similarly, the "hot seat," a setting in which one person has motives, tensions, and problems evaluated and interpreted by the leader and other group members, can be more stressful than helpful, especially if the leader is particularly aggressive or the participant is particularly vulnerable. A further difficulty is evoked when the leader or group members encourage physical affection, hostile aggression, or overtly sexual behavior, either directly or indirectly. With effective leaders and personally stable members, all these difficulties can be averted. A sensitive leader can help upset participants work through their feelings or else can enable them to refrain from participating; stable group members can decide to behave as they wish, regardless of group pressures, or can decide to abide by the group pressures, recognizing that they have the personal strength to withdraw if at a later time they become sufficiently uncomfortable. However, casualties are inevitable when the needs of the facilitators for personal power, status, or expression of hostility or sexuality are too great or when the personal adequacy of a participant is less than required for a demanding group experience.

Various authors have suggested guidelines for encounter groups. These guidelines include the following:

1. Participation should be completely voluntary (for example, professors should not turn a class into an encounter group, nor should industrial supervisors bring any pressure on their staff to participate in group experiences).
2. All participation should be based upon informed consent with respect to the purpose and goals of the group.
3. Some screening of participants should occur, so that those most likely to be casualties may be screened out early.
4. Participants need to understand what types of behavior are permissible in the group. One program, for example, banned the use of marijuana and other drugs, nudity, intimate sexual behavior, and any

physical violence that might produce serious pain or injury. That these things had to be explicitly ruled out indicates the variety of occurrences that can take place in encounter groups.

5. All members should be followed up after the end of the sessions so that leaders may ascertain whether any require additional therapy or help.
6. Organizers should not make unverified claims for the success of the group.
7. Leaders should remain aware of the extent to which their own values and motives influence their performance, especially in regard to encouraging strong emotional expression and physical actions (crying, physical aggression, sexual responsiveness).
8. The opportunity for privacy and anonymity should be provided [based on Jaffe & Scherl, 1969; Lakin, 1969].

## BODY THERAPIES

There are innumerable schools of psychotherapy. Each makes assumptions about human behavior and how to alter that behavior; each has its own training programs and its own qualifications for practitioners; each is directed at a somewhat different segment of the potential universe of users of psychological help.

One group of schools, however, differs from the others in its focus on the physical body rather than on psychological feelings. Practitioners of these schools do not necessarily ignore feelings, cognitions, and early experiences—indeed, for the most part, these are extremely cogent in the therapeutic process—but they get through to these feelings through the physical body. The relevant schools include rolfing, biofeedback, bioenergetics, and dance and movement therapies. In addition to these therapy schools, some kinds of programs not directly therapeutic but very much concerned with the body have also come into prominence. They include body massage, meditation, deep breathing, deep body awareness, and an emphasis on physical exercise for psychological well-being. Nutrition and diet have also been recognized as related to personal feelings and life satisfaction. One point in favor of such approaches is that the interconnectedness between the body, which often carries the tensions resulting from daily stress, and feelings, values, and thoughts is so great that we can often conceive of them as being one and the same.

## OTHER SOURCES OF HELP

The variety of possible resources for persons needing to reduce stress or wishing to enhance their lives is great. In addition to those mentioned, we will take brief note of some other sources of help.

*Total Institutions.* For some individuals, stress is so great that only total care in an institutional setting, away from the stresses of their ordinary existence, is sufficient. The present trend is to return people from these institutions to their own communities (although precautions to make certain that the local community can provide adequate resources often are insufficient), but institutional care of some sort will continue to be required for some people for the foreseeable future. Although institutions have undoubtedly helped many persons and do serve the function of removing the problem from society's scrutiny (undoubtedly part of the reason for their original popularity and part of the reason for their failure), there is considerable doubt whether the institutional atmosphere is conducive to improvement. The entire approach of most institutions tends to increase the patients' helplessness by substantially reducing those areas in which they retain decision making power and to increase their image of themselves as incapable and too disturbed to function effectively by treating them in just such a fashion. In recent years, some institutions have tried to break out of this mold, but their very physical structure—barred windows, locked doors, white-coated aides who carry keys—all attest to the prevailing attitudes toward patients.

*Halfway Houses.*   Many people can function successfully outside of institutions but are not successful in being completely on their own. A variety of halfway houses have been established with mental-hospital patients, ex-convicts, alcoholics, drug addicts, suicide attempters, and others, where they can live and have access to some services but work and enjoy leisure in the general community.

*Clinics, Free and Otherwise.*   In many cities clinics have been established to provide a variety of helping services. These clinics may provide medical care or be limited to counseling; they may be free, or they may charge a sliding scale of fees; they may be based on volunteers, or they may operate under the auspices of some community agency. Some of the kinds of help they offer are: general medical care and, when needed, referral to appropriate physicians; sex-related counseling, counsel regarding care of venereal diseases, and birth-control information; counsel regarding drug abuse and referral to appropriate care agencies; counseling on legal rights, especially regarding sex and race discrimination.

There are still other sources of help. Churches, schools, and colleges maintain counseling centers and frequently employ consulting psychiatrists or clinical psychologists. Alcoholics Anonymous, Gamblers Anonymous, and a variety of self-help groups are available. Chemical relief for stress is found by some in tranquilizers, sleeping pills, and other drugs (some would include marijuana in this list, while others would include alcohol or tobacco), although these have their own potential dangers, some of which are still being uncovered. And sometimes the best medicine for stress is a good night's sleep, an improved diet, a vacation, a change in jobs, dropping out or dropping back in, or an attempt to apply one's own logic to the situation or to use one's own will power.

# REFERENCES

Aronson, E. *The social animal.* San Francisco: W. H. Freeman, 1972.

Coleman, J. C. *Abnormal psychology and modern life* (4th ed.). Glenview, Ill.: Scott, Foresman, 1972.

Gurin, G., Veroff, J., & Feld, S. *Americans view their mental health.* New York: Basic Books, 1960.

Jaffe, S. L., & Scherl, D. J. Acute psychosis precipitated by T-group experiences. *Archives of General Psychiatry,* 1969, *21,* 443–448.

Lakin, M. Some ethical issues in sensitivity training. *American Psychologist,* 1969, *24,* 923–928.

Lieberman, M. A., Yalom, I. D., & Miles, M. B. *Encounter groups: First facts.* New York: Basic Books, 1973.

Maslow, A. H. *Motivation and personality* (2nd ed.). New York: Harper & Row, 1970.

# CHAPTER 18

## MENTAL HEALTH: IMPLICIT VALUES AND ASSUMPTIONS

Two undergraduates were having a heated argument over whether Vincent Van Gogh would have been as exciting and innovative an artist if he had undergone psychotherapy and received general mental-health attention. One contended that, had Van Gogh been at peace with himself, he could have put more of his energies into his art; the other insisted that psychotherapy would have removed Van Gogh's intense motivation for self-expression and that his paintings would then have engendered little excitement. Finding their views on this matter irreconcilable, they never did move on to the next logical question: would society in general or any person in particular have either the right or the obligation to provide a Van Gogh with psychotherapy, if it was assumed that such treatment would substantially reduce his artistic abilities?

## THE MORALITY OF INTERVENTIONS

What are our rights with respect to intervening in others' lives? When are we morally entitled to do something in an attempt to influence another person? What are the outer bounds of these rights? As authors, do we have the right to assert our own beliefs? Even in a textbook? Does a professor have the right to give a student a failing grade? Even knowing that failing grades might cause the student to be dropped from college? As parents, do we have the right to restrict our teenage children's social life because they use language we don't like? What if they use it while speaking to the school principal? As citizens, do we have the right to encourage the state to execute a convict? What if the convict has perpetrated several horrible murders and announced an intention to commit others? Is a psychology professor entitled to require students to participate in research studies? Even if the research involves the study of pain thresholds or the effects of embarrassment?

In what situations do *you* feel justified to intervene? Only in the name of social justice? To fight oppressors? To improve the human condition? Intervening in the lives of others frequently turns out to have unexpected results. The United States intervenes in the affairs of a small nation in Asia, ostensibly at the request of the nation's leaders, and finds itself mired in a ten-year war that endangers the stability of Asia, the United States, and the entire world. A policeman tries to break up a fight between a husband and wife, and they both turn on him, resenting his interference. A young man counsels a friend to hold on to his marriage, then is blamed when the marriage breaks up a year later anyway. You recommend a restaurant, a film, a friend, a vacation spot, or a book to a friend who doesn't like it and holds you responsible for wasting his time and money.

We cannot exist without intervening, but we can become aware that we are indeed intervening and that interventions have hazards as well as favorable outcomes.

## PSYCHOTHERAPY AS INTERVENTION

Almost nothing that we do is totally free of implicit and explicit values. Some people believe that psychotherapy is value free; some people still insist that science is value free. It will come as no surprise that we strongly believe that both contentions are wrong. A psychotherapist who would have treated Van Gogh would have implied that it was worth risking the loss of the artistic enjoyment of the rest of the world to save the man's emotional well-being. A prison psychologist frequently intervenes to reduce tensions among inmates, with the result that they are easier to manage, more docile, less likely to riot. But what if prison riots are in fact the best way to introduce much-needed changes? Can we still contend that the therapist is functioning in a value-free fashion?

A soldier returns from battle, deeply angry over what he has seen and determined to join the peace movement. A young Black is driven to fury by the discrimination encountered by his people. A woman, kept from a job because of prejudice against her sex, is ready to explode. The son of a well-to-do Protestant couple decides against joining his father's law firm and instead becomes a Jesuit priest. A middle-aged woman, married for 12 years and with two children, leaves her husband and takes another woman as a lover.

What is the proper role of the social system in these instances? To get these people to psychotherapists? To encourage them along the paths they have taken? To do nothing, which suggests tacit acceptance of the paths they have selected—or their right to select them? And what is the role of the therapist, should they seek therapy for whatever reasons? Therapists are not helpless pawns in the hands of an overpowering technique. They are fully capable of functioning so that—at least to some extent—the individual is encouraged or discouraged from following certain paths. They may find that psychotherapy is removing the motivation from the soldier, the Black, the women, the Jesuit novice, permitting them to draw back into more passivity. We all know that catharsis, the opportunity to talk things out, frequently reduces the intensity of anger and frustration, but we normally assume that catharsis is helpful. It may well be—depending on what you are trying to achieve. For example, Rennie Davis was, in the 1960s, one of the nation's strongest advocates of revolutionary action to produce extensive social change. In the early 1970s, he found peace and joy through a guru, and he lost his revolutionary fervor. Robert Lindner, a Jewish psychotherapist, records in some detail his work with an anti-Semitic fascist who eventually—undoubtedly as a result of the therapy—dropped out of the American Nazi party and became much more liberal.

In other words, whether by intent or accident, commission or omission, psychotherapy does not operate in a value-free way. This is equally true outside the area of political values. A therapist working with an unhappily married man or woman might try to ameliorate the difficulties between client and spouse in order to keep the marriage intact. Or the therapist might emphasize the need of the client to make his or her own decisions, without particular feelings of responsibility for the others involved. That is, the therapist may emphasize responsibility to one's self, to one's own growth, rather than to other persons, to future generations, to the maintenance of a cohesive family or a stable society. The choice between these alternatives is clearly based squarely on values.

Another example: a psychotherapist learns that a client has committed felonies—pushing heroin, robbing supermarkets, mugging elderly women for their welfare checks, or extorting money from children. What responsibilities does the therapist have? To whom? What if there is good reason to believe the criminal behavior will continue? Again, the therapist does not exist in a value-free world and cannot maintain a value-free practice.

Psychotherapists tend to see themselves as politically and socially liberal, even radical. They are more likely than most professionals to take stands favoring equal rights, affirmative actions, innovative welfare programs, and environmental protection. Yet they are frequently seen by others as stalwarts of the Establishment, trying to manipulate people into accepting the world as it is rather than demanding meaningful change. Whether they indeed wish to do this, whether they are doing it, or whether they could accomplish this goal if they wanted to: all these are unanswered questions but not irrelevant issues.

## MENTAL HEALTH: AN ULTIMATE GOAL?

The entire mental-health movement has come under attack from both the extreme political left and the extreme political right. Representatives of the latter ideology have claimed that mental-health professionals are trying to inculcate Communistic, anti-American, and anti-Christian thoughts, to turn children away from their parents, to encourage the break-up of homes by presenting divorces as a way out of difficulties, to set the stage for sexual immorality, to defend pornography, to enhance a socialistic welfare state.

The left, on the other hand, sees the mental-health movement as diverting funds, energy, and involvement from the real causes of social discontent to what they feel are superficial matters, such as an individual's "mental health." While rats infest bedrooms, while too few jobs are available, while welfare recipients are harassed by petty regulations, the mental-health movement is charged with encouraging social workers to help people adjust to their situations rather than to fight for rapid change. Since mental-health workers are paid—and often well-paid—by the existing power structure, it is difficult for many to believe that these persons sincerely wish to change the power structure.

Counseling is thus often perceived by members of racial and ethnic minorities and by women as trying to mold them to the demands of society rather than as trying to alter society, to get them to train for an available job rather than to place pressure on the political and economic systems to open up all jobs to them:

> ... ethnic minority people seem to have reached a critical social-psychological point where a growing number feel that the majority group has neither the will nor the ability to deal with legitimate social problems stemming from race and social class. These circumstances have contributed to the growing pessimism of Afro-American students and an increasingly expanding number of their middle aged, middle income elders about the hope for real social progress [Thomas, 1970, p. 423].

But you do not need to take either extreme political position to question the extent to which mental health should have priority over other demands. Kalish has referred to the United States as a *healthocracy*, implying that physical health and, to a slightly lesser extent, mental health are our dominant values, to which all other values are made subservient. Anyone who chooses to smoke, to avoid exercise, to overeat, to over-work, to endanger his or her longevity in other ways, is violating the social norms and looked on as suspect. Similarly, persons who are extremely intense, who don't value emotional well-being, who place achievement ahead of mental health, are also cause for suspicion.

In order to assure physical health, we require school children to be vaccinated. Is there an emotional correlate? Many schools have required that hyperactive children take medication, although this matter has stirred considerable controversy. What rights and privileges are people willing to forego in order to maintain health and emotional well-being? If you were in physical pain and probably dying, would you wish to be sedated so that you could live out your remaining days without pain *and* without much awareness of what was going on? Should a government hold back bad news from its citizenry because it might upset their emotional health? Would you avoid a love affair if you felt the odds were high that, in the end, you would be hurt? Would you avoid becoming emotionally attached to someone who was scheduled to leave the country shortly? Would you forego an opportunity for significant personal growth if you had to risk a fair amount of emotional pain?

Where do your basic priorities lie? With mental health for the individual? With societal stability for the community? With personal growth and primary responsibility to the self? With the need for rapid social change? With happiness for the majority? With the elimination of oppression? With the reduction of deviant behavior? With maintaining the legal order? With reducing anger and violence within individuals?

These are goals that can often be achieved simultaneously, but there are occasions when the achievement of one conflicts with the achievement of another. Social stability for the community may be higher if people subjugate some of their growth-directed actions to responsibility to community problems: what right do you have to meditate when your energy and time might be spent helping a crippled child gain some enjoyment from life? The reduction of what is interpreted as deviant behavior might conflict with elimination of oppression: if most community members feel more relaxed when homosexuals are removed from the area, is it the obligation of the authorities to harass the gays into changing their behavior—or their homesteads? These are not questions for immediate answer; they are questions that deserve careful thought, since their answers are complex and not obvious.

# THE EFFECTIVENESS
# OF INTERVENTIONS

To determine whether an intervention is successful, we need to know what we expected of that intervention in the first place. Is prison successful? For whom? To accomplish what? If your goal is to punish people, prison is undoubtedly very successful for most inmates; if your goal is to keep potentially dangerous persons away from society, prison is moderately successful; if your goal is to make the inmates feel guilty and repent, prisons in the United States probably are not successful; if your goal is to cause inmates to emerge improved people who can subsequently lead better and more productive and more socially acceptable lives, prisons may well be counterproductive. Other interventions need to be evaluated in the same fashion: federal housing programs, elementary school remedial-reading programs, nutrition programs for the elderly, corporation public-relations programs, new law-enforcement programs.

Just as interventions may lead to unanticipated moral issues, they also may lead to unanticipated outcomes. Thus, introducing more street lights into a suburban community reduces crime in that community, so the intervention appears to have succeeded; but a subsequent investigation shows that crime has increased in adjacent communities. Apparently the criminals have simply moved their operations. So has the intervention worked after all? A well planned and well conducted program to have mothers of terminally ill children spend considerable time in the hospital caring for their children did a great deal to help the children and the mothers and was even admired by the hospital staff, so the intervention was highly successful—for these people; but the brothers and sisters of the dying children resented the absence of their mothers and felt guilty that they should harbor such feelings when their siblings were dying. For them, the intervention did not work (Hamovitch, 1968).

Turning to psychotherapy, let us take note of a remark of Howard and Orlinsky (1972): "No area of psychotherapy has suffered so much from simplistic thinking in the guise of tough-minded pragmatism as has research on therapy outcome. The insistent demand to know if therapy 'works' has obscured the extreme subtlety of the question . . ." (p. 645). These authors point out that the success of a psychotherapeutic intervention must be measured against the goals established for that intervention. If the psychotherapy is with a mental patient or a highly disturbed person, the goals implicitly are to reduce or eliminate the symptoms *and* their underlying causes.

The first step in determining the effectiveness of psychotherapy, then, is to define with reasonable precision what the goals of the therapy are. We have already discussed the impossibility of doing this in a value-free context, so we need to make some decisions on priorities, such as personal growth versus family stability, achievement and productivity versus "doing one's own thing." True, these do not necessarily come into conflict, and we could decide to make them all goals of equal value.

Howard and Orlinsky (1972) have suggested a number of criteria on the basis of which the success of psychotherapy might be judged:

- Individual well-being: somatic functioning (health versus sickness), affective functioning (happiness versus unhappiness), ideational functioning (sanity versus insanity).
- Social adjustment: instrumental norms (competence versus incompetence), situational norms (propriety versus impropriety), political/legal norms (lawfulness versus criminality).
- Self-actualization: developmental norm (maturity versus immaturity), aesthetic norm (creativity versus banality), moral norm (virtue versus sin).

Any or all of these nine criteria could be utilized to evaluate therapeutic effectiveness. Or we might prefer another kind of criterion, such as reduction of the economic cost to society in terms of less absenteeism at work or elimination of the need for confinement in a mental hospital. Or perhaps we would be satisfied merely to know that when people stop going to see psychotherapists, they believe they have been helped; in other words, perhaps a totally subjective evaluation should suffice. Regardless of our criteria, we might wish to learn whether there are alternatives to psychotherapy that can achieve the same goals while causing less personal discomfort, taking less time, and costing less money.

# THE MODELS OF INTERVENTIONS

Not very long ago, sophisticated and aware persons would have agreed that the behavior of alcoholics, of those who attempted suicide, or of the mentally disturbed was not evil or willful or criminal, but *sick*. Recently, however, the assumption that illness is a proper way to look upon these kinds of behavior has come under strong attack.

## MEDICAL MODEL OR SOCIAL LEARNING?

Which of the following two accounts is more accurate?

A. Mental illness, emotional pressures, and feelings of tension all need to be understood in the same way that physical illness, physical pressures, and feelings of physical tension need to be understood. They have a biological basis and biological symptoms, although thoughts, anticipations, and other forms of cognitive functioning obviously enter in. Being biologically based and, equally important, being types of illness or precursors of possible illness, these concerns must be dealt with by physicians. In many instances, some form of biological treatment (pills, shock, operation) is most appropriate, although there are occasions when verbal interactions with a medical psychotherapist are the treatment of choice.

B. Inappropriate and confused behavior patterns, emotional pressures, and feelings of tension all need to be recognized as resulting initially from improper learning situations—in other words, from improper socialization. Although symptoms can be described in biological terms and a biological basis for these concerns can also be described, the essential origins are best understood through knowing what the individual has learned, perceived, and felt. Since the basic causes are social, these concerns can best be dealt with by persons whose training and experience focus on the processes of socialization. Although biochemical treatments can reduce the immediate effects of the difficulties, in the long run it will be necessary for the individuals to learn new responses to stimuli. For example, instead of reacting to thoughts of self in a deprecatory fashion, they must learn to regard themselves positively.

Some forms of stress are obviously physiological and find a physiological response in the organism. Loss of blood, exposure to extreme cold, and a painful leg injury are examples. Each, of course, has psychological side effects, but the direct outcome of physiological impact is physiological change. Other stress forms can be termed social, psychological, or—perhaps—environmental. These result in changes in behavior, either overt or covert, including feelings, thought, and fears. In these instances, the stressful conditions may be looked upon as stimuli and the behavior as response. In essence, the individual has learned—perhaps over a period of time and through many reinforcing occurrences—to behave in a particular fashion when faced with a particular stress. Although the behavior is mediated by physiological changes and is directly caused by biochemical changes in the brain, nervous system, sensory-motor system, and so forth, these biochemical alterations are themselves the organism's response to its perceptions of its environment.

To repair the deleterious impact of physiological stress, we usually have recourse to medical treatment, from Band Aids to surgery. Although we may recognize the probable importance of tender loving care, or will-to-health, or patient cooperation, our main emphasis is upon a medical model.

When it comes to repairing the deleterious impact of psychosocial stress, the path is not so clear. Often the medical model prevails. The sufferer seeks care in a medical institution or from a medically trained person, is given medication that affects body biochemistry, refers to the difficulties as mental or emotional *illness*, and talks about getting better or worse. In all these respects, the patient resembles the sufferer of physiological stress. This resemblance has an obvious legitimacy in that his or her body has undergone simultaneous and interacting biochemical and behavioral/attitudinal change.

On the other hand, the crux of the problem lies in learning and feeling patterns, in the way the sufferer has learned to respond to stress-producing situations, in the way he or she has learned to relate to others and to feel about himself or herself. The biochemistry of the body can be changed, but, when the effects of biochemical medication wear off, previous learned responses remain. And so do problems. If the tension is caused by an acute stress—for example, an extremely important job interview, an early morning airplane trip, an impending operation—the medication can help a person through the tension until the stimulus has passed. However, if the stress is more chronic, if it lies within basic feelings, relationships, and life-styles, then the temporary effects of the pill will need to be repeated frequently. Thus we have people who exist from tranquilizer to tranquilizer.

For meaningful change to occur, relearning must occur. Those who suffer need to feel differently about themselves, about others, about the world, about their abilities and their relationships and their meaningfulness. Only occasionally can this change occur in isolation. Most commonly, the relearning requires clients to be doing things and being with others and experiencing the world, so that they can learn first-hand that their previous learning was faulty. This task is not as simple as it may sound. Such relearning can be painful, highly threatening, and sometimes impossible.

## ALBEE, MOWRER, AND MASLOW

George Albee, past president of the American Psychological Association, has made a very strong case for the social-learning model. He remarks: "Most disturbed behavior consists of learned . . . anxiety-avoiding responses. The origins of the anxiety to be avoided are to be found in traumatic social interaction of infants and children with the parents or parent surrogates" (1968, p. 319). As you might anticipate, we would extend Albee's comments beyond the period of infancy and childhood. Albee makes the additional point that the best persons for the task of re-education may not be professional psychotherapists: "I find it astonishing that all of us as parents . . . are willing to send our children . . . to school teachers trained essentially at the bachelor's level, and yet we insist that professionals dealing with our emotionally disturbed and mentally retarded children and adults must have far more training than teachers for their face-to-face intervention" (p.

319). By moving from the medical model to the social-learning model, Albee gets away from the insistence on using health personnel, especially physicians, for major roles in the mental-health movement, and points to the use of teachers and educators.

Another implicit element in the social-learning model not found in the medical model is the potential of individuals to learn how to overcome the destructive components of stress under their own power. The medical model implies that, if you put yourself in the hands of the healer, you will be healed—although you must do some of the things the healer recommends. If, however, the pathway to overcoming stress is through learning new forms of behavior, you have two alternatives: either you can follow carefully and unquestioningly the advice of the teacher, which parallels the passive nature of the medical model, or you can be an active agent in the relearning process.

Another attack upon the medical model was made by O. H. Mowrer two decades ago. Although it received considerable attention at the time, it had little subsequent impact upon the field of psychology. Nonetheless, Mowrer's thinking represents an important historical theme and may well re-emerge as consequential. Mowrer criticized the traditional psychiatric view that guilt was merely a matter of pathology that a helpful therapist should dissolve so that the individual can return to responding freely to impulses. Rather, Mowrer contended, the concepts of right and wrong, good and evil, sin and virtue should be brought back into psychology (Mowrer, 1960). Mowrer's form of treatment includes having the person confess sins, serve some form of penance, and alter behavior.

The views of Abraham Maslow would also support Albee, although from a somewhat different vantage point. "It will be seen that gratification of the basic needs is an important (perhaps the *most* important) step along the path to the ultimate, positive goal of all therapy, namely, self-actualization" (Maslow, 1970, p. 242). In Maslow's lexicon, basic needs are defined to include not only the survival needs (food, liquid, air, temperature regulation) but also safety, belongingness, love, and respect. Since the satisfaction of these needs for the most part requires human relationships, "therapy must take place mostly on an interpersonal basis" (p. 242).

The common thread that Maslow hypothesizes as running through many, although perhaps not all, successful therapeutic contacts is the communication from the therapist that the client has personal worth and integrity. Clients then learn to view themselves as valued people in a social context. But psychotherapy is not always necessary to gain these ends. A close personal friendship may accomplish the same goals. Success can also be highly therapeutic: entering a satisfying socio-sexual relationship, doing well in school or on the job, winning some sought-after award, rising to some challenge (personal, work, interpersonal, whatever) and being successful.

Albee emphasizes re-learning; Maslow focuses on improved self-worth; Mowrer discusses altered behavior through acceptance of sin and penance. They all fall back on a psychological model, rather than a medical model; they all emphasize the need for decision making that emanates from the individual, rather than from a strong therapy figure; they all focus on concepts such as *self*, *worth*, and *re-socialization* rather than illness and health.

## MENTAL ILLNESS: A POLITICAL ARTIFACT?

Albee, Maslow, and Mowrer are pro-Establishment (i.e., psychotherapeutic Establishment) gentlemen compared to the militant, anti-Establishment psychiatrist Thomas Szasz. Szasz (1960) attacks the entire concept of mental illness, insisting that—except for instances in which organic impairment can be established—mental illness is merely deviation from a socially accepted standard. Not only is Szasz opposed to the medical model of mental illness as a health concern; he challenges the basic notion that mentally ill behavior is any more than lack of agreement with the social definitions and demands of a powerful elite who determine for their own satisfaction the nature of reality and unreality. What is called mental illness should be regarded as expressions of our struggle with the problem of how we should live.

Szasz argues that the mental-health movement is, in many ways, a contemporary version of the 15th-century Spanish Inquisition. People who exhibit views that the rulers deem unpopular or dangerous or out of touch with reality are placed in custody. Their loss of freedom arises not because they are dangerous to the health of themselves or of others but because they are dangerous to the morality upon which the political system is based.

Many articles have described how Russian intellectuals opposed to the regime have been hospitalized as mentally ill, not only to remove them from the scene but to discredit their views. To attack the views of another person, you are more likely to call him "nuts" or "crazy" than you are to call him "evil" or "wrong." The latter terms imply a strong difference in values, which is usually the intellectual crux of an argument, but it is simpler to brush another's views aside by invalidating his or her mental and emotional processes. In the Middle Ages, the task was accomplished by insisting that such people were inhabited by the devil, so that their expressions were evil. In order to get the devil out of them, exorcism was required; if that failed, they had to be removed from society (to save society) and had to undergo a variety of treatments (purges, exhortation, whippings, and perhaps burning) so that their souls would be redeemed. Alternatively they might remain in a dungeon. The parallels with the psychotherapy and hospitalization of today's mental-health movement are said to be obvious (Keen, 1972).

That contemporary patients may agree with the diagnosis of the mental-health professional is irrelevant. How else can they interpret their behavior, in the face of the mental-health inquisition? Many witches of earlier times confessed their witchcraft, sometimes after torture, but often because they sincerely believed they were witches. Put yourself into this situation: suppose that each time you raise your hand straight up in the air, the telephone rings and your recently deceased grandfather is on the other end; however, no one else can hear either the telephone ring or anything on the other end except a buzz. What do you do? What do you think and feel?

Szasz would contend, in the situation described above, that your belief system differs from the belief system of most other people. Any attempt to institutionalize you or to subject you to another form of treatment would arise from the desire of those who disagree with your views to coerce you into accepting their views of reality. It is your right, he feels, to have these views, and any impingement upon this right is a violation of individual freedom.

Depriving people of liberty through jailing them requires considerable legal procedures; depriving people of liberty through placing them in mental hospitals has often been much easier, sometimes necessitating only the signature of a physician. Szasz has contributed greatly to the efforts of political reformers to give persons accused of mental illness the same rights as those accused of criminal behavior (Keen, 1972).

Szasz also assumes that those accused of mental illness are neither dangerous to themselves nor to others. Rather, they are reminders to the rest of society of its failures of socialization. Therefore, as with so many failures, they are removed from sight (Keen, 1972).

Even supposing that some persons are dangerous to themselves, should this preclude their being free to harm themselves if they choose? And who is to define harm? Are you mentally ill if you decide to smoke two packs of cigarettes a day? Should you be legally prevented from doing so? What if you decide you wish to risk your life to protect your country? Does that action define you as mentally ill? If you decide to live with the poor and diseased of another nation to provide them with the means to better health, is your assumption of that risk psychotic? Should you be forcibly restrained from so acting by laws and incarceration? It becomes apparent that the issue is not *whether* people should be permitted to risk or sacrifice their lives; rather it is *the circumstances* under which they should be permitted to do so.

The same line of thinking can be extended to harming others. If you are accused of being a paranoid schizophrenic, you will be hospitalized in part because your so-called paranoid delusions might make you dangerous to others. Are you more dangerous than the surgeon who encourages operations that are not necessary? Or the producer of pharmaceuticals who permits a potentially harmful drug to remain on the market because the proof of its detrimental effect is inadequate to satisfy the FDA? Or the student who drives home after several drinks or several joints?

How can we argue back with Szasz? A possible first step is to notice how radically Szasz differs from, say, Albee on philosophical beliefs, especially concerning the nature of reality and the relative importance of common and individual realities. One might take the position that there is an objective reality, although our grasp of it is at best imperfect. People whose perceptions of this reality are so different that they appear to have difficulty in functioning within the reality are entitled to receive help. Not to give help would be morally wrong, as well as pragmatically wrong. Even though knife-happy surgeons and greedy manufacturers are as likely to cause harm as paranoid schizophrenics, we must place them in another category. Moreover, both observations by others and self-reports by the mentally ill indicate that they suffer from the effects of their stress and that their life satisfaction improves when they are freed from the stress. In other words, it can be argued that true freedom for these persons cannot be realized until they can function effectively in the real world and that the liberty that Szasz discusses is the fantasy of a polemicist. No one so encumbered by fears, guilt, anxiety, and conflict can have meaningful freedom.

Ironically, Szasz, who has emphasized the political nature of the mental-health movement, has seen his views serve the political ends of others. Persons who adhere to a very conservative political position have long resented the mental-health movement. They dislike its use of tax money. They feel that mentally ill or emotionally disturbed persons could get better if they really wanted to. They see heavy drinking, criminal behavior, sexual promiscuity, drug addiction, and so forth solely as moral transgressions for which those involved should be punished. The mental-health approach that people exhibiting these behaviors need additional (and expensive) services, or that they are not really doing anything wrong, strikes the more conservative as immoral in itself. They resent the idea that behavior is controlled by forces over which we have no power—the determinism of both behavioristic and psychoanalytic psychology.

These ultraconservatives have rallied to support Szasz, in the hope of reducing the power of psychiatrists and other mental-health professionals. More recently, persons to the left of center have also advanced to the Szasz banner, although with somewhat different motives. These persons are primarily concerned with the need for due process before anyone is deprived of freedom. Some of their concern has undoubtedly evolved from observations that those without power—the poor, the ethnic and racial minorities—are in greatest danger of being hospitalized without due process. They recognize, along with Szasz and the conservatives, that what is considered disturbed behavior may merely reflect moral or social views at variance with those of the decision makers of society.

Consider this anecdote:

> After three months of sharing an apartment with Laura, Jeannette announced that her brother was arriving from Portland and asked whether he might live with them for the two weeks he would be in town. Laura agreed without particular reservation. Within a few hours of Randy's arrival, both girls realized something was wrong. He was moody, went for hours without saying a word, would talk about how godless his sister had become, then would return to silence. On the third day, Randy and Jeannette had an argument about some trivial matter, and Randy began to throw dishes and glasses at his sister. Laura was eventually able to quiet him, although Jeannette could not get near him. At that point, Randy began to talk more freely about Jeannette's being promiscuous with anyone who wished her, eventually suggesting that she had even propositioned him; then he called her names and struck her with his hand. His conversation became increasingly difficult to comprehend, and he made many allusions to Jesus; sometimes he would stop in the middle of a sentence, as though he were listening to an unheard voice.
>
> At this point, Laura went to a psychologist, who agreed that Randy needed immediate attention and called a good friend who was chief psychologist at the state mental hospital. How could they get this young man the proper care? They were asked whether Randy's sister or parents would request institutionalization. The answer was negative; his sister refused either to ask for professional help or to notify their parents. Then, they were told, nothing could be done unless he broke a law and was arrested, at which point he might be sent to the mental hospital.

How might Szasz respond to this story? He might argue that Randy had not really hurt anyone; that lots of brothers probably call their sisters names and throw things; that the intent to hospitalize him was just a manifestation of other people's discomfort with Randy's views about how to react to a sister; that, since no one had yet suffered serious injury, no one was likely to in the future; that, if Randy broke a law, he should be treated like any lawbreaker. Furthermore, Szasz would probably condemn the immorality of a law that would permit a young girl to have her brother hospitalized merely because she happened to dislike the way he treated her. What is your view of these arguments?

Albee, Szasz, Maslow, and Mowrer begin at very different points, but they join forces in seeking models for explaining and changing response to stress outside the traditional boundaries of mental *health*. Each emphasizes the need to understand social learning, to see the individual in the context of the community, to focus upon the strengths of the individual rather than upon his or her helplessness (see Albee, 1969; Mowrer, 1960; for Szasz, see Keen, 1972). Each points to a different aspect of a very real concern in terms of human values.

We began this book with a discussion of meaning, and we end it with a discussion of the meaning of mental health. In between we have discussed many meanings, purposes, and values. Now we encourage you to consider where you go from here, what town you want to visit, and whether that town is where you will be comfortable. If you feel considerably more confused now than when you began this book, we would say that our program has been successful; if you feel considerably less confused now than when you began, we would again say that our program has been successful. We have failed only if you decide that you haven't changed at all.

# REFERENCES

Albee, G. W. Conceptual models and manpower requirements in psychology. *American Psychologist*, 1968, *23*, 317–320.

Albee, G. W. Emerging concepts of mental illness and models of treatment: The psychological points of view. *American Journal of Psychiatry*, 1969, *125*, 870–876.

Hamovitch, M. B. *The parent and the fatally-ill child.* Los Angeles: Delmar, 1968.

Howard, K. I., & Orlinsky, D. E. Psychotherapeutic processes. *Annual Review of Psychology*, 1972, *23*, 615–668.

Keen, E. *Psychology and the new consciousness.* Monterey, Calif.: Brooks/Cole, 1972.

Lindner, R. *The fifty-minute hour.* New York: Bantam, 1954.

Maslow, A. H. *Motivation and personality* (2nd ed.). New York: Harper & Row, 1970.

Mowrer, O. H. "Sin": The lesser of two evils. *American Psychologist*, 1960, *15*, 301–304.

Szasz, T. S. The myth of mental illness. *American Psychologist*, 1960, *15*, 113–118.

Szasz, T. S. *The manufacture of madness.* New York: Harper & Row, 1970.

Thomas, C. W. Black-white campus issues and the function of counseling centers. In F. F. Korten, S. W. Cook, & J. I. Lacey (Eds.), *Psychology and the problems of society.* Washington, D.C.: American Psychological Association, 1970.

# CODA

The word *coda* comes from the Latin word *cauda*, meaning "tail." In music, a coda is a separate section added to certain works as a sort of tail-piece to close things off satisfactorily. It keeps the hearer from falling off the edge, so to speak. These next few pages are our coda, the tail of our book.

We've covered a lot of territory, both philosophically and psychologically, but there is a lot we've left out. For example, consider the function of work. Is it a purpose in life? Of life? Neither? Is it an unfortunate necessity to be avoided whenever possible? How do your philosophical predilections lead you to answer these questions? What about your beliefs about human psychology? These are leading questions that would start the book all over again from a rather different perspective. Or again, we could have written the book taking sex as our leading problem. And the same kinds of questions about values would have arisen.

We chose the problem of human development as our leading problem because it interests us and because it is very important to us all as human beings, citizens, and professional people. Other problems are just as important, though, and lead to similarly intricate and fascinating questions.

Our program has involved an implicit assumption about the subjects usually called "philosophy" and "psychology," and now it is time to make that assumption explicit. In our view, the division of human wisdom into all the various academic slots and pigeonholes is quite artificial and is made essentially for administrative convenience. But that convenience is sometimes blinding. It can suggest, for example, that psychology and philosophy have nothing to do with each other. We would maintain, however, that wisdom is not so easily divisible into compartments. It is a whole, self-contained and immense. To suppose that psychology (or philosophy or any other "subject") exists solely by and for itself with no borrowings from anywhere else is not unlike, to borrow an image from Ursula K. LeGuin, supposing that the palm of your hand exists without the back of your hand. Each is essential to the other. To have one, you must have the other. Just so, psychology is not separable from philosophy, or from history, or from sociology, or from music, literature, biology, or any other subject you care to name. Nor are these subjects separable from psychology.

Look carefully at the accompanying illustration, and ask yourself which section is the "real" figure and which is the ground. It is impossible to tell, because it depends entirely on how you look at it. Wisdom is like that. We suggest that you cannot tell which is "really" psychology and which is "really" philosophy or history or drama. These "subjects" create each other. They are separable when you look at them in a certain way, but a deeper understanding reveals that each has roots in every other.

This observation suggests other ways to write not only this book but a whole curriculum. Imagine attending a school in which all the books and courses made this assumption: the various "subjects" studied interpenetrate and cross-fertilize one another; to grasp the full impact of a subject, you must understand this interpenetration and see the cross-fertilization at work. At such a school, you wouldn't study English, then history, then psychology in the way a child wanders down a beach picking up one pretty pebble, discarding it, then picking up another. Instead, you would study in the way a painter creates a landscape, adding and blending colors in order to make a complete and meaningful whole in which each patch of color contributes to the painting. We can't imagine a more exciting prospect. Our fondest dream for this book is that it might inspire other books like it that would make such a curriculum possible.

One final word comes to mind. We want to echo a thought we expressed at the start of this book. Some readers might think that we have taken a crassly relativist position—namely, that to say that something is valuable is to say that a certain society (or even a certain individual) approves of it. We do not believe that. What we do believe is that people *act* not on what *is* the case but on what they *believe* to be the case. Since there is a difference between what is true and what people believe, people can be wrong, and their actions can be completely wrong-headed. Our challenge to you is to acknowledge this and to take responsibility for your decisions and actions, in the full awareness that you may be wrong.

In Carlos Castaneda's book *Journey to Ixtlan*, Don Juan makes this same point. He says this:

> When a man decides to do something he must go all the way, but he must accept responsibility for what he does. No matter what he does, he must know first why he is doing it, and then he must proceed with his actions without having doubts or remorse about them. . . .
>
> I have no doubts or remorse. Everything I do is my decision and my responsibility. The simplest thing I do, to take you for a walk in the desert, for instance, may very well mean my death. Death is stalking me. Therefore, I have no time for doubts or remorse. If I have to die as a result of taking you for a walk, then I must die.

That is the responsibility we mean. We must decide, and we must act. And we must act knowing that our knowledge is incomplete, our wisdom insufficient. We will make errors. To be educated is to be aware of our fallibility, to take responsibility for our errors, both factual and moral, and to go on without becoming discouraged or sliding into the view that the pursuit of what is truly real and valuable is futile.

This kind of responsibility demands both courage and integrity—the courage and integrity of a Socrates. It was Socrates who said "The unexamined life is not worth living." To which we might add that unexamined values are not worth having.

# INDEX